Big Bill of Chicago

BIG
BILL
OF CHICAGO

By
LLOYD WENDT
and
HERMAN KOGAN

Foreword by **RICK KOGAN**

NORTHWESTERN UNIVERSITY PRESS
EVANSTON, ILLINOIS

Northwestern University Press
www.nupress.northwestern.edu

Foreword copyright © 2005 by Rick Kogan. Copyright © Herman Kogan
and Lloyd Wendt. Published 2005 by Northwestern University Press. Originally
published 1953 by the Bobbs-Merrill Company, Inc. All rights reserved.

Printed in the United States of America

10 9 8 7 6 5 4 3 2 1

ISBN 0-8101-2319-3

Library of Congress Cataloging-in-Publication data are available from the
Library of Congress.

∞ The paper used in this publication meets the minimum requirements of the
American National Standard for Information Sciences—Permanence of Paper for
Printed Library Materials, ANSI z39.48-1992.

CONTENTS

CHAPTER   PAGE

Part I—The Education

Part II—The Reign

CONTENTS—*Continued*

FOREWORD TO THE NEW EDITION

Rick Kogan

Chicago has had forty-five mayors. The latest, Richard M. Daley, seems like a decent enough guy, especially in those moments, rare as they might be, when he isn't being asked to defend or explain himself.

One such moment took place in his fifth-floor office in City Hall last year when I showed him a photo from 1955. His father, Richard J. Daley, had just won his first term as mayor, and in the photo he is at Comiskey Park, in conversation with White Sox manager Marty Marion and Cubs skipper Stan Hack. There, standing next to him, are his boys: William, Michael, John, and Richard.

As the mayor looked at the photo of himself as a child, a smile began to cross his face. "Oh, yeah . . . Oh, boy . . . ," he said. "I was in seventh grade. I played baseball all the time. Spring, summer, and fall, we were always playing, baseball and some softball, pickup games. I played catch with my dad. I was the pitcher, he was the catcher, or sometimes it was the other way around. I was four or five, and we were always in the backyard throwing the ball."

Fathers shadow their sons in so many ways. Sitting there with the mayor, I remembered when my father and I played catch, and then, as with almost all memories of my father, I started to hear the sound of a typewriter. It comes from a small room, an office that was in the apartment in which I grew up in Old Town. It is the sound of two fingers pounding furiously.

My father, Herman, was a newspaperman in love with Chicago and its history. Vividly, often in collaboration with his newspaper pal Lloyd Wendt, my father wrote books about that history. He and Wendt wrote *Lords of the Levee*, the story of First Ward bosses John "Bathhouse John" Coughlin and Michael "Hinky Dink" Kenna (reissued by Northwestern University Press); *Give the Lady What She Wants!* a history of Marshall Field and Company; *Bet a Million!* the

5

biography of industrialist/gambler John W. Gates; *Chicago: A Pictorial History;* and the book you are holding, also courtesy of the fine folks at Northwestern University Press.

I have read all of these books and the many others my father and Lloyd wrote on their own or with others. But before I was old enough to read most of them, my father wrote books in my head and on my heart. Through his stories, he made me feel the pulse of the past and convinced me for keeps that the past never really vanishes. It echoes through the years. History courses through this city's veins. It cannot be destroyed by bulldozers driven by corporate greed, political expedience, or forgetfulness. There is not a day that passes that I do not find my head filled with images from Chicago's history. They may come from pictures, from words in books, from stories told and sights seen, or from some weird combination of all those things.

Before I would ever meet William Hale "Big Bill" Thompson in print, I met Paddy Bauler in the flesh. He was, of course, the alderman of the Forty-third Ward, ever famous for uttering that catchy phrase on the night Richard J. Daley was first elected mayor: "Chicago ain't ready for reform." Ty Bauler, Paddy's grandson, was my childhood friend. Often he would take me to "Grandpa's place," the saloon Bauler owned on North Avenue, just west of Sedgwick Street. These visits lasted about ten minutes. Paddy would ask about school, after which Ty would ask him to give us money. "Here, kids, here's two dollars, go get some ice cream," he would say, peeling the bills from a huge roll of dough.

One day when we were sitting at the back of his saloon, a man walked in and, after talking with one of the hulking minions who always seemed to be around, was brought back to see the alderman.

"My garbage can was stole," the man told Paddy.

"You need a new one, then?" said the alderman.

"I gotta have one, Alderman."

"Take this," Paddy said, digging twenty dollars from his roll.

"Thank you, thank you, thank you," said the man as he was ushered out.

"That's how you win elections," Paddy said to us. "You gotta take care of the people in your ward, even the little ones."

This was a vivid early lesson in Chicago politics, but it did nothing to prepare me for the extraordinary, extravagant, and complex Big Bill.

Among Chicago's mayors has been one woman (Jane Byrne) and one African American (Harold Washington). There have been some honest mayors and some crooks. There were also—and this will surprise anybody born after about 1930—some Republicans.

The last Republican mayor was William Hale Thompson, a man for whom the adjective "flamboyant" seems pale. Oafish, bombastic, and colorful (in the best and worst sense of that word), he once staged a minirodeo in the city council chambers. He always wore a cowboy hat and, in winter, a heavy fur coat. He let gangsters run free. He threatened to punch England's King George V "in the snoot." He was a man whose biography deserves the fairy tale–like beginning that my father and Lloyd give it: "Once upon a time there really was a Big Bill Thompson." Some 350 rollicking pages later, they conclude that "neither myth nor legend can ever match the fact and reality of that lusty and uproarious life."

Reading *Big Bill of Chicago* again, I feel enriched and enlivened. I feel again connected to the city. I can hear those typewriter keys pounding.

The Education

1 ||| A Noisy, High-Spirited Boy

ONCE UPON A TIME THERE REALLY
was a Big Bill Thompson. And he was the tumultuous mayor of the
city of Chicago in wild and incredible years.

In the beginning he was a fearless hero, by chance a champion
of reform, and he strutted and shouted his way into the city's heart.
Chicago was young then, as great cities go, and complex and contradictory. Flirting behind a china teacup or an ivory fan or the
door of a Levee panel house, Chicago asked only to be pleased. Big
Bill knew the arts of pleasure, and his raw voice called for fun while
his hired minstrels and professional praise-shouters sang his fame as
a builder of golden dreams.

While he carried on his romance with the city and had his way
with her, it became clear to many that he was loud and boisterous but
neither hero nor reformer. Chicago, they said, was a dissolute har-
ridan who deserved to be fooled. And there were defenders who
spoke up for Big Bill's and Chicago's good names. The din of the
cries echoed far. Removed in distance and time, many marveled
that one city could arouse so much evil report, that one man could
evoke such fervent loyalties and unquenchable hatreds.

Some said of him: "God made just one William Hale Thompson
and forgot the mold. Truth, courage, consecration, ideas of right,
ideas of justice—all are in him. Call him a Napoleon, call him Abraham Lincoln—when history is written, they will write high in the
blue sky above all of them the name of William Hale Thompson!"

And others: "He has given the city an international reputation for moronic buffoonery, barbaric crime, triumphant hoodlumism, unchecked graft and a dejected citizenship. He nearly ruined the property and completely destroyed the pride of the city. He made Chicago a byword of the collapse of American civilization."

Big Bill Thompson? A master politician, a firm patriot, a defender of American ideals, a friend to the oppressed, a supreme showman, a great sportsman, a prince of good fellows, a humanitarian who yearned only to do miracles for the city he ruled.

Big Bill Thompson? "He is indolent, ignorant of public issues, inefficient and incompetent as an administrator, incapable of making a respectable argument, reckless in his campaign methods and electioneering oratory, inclined to think evil of those who are not in agreement or sympathy with him, and congenitally demagogical."

Big Bill Thompson? They called him a charlatan and a genius, a knave and a saint, a rogue and a knight, a builder and a despoiler, a mountebank and a gentleman, a P. T. Barnum and a George Washington, a churl and a gallant, a petulant child and a canny thinker. "Bill Thompson's the man for me!" sang some, and others answered, "He has the carcass of a rhinoceros and the brain of a baboon!" Some cried, "Big Bill's heart is as big as all outdoors!" and others replied, "The people have grown tired of this blubbering jungle hippopotamus!"

When this romance started, Chicago was a city of opportunity, no place for the weak, the docile or the squeamish. Its workers slaughtered more pork and beef, loaded more grain, made more soap, tanned more hides, poured more steel, built more plows and railroad cars than any other place in the land. Most of these workers had not journeyed to the city to create a political utopia. They came to make homes and to make money. They created what was needed for the vast commerce that grew up in the wilderness they had opened: houses and bridges and streets, factories, hotels and skyscrapers. They dispatched buyers and sellers, promoters and schemers. They sent out mail-order catalogues and to produce them they set up massive printing plants. When their tasks were done they were weary, most of them, and they left the chores of politics and politicking to those who hungered for power and prestige.

Big Bill came riding home from the West at a time when the city seemed ripe for the kind of man he was. In his affair with Chicago, he was sometimes tender, sometimes rapacious. Those who loved him praised even his faults. Those who hated him denied even his virtues. But no one could say that Big Bill gave sparingly of his ardor. Nor was his romance with the city of Chicago ever dull.

2

William Hale Thompson was born in Boston, on Beacon Street, the first son of a wealthy man. These were twin misfortunes for a boy destined to political life in the rough town of Chicago, for that city even then, in 1867, was famed for its obstreperous ways, its dislike of the East, its preference for poverty in those who yearned to serve the people.

But there were compensations. Thompson came from a long line of warriors and malcontents, who were among the first in America to feud with the English crown. Robert Thompson, founder of the family in the New World, arrived in Boston from England in 1700, settling later on the frontier near Durham, New Hampshire. For his prowess as an Indian fighter, he was awarded bounties totaling five pounds by the Provincial Assembly at Portsmouth. The Assembly encouraged him toward more forays, but there is no record that Thompson offered other scalps for additional bounty payments. Instead he occupied himself in his later years with warfare against the constitutional authorities who sought to dispossess him from his great landholdings on dubious New Hampshire grants. By 1737, when his son, Ebenezer, was born, Robert Thompson, victorious in these land wrangles, was a rich and respected citizen.

Trained in medicine, Ebenezer hung out his shingle as a "physition." But he showed more talent for politics than bleeding and leeching. In 1757, when he was only twenty years old and had yet to treat his first patient, he was chosen one of Durham's selectmen, an unusual honor for such a young man. Until 1766 he was re-elected annually. Then he became the Durham representative in the New Hampshire General Assembly, where he started an active career of opposing King George III. Seizing the leadership of the forces opposed to John Wentworth, the King's governor, he incurred Wentworth's wrath when he asserted he had been elected to serve the people and not the King. In 1774 he and a dozen other men from Durham helped to seize the powder stores in Fort William and Mary, His Majesty's outpost at Newcastle. This daring raid, on December 14, was one of the first overt acts of war in the Revolution, and Governor Wentworth had Thompson indicted for treason. A reward was offered for Thompson's capture, but friends sheltered him. Late in 1775 he was one of five men commissioned by the insurgent General Assembly to "draw up a plan for the government of the Colony of New Hampshire during the contest with Great Britain." He accepted this task eagerly, and throughout the war his rebellious activities matched those of Samuel Adams, of Boston, although, in the remote New Hampshire hills, they won less attention. He served, at the war's start, as Councillor of State for his colony, then as a member of the Committee of Safety, that most pernicious thorn in Britain's crown, and finally as New Hampshire's secretary of state. After the war he was named judge of the Superior Court of New Hampshire, although he had no legal training, and as presidential elector from New Hampshire he helped to elect George Washington the new republic's first President.

His son, Ebenezer, Jr., carried on the family traditions as an officer of the New Hampshire militia, strenuously opposing the efforts of the state of New York to seize the New Hampshire land grants. New York's claims were based on royal patents which the son, like the father, refused to recognize. Rich in New Hampshire lands, he married Elizabeth Hale, daughter of a Portsmouth war veteran and Latin teacher. One of their children, Ebenezer Thompson III, continued the family's tradition of fighting the British by serving as a captain in the United States Navy in the War of 1812. And Captain Thompson's son, William Hale Thompson, Sr., continued the seagoing tradition.

Born in 1838, this Thompson—Big Bill's father—shipped on the crew of the *Emily Farnum* when he was only nineteen, two years after his father died. He quickly rose to be ship's second officer but was injured so badly when he fell into the hold in dock at San Francisco that he had to give up his active sea service. He returned to New England and in Boston entered the counting room of Cummings and Lee, East India commission merchants. Able in business and rich from his inheritance of New Hampshire land, he bought a mansion on elm-lined Beacon Street and joined the fashionable Boston Tigers regiment of the state militia. When the Civil War broke out Thompson expected to fight with his regiment. But an uncle, Senator John P. Hale, chairman of the United States Senate Naval Committee, urged him to apply for a naval commission. Second in his examinations, Thompson was ordered, on October 2, 1861, as a lieutenant to the sloop-of-war *Mohican*. His duties were those of ship's paymaster. Eight months later he was promoted to lieutenant commander and assigned to the staff of Admiral David G. Farragut, an affiliation of which his worshiping son made much in later years. Big Bill always called boastful attention to his father's service with Farragut in major engagements. The record shows that the elder Thompson was not at the thundering guns, but with the ship's gold and precious papers. He performed this unheroic duty ably, was commended and promoted to paymaster of the fleet, and resigned with honors in 1866.

While on leave in January 1864, Commander Thompson married Medora Gale, member of a pioneer Chicago family. Her father, Stephen, was one of the thirty-eight incorporators of the town of Chicago, and her grandfather, Theophilus Smith, was a Justice of the Illinois Supreme Court. Their first child, Helen, was born in Portsmouth in 1866. On May 14, 1867, their second, William Hale Thompson, Jr., was born.* Later there came two more sons, Gale, in 1871, and Percival, in 1876.

3

A year after young Bill was born, his father grew unhappy with Boston and his chores at the countinghouse. Using as a logical ex-

---

* Later, when he was in politics, Thompson sheared off two years, claiming he was born in 1869.

cuse the need for settling his wife's inheritance in Chicago, he went
to the bustling town to look it over.

In 1868 Chicago boomed with a noisy exuberance that easily
won this sailor's heart. Splendid factories, stores and office buildings were being built. The new cobblestone streets, raised from
the mud by a young Boston engineer named George Pullman, were
packed with carts, wagons, fine carriages and clattering bobtailed
streetcars. Along the Chicago River the wharves were lined with
ships of the Great Lakes fleets, lumber schooners from the north,
barges from New Orleans, big freighters from European ports.
Thousands of homes were going up, from the tiny shanties to the
elegant mansions of the newly rich, the packers, the traders, merchants and railroad promoters. Chicago sprawled west, north and
south, along plank roads and stretches of rail knitting the new
metropolis to a region of prospering farms and thriving towns.
Some of the homes on Michigan Avenue's Terrace Row and many
of the Lake Street stores exceeded in grandeur those in Boston or
other big cities of the East. The sprawling McCormick reaper works
and the giant packing houses and grain elevators lining the murky
riverbanks were sights that thrilled Thompson. He soon learned,
too, that fortunes were being made in record time in Chicago. Who
had not heard of Potter Palmer, the amazing dry-goods wizard, a
multimillionaire at thirty-nine? And of Cyrus McCormick, the
reaper king; of Marshall Field and Levi Z. Leiter, the merchant
princes; of such promoters and dealers in real estate as William
Ogden, Isaac Arnold and Walter Newberry, whose sumptuous
homes stood in the quiet groves just north of the river?

Thompson decided to settle in Chicago, and he selected the real-
estate business in which to prosper. To his wife's holdings he added
several lots in the block bounded by Madison, State, Washington and Dearborn streets. He returned east to dispose of his New
Hampshire farm and other land and by 1869 he and his family were
in Chicago for good. He bought a house at 48 South Sangamon
Street in a quiet residential district and began the erection of the
Thompson Block, a solid, four-story brick building on West Madison Street. Only a few months after it was completed the Great
Fire of 1871 scourged most of Chicago. Almost the entire business

and industrial area was destroyed, but the section where Thompson's new building stood went unscathed. As owner of one of the few good business buildings—nearly 18,000 houses and commercial structures had been razed by the flames—Thompson could command premium rentals, and did. He also joined the civic-minded in welfare work, and he kept busy buying up land and leases from his less fortunate neighbors. By the time his husky young son, Billy, was ready for elementary school, Commander Thompson was on his way toward his first million dollars.

Developing a taste for politics, Thompson, Sr., was elected as a staunch Republican to the Illinois legislature. Among his remembered accomplishments were his sponsorship of the first Illinois law for the prevention of cruelty to animals, and his orations for a measure to establish a state militia. For the latter service, Governor Shelby M. Cullom appointed him his military aide, with the rank of colonel. Thereafter Commander Thompson preferred to be known by his higher-ranking title.

4

Colonel Thompson had attended Phillips Exeter Academy and hoped that his son Billy would go there too, eventually enrolling at Yale University. But Billy, a noisy, high-spirited boy with more energy and length of limb than he could conveniently use, had few intellectual interests beyond reading eagerly the tales of the Western range in *Big-Foot Wallace* and *Buffalo Bill* and other paperbacked thrillers.

Chicago was a good town for the sons of rich men. Around the Thompson house, white, spacious and gabled, there was plenty of room for stables, a barnyard, a poultry house and gardens. Sons could be put to work at home; they had horses to ride, cows to milk, chickens to feed and plots of vegetables to weed. Bill preferred even these chores to schoolwork, but most of all he enjoyed riding about the town on his pony with his cronies, the Pike brothers, Eugene and William.

He also dared to invade the dangerous regions that adjoined the Sangamon Street home. To the west the city was sparsely settled.

The area was still swamp, and in the spring was usually flooded all the way to the Des Plaines River. To the south, on Twelfth Street, was an Irish settlement clustered about the Jesuit church. The tough Irish boys hated rich men's sons; when Billy Thompson and his friends hunted railroad spikes along the Chicago, Burlington & Quincy right of way, they expected to fight their way back, and usually did. To the north was St. Columbkille's parish, where the Irish were even tougher. They waylaid rich boys venturing into the woods beyond Whisky Point Road, or fought them when they swam in the district's limestone quarries. Young Thompson led expeditions into these areas. He could hold his own in a fight, and he enjoyed the excitement and angry action.

When he was not fighting or reluctantly attending his classes at the Charles Fessenden Preparatory School, popular with wealthy families on the city's West Side, young Thompson was racing about on his pony. His flair for dramatizing scenes of the Western range he had read about in the dime novels often involved him and the Pikes in trouble. Once their untended campfire destroyed several trees in new Lincoln Park. Sometimes the boys shot at birds in South Park, which the local constabulary seemed to regard as a bird sanctuary. The lads frequently invoked the anger of bridge tenders when they pursued imaginary outlaws and Indians on their ponies across the rickety spans with noise and extra bursts of speed. It was this kind of prank that won Bill Thompson his first notice in the local newspapers.

It happened early in April 1881. The Chicago River was at its flood stage, and the bridge guards worried about their fragile structures, most of which had been rebuilt hastily after the Great Fire. Thompson and his companions, riding toward an imaginary battle with Indians in Lincoln Park, approached the State Street bridge at a rapid gallop. They ignored a first warning to slow down, and rode on. At the other end, however, Edward Kehoe, the bridge tender, seized Thompson's bridle. There was a short but violent tussle that brought police from the near-by Chicago Avenue station. Bill Thompson was dragged to the station and thrown into a cell with a fifteen-year-old razor wielder, a pickpocket and a man beaten in a saloon brawl.

It was two o'clock in the morning before Colonel Thompson learned where his son was. He charged into the station, secured Bill's release and berated the police. On the next morning he was in the City Hall office of Mayor Carter H. Harrison, Sr. "I want satisfaction!" he yelled. "I want you to discharge every policeman who laid a hand on my boy. What kind of a town is this, sir, that an innocent citizen cannot go about his business without being basely assaulted? What kind of ruffians do you employ, sir, who let thieves and robbers run wild while they arrest innocent children?"

Mayor Harrison summoned Police Chief William J. McGarigle and Lieutenant Homer Schaack of the Chicago Avenue station and gave them a curt scolding. After they apologized, Colonel Thompson was placated. As for the boy, he made a decision: he would send Bill to a boarding school where the discipline was rigorous and would subdue the energies of his six-footer son.

But Bill saved himself from this fate. While his father was in the City Hall he found a job in a grocery at Peoria and Madison streets. He wanted to go west, he told his father, and he was going to earn enough money in his job to become a cowboy or, better yet, a rancher. He spoke eagerly of the horses he loved, of camp-fires, of life on the open range. His brown eyes sparkled as he talked of the adventure and opportunities in Deadwood or Cheyenne. And he won out. If he behaved and saved seven dollars of the nine-dollar weekly wage he would receive at the grocery, said Colonel Thompson, Bill could go west next fall, paying his own way.

2 ||| Cowboy Bill

I

IN THE CABOOSE OF AN EMPTY CAT-
tle train, Bill Thompson, gangling and ruddy but not yet fifteen
years old, was soon on his way to his exciting land of the dime
novels. At Omaha he took a job as an assistant brakeman on the
Union Pacific and hit Cheyenne, Wyoming, at the peak of the
Black Hills gold rush.

Cheyenne was the place where fortune hunters took stagecoaches
to look for gold in the hills. It was near grazing lands on which
Texas longhorns, driven up the Chisholm Trail, were fattened on
buffalo grass for shipment to Chicago and other markets. To Cheyenne came the bullwhackers bringing their freighters down the
Bozeman Trail, cow hands from the ranches, and drawling Texans,
all parched and rambunctious after three months of herding cattle
north from San Antonio. It was the capital of sutlers and provi-
sioners who supplied the Federal troops fighting the Indians, supplied arms and whisky to the Indians, and hustled a dollar when
and where they could.

To young Thompson it was his play dream come true. Cowboys
swaggered through the streets. Cow ponies stamped at the hitching
rails. On both sides of Main Street, from the Inter-Ocean Hotel to
McDaniel's Variety Hall, stood saloons and wide-open gambling
hells, each with cribs upstairs for rendezvous with the painted
ladies. By night, when the dusty stagecoach rolled in from Deadwood, gold hunters returned, tenderfeet piled from the Omaha

train and cowboys and soldiers gathered for an evening's pleasure, Main Street rocked with the noise and clamor of a lurid carnival. Lanterns and torches lighted the way to the saloons and gambling dens. Pitchmen and touts shrilled their spiels. Women called from doorways, pianos tinkled and melodeons wheezed in the barrel houses. All night there was song, shouting, cursing and laughter, and often the sound of gunfire.

Bill had saved eighty dollars during the summer to earn his way west, but three days after he reached Cheyenne he had only eighty cents in his pockets. Meals were a dollar each and a cot in the Inter-Ocean Hotel cost four dollars a night. Premium prices were paid for transportation into town or out of it. To rent a horse or sidecar buggy cost fifteen dollars a day. The card sharps and hustlers were ruthless. Bill's money had gone fast, and he needed a job. He applied for one to R. M. Allen, assistant manager of the Standard Cattle Company ranches. Despite his lack of experience, Thompson managed to convince Allen he would be useful as the "hood" on a ranch, the driver of the hoodlum wagon used to carry cow hands' bedding and to haul wood and water, and assist the ranch cook. He got the job at twenty dollars a month and keep, which permitted him to sleep in the wagon and supplied him with all the cowboy fare he could eat—corn bread, bacon, sow belly, treacle and onions. He had never cooked a meal in his young life, so he spent half of his eighty cents for a cookbook, and when the Standard provision wagon left Cheyenne, Bill was aboard, riding the high spring seat.

2

Thompson was assigned to the 101 Ranch, which ranged on the Chugwater and Horse creeks in Wyoming. As the "hood," he drove the wagon to the cowboys rounding up the cattle on the range from Fort Laramie all the way to the Black Hills divide. At three o'clock every morning he rolled out of his blankets to re-build the fire, haul water or gather wood. Then he helped the cook cut meat for breakfast or bake the day's supply of bread. These cowboys were not epicures, but they demanded and got a fresh supply of bread every day during roundup time.

By that winter, when the range riders took to their bunkhouses and Bill reluctantly obeyed his father's written order to return home, he had acquired bits of special knowledge. He knew the heat values of the various kinds of wood available on the prairies, and of buffalo chips, called "prairie coal." He could build and hold a fire, spot a water hole, pack cooking gear for the trail, bake bread and broil steaks. Sometimes he had ridden with the hands as they tailed up mavericks from canyons, gulches and ravines, and he had learned to rope and tie a steer.

As he stood before his father, he was determined, this lithe, tanned youth with loud voice and plainsman's vocabulary, that he wanted forever to live the life of a Western rancher. He told Colonel Thompson how some boys, little older than himself, were already getting rich by laying claims to their share of unbranded cattle in the roundups. All he needed was money to buy a *remuda* of horses, a saddle and cowboy equipment so he could ride with the cowboys. Land out West was cheap. Perhaps he could find a ranch and build on it. His father was impressed. "Spend your winters in school in Chicago and your summers out West and perhaps we will find something" was his promise.

In the next six years Bill attended classes at the Metropolitan Business College for three months each winter and spent the rest of the year on the Western range. With every return to Chicago he knew something more: how to handle a gun, how to rope a calf on order of the roundup foreman, how to wrestle a steer for the branding iron, how to pick the finest of the mavericks when the cow hands had the chance to choose from the stray cattle. In Chicago he went about in cowboy garb: a bright wool shirt, blue denim pants fitting snugly about the hips and legs and with pockets straight down the front ("You lose too much change from side pockets when you sit in the saddle," he casually explained to his citified friends), a twenty-dollar beaver Stetson and a pair of eighteen-dollar hickory peg boots. He displayed his Colt .44 single-action revolver and told stories of the roundup camps and of hunting mountain lions and Indians. In the fashionable clubs at Christmas-party time he could be found in the center of a cluster of boyhood friends, now pale-faced students in Yale or Harvard, and he talked jovially and happily of the thrilling world in which he lived.

3

In the spring of 1888, when Bill was in Cheyenne, he received a telegram from his father: BOUGHT RANCH AT EWING, NEBRASKA. YOU TAKE OVER.

Bill was overjoyed, for older cattlemen had told him Nebraska, with acres of good feeding grass, was ideal for raising herds. He could not find Ewing on a map, but he rode happily out of Cheyenne with a string of cow ponies to follow the Union Pacific tracks eastward. He was certain Ewing would lie somewhere near a shipping point on the railroad, and he intended to enter his new home town in true cattleman's style, at the head of his string of horses.

Before he reached his destination, he came across the town of Sidney, Nebraska, and there acquired quite innocently a reputation that pursued him all the way to Chicago.

Sidney, despite its tiny size and population of only eight hundred, was infamous as one of the West's most depraved towns. Even its only minister, a Reverend Mr. Benton, later turned out to be a confidence man named Simpson, who assumed clerical garb to expedite his swindles. Every Saturday night the population trebled when teamsters, cowboys, herders and assorted outlaws trooped in to drink, gamble and patronize the prostitutes, called by the *Telegraph* with some pride, "our Nymphs du Pave."

Not only did the gamblers and whores ply their respective trades, then enjoying a peculiar respectability in the West, but they engaged in more reprehensible activities, including murder. In one notorious establishment, the Lockwood House, so many honest cowboys and gold miners had been slain in cribs that the lesser criminals formed a vigilante group and hanged five of the Lockwood House operators. Thereafter its girls' embraces proved less lethal, but its Saturday-night dances were still wildly unrestrained in morals and mayhem. At one such affair three men were slain. First a soldier, back from chasing the Sioux, shot himself. "The body," reported the *Telegraph*, "was dragged in a corner and the dance went on." Then a Sidney citizen named Jack Page, after an argument, shot and killed a cowboy. "The merriment did not abate," related the newspaper, "until a third man was killed in a fight. This broke up the dance. Daylight found some sleeping off their drunken slumber. The others had gone to bury the dead in the Boot Hill graveyard."

When Bill Thompson, dusty and hungry, rode into Sidney, he went to the Lockwood House, unaware of its reputation. As he stood at the bar someone asked him his name. "Billy Thompson, they call me," he responded, with a wide grin.

Men's hands shifted toward their guns. Dance-hall girls skittered to the safety of their cubicles. Thompson stared at the assemblage and blinked. In a few minutes Deputy Sheriff Jack Southers, an official who had himself killed four men in a gun fight, strolled in to advise Thompson to behave himself.

"But I don't want trouble," Bill insisted. "I'm on my way to Ewing."

Still the men in the barroom eyed him coldly. "C'mon, I'll buy drinks on the house!" Thompson yelled.

At this the cold tenseness vanished. Drinks were set up and Jack Southers offered an explanation. Only a week before an outlaw named Billy Thompson had killed a sheriff at Ellsworth, Kansas, and was reported heading toward Sidney. "Billy Thompson," the *Telegraph* had reported, "has the reputation of being a really bad man. He has come into this territory to look for the man who killed his pal, Billy Phebeus. He believes in the unwritten law, 'Get the man who gets your friend.'" Chicago's Bill Thompson had, of course, been mistaken for the killer. But his offer to buy drinks for the house and his friendliness had saved him from embarrassment, and worse. A false move by Thompson in that wild little town that night might easily have led to the inevitable necktie party and the tribute always given by the *Telegraph* to such lynching victims: "In some ways he was a bad man, and in others he was a damsite wuss."

Bill laughed at the incident as he continued on his way, and wrote about it to friends in Chicago, who promptly garbled the details so that even when Thompson's Western years were far behind him there was always the whispered story that Bill Thompson actually had killed a man, or several.

4

The ranch Colonel Thompson had bought was on Goose Lake, southwest of Ewing. Its capable foreman was a veteran cowboy, Frank C. Heinz, and the hands were skilled in the ways of the West. They feared the worst when they were informed that the son of the new Chicago owner was to be their manager.

But they soon changed their opinion. Shortly after Bill arrived he proved himself as hard-riding and hard-drinking a cowboy as any of them. On one Saturday night he led a pack of his cowboys on a wild race through Ewing's Main Street and past the swinging doors of the Ewing Saloon to demand drinks. On another they roamed through the town after a session in the saloon, firing their revolvers into the night air before riding back to the ranch. Every summer Thompson invited Chicago friends to the ranch, and among the guests was Florenz Ziegfeld, later the musical-comedy producer. For such visitors Bill and his cowboys staged mock gun fights and kidnapings and sometimes scared the tenderest of them by pretending to plan to rob the Ewing State Bank.

In his second summer as ranch manager, Bill had trouble hiring extra hands. He gathered up every available man, including some claimed by a neighboring rancher named John Carr. Carr circulated a story that Bill had lured the men by importing a group of prostitutes from Omaha and maintaining them in the bunkhouse during the haying season. This led to a furious fight one night when Carr and Thompson met at the Ewing Saloon. When Thompson upbraided Carr for spreading the false story, Carr reached for his gun. Thompson hurled a whisky bottle at him, then knocked Carr to the floor with a single punch. Carr's friends leaped at Bill, but he retreated to a pool table, grabbed a cue stick and flailed away. Three men lay unconscious when the brief battle ended. There was no further trouble with Carr, who later killed a man at Stafford, Nebraska, and became a fugitive. "He's a four-square guy any spot or place, bronco busting, roping or dealing poker," the cow hands said of Thompson when Chicago visitors spoke with them about him.

Despite all the high jinks, Thompson tended to business. He bought yearlings at Kansas City or Omaha and shipped them to the 3,800-acre ranch, fattening them on Nebraska grass and corn for sale in Omaha, Sioux City and Chicago. He bought well-bred Herefords to improve his herds. He made improvements in the bunkhouses and swelled the yield from the hay and corn fields. At the end of three years, his books showed a total profit of $30,000.

5

This joyous phase of Thompson's life ended abruptly in November 1891, when his father died of pneumonia. Bill was still in cowboy dress when he hurried back to Chicago where Colonel Thompson lay in state at the family mansion. He had just time enough to be fitted for a suit of black at Nicoll's, the fashionable tailor at Clark and Adams streets.

At the funeral service young Thompson learned how respected a man his father had been in the community. Men in uniform from the Union Veterans Club, the Ulysses S. Grant Post of the Grand Army of the Republic, the Knights Templar and the Farragut Association of the United States Navy marched in the funeral procession. Unity Church was banked with flowers from dozens of organizations. Staring at the casket covered with a blanket of roses surmounted by a snowy dove, Bill heard the church's pastor, Dr. John Milsted, offer a prayer and the Reverend Dr. William Thomas praise his father "as one of the builders of Chicago and one of Chicago's finest citizens."

As the services ended, Bill also heard his mother put an end to his carefree life out West. Although Colonel Thompson had left her well provided, with over $2,000,000 in real estate, and the Madison Block was being well managed by his former bookkeeper, Frank E. Locke, Medora Thompson sobbed and clung to her son's arm. "You can't go back out there again," she said tearfully. "You're the oldest, and your father expected you to carry on. He was so proud of you."

Unsmiling and depressed, dismayed at the new responsibility of handling his father's vast interests, Big Bill pressed his mother's hand in his. By the time the cortege started down the street between crowds of friends and the curious, he gave her his promise to remain in Chicago.

3 ||| An Athlete Clean and Pure

I

BILL THOMPSON YEARNED FOR SOME-
thing to fill his days with the excitement he had known on his
ranch. Dutifully he devoted himself to his father's business affairs.
But Locke and the office staff had these so well in hand that there
was little for him to do but collect his weekly salary. His mother
thought she knew the answer: marriage. True enough, mused
Medora Thompson, Bill still retained those frightful habits he had
acquired out West. He talked too loud. He rolled his own cigarettes. He sometimes cursed. He was awkward in the company
of young women; when he went riding with her on Sundays in
their rakish new Studebaker buggy in Lincoln Park he blushed
furiously whenever she paused to talk with some society girl in
an adjoining cart. But, still, he was twenty-four, robust, handsome
despite a slightly crooked front tooth, wealthy, a real catch for
the right girl. In time, when the mourning period was over and
she could entertain, she would have to speak to Bill about finding
a nice girl from a nice family to settle down with.

In this restless period Bill sought the company of the Pike brothers. They were rich, too, and lived in a fine home on Prairie Avenue, street of the millionaires. The Pikes, Willie and Gene, were
gay fellows now. They were steady patrons of the Levee, the
world-famous district of brothels and taverns, and they invited
Bill to come with them. One of their favorite haunts was Frank
Wing's establishment, where they took Bill for oyster suppers and

28

musical entertainment by the talented girls of the house. Even with these girls and their free and easy ways, Thompson was not at ease. Often, instead of going with one of them to an upstairs room, he sat and talked about his life on the ranch or told stories of wild nights in Cheyenne or Ewing, or gorged himself on delicacies prepared by Wing's Chinese chefs.

Through Gene Pike, however, Bill did plunge into other activities which helped him forget some of the yearnings for the Nebraska ranch. Pike, a Yale graduate, was one of the outstanding members of the Chicago Athletic Club and he persuaded Thompson to join. Bill's athletic endeavors since his return had consisted, besides regular horseback rides in Lincoln Park, of occasional games with the Marquette indoor baseball team to which his sister's fiancé, William Pelouze, belonged. He readily joined with Pike, who introduced him to the club's water-polo coach, John Robinson.

"Ever do any swimming?" Robinson asked.

"Used to, but not lately. Not much water in Goose Lake."

"Well, get into the pool and see how you do in water polo."

Thompson had never played this rough game. But he quickly saw what was wanted, and he swam with strong, sure strokes. His attack was furious, his competitive spirit keen. In the third quarter he struck Bert Alvord, the team captain, while diving for the ball, and Alvord sank to the bottom of the pool. He was dragged out and revived and insisted on shaking hands with Thompson. "You're a wonder! We want you on the team." He looked Thompson over. "And I'm captain of football! We want you on that too."

2

Bill Thompson now began an amazing career as an all-star athlete. The Chicago Athletic Club competed not only with other private clubs but also with teams from Harvard, Princeton, Yale and leading Midwestern colleges. Most of the C.A.A. athletes had been stars in college, but Thompson, learning their games for the first time, was the equal of any and better than most.

Within a year he was captain of the water-polo team and led it to victories over Yale, Harvard, Princeton, and the Boston and

New York athletic clubs. One year his team won its way into the finals of the national water-polo championships against the New York Athletic Club, the titleholder. Out to eliminate Thompson early in the contest, W. E. Dickey, New York's star, crashed into Bill. "Thompson's blood crimsoned the water," reported the *Cherry Circle*, the C.A.A.'s magazine. "Then out went his fist, square on Dickey's nose. There were cries of foul, but the referee, who witnessed Dickey's offense and its punishment, smiled and said, 'Play on!'" Although Chicago lost the match, Thompson returned to his city a hero. "Fighting Bill" the club members called him, and others, casting their eyes over his well-built six feet and great reach, took to calling him "Big Bill."

He soon proved himself adept in other sports. He was a star at baseball, won the club handball championship, acquired several swimming and diving trophies, and even became skilled in aerial trapeze exhibitions. But it was as a football player that he won his greatest athletic fame.

In 1894 he was the C.A.A.'s left tackle, called by the *Cherry Circle* the club's strongest player. In that year the C.A.A. defeated Princeton and Dartmouth and lost to Yale and Harvard in rough games. By 1896 he was captain of the team, determined to have a national championship. He hired Fred Stone as trainer and assembled a squad of former college stars, including Laurie Heyworth of Yale, W. H. Aldrich of Purdue, H. G. Hadden of Michigan, E. B. Camp of Pennsylvania and Ralph Hoogland of Princeton.

Acting not only as captain but as coach, strategist and manager, Thompson led the team to victory after victory. By the week of Thanksgiving the Cherry Circle players were hailed as champions of Western athletic clubs. On Thanksgiving Day they were scheduled to play Boston Athletic Club for the national championship. But on the night before the game Thompson was confronted with a near-disastrous problem. Some member had turned in a report that another member had been providing free meals for six of the C.A.A. players, a boon strictly forbidden by the Amateur Athletic Union.

"Fellows," said Bill hoarsely to his fellow C.A.A. directors,

Big Bill the Cowboy (left) in his young days out west, with two visitors from Chicago.

Big Bill the All-American Boy, when he was captain of the
Chicago Athletic Association football team.

"there's only one thing to do. We want the championship, but we've got to expel those men."

On the morning of the game the *Tribune* commented: "Thompson says the Chicago Athletic Club has taken a stand before the world for clean football." Thompson's sacrifice was more than offset by the rest of the team. Big Bill himself made the first touchdown before a crowd that cheered him in a downpour. Early in the second half, Phil Draper, assistant captain, added another. That night, with Boston defeated without a point, Thompson was toasted and hailed at a victory banquet. "Captain William Hale Thompson has done more for the Chicago Athletic Association than most of our members realize!" cried Lincoln Placand, a C.A.A. official. "It was not only the great victory of defeating Boston, or of letting out the players who might have caused him to blush for pure amateurism, of which he is the leading disciple. It was the patriotism that he instilled in each player for the C.A.A.! They felt as he did!" From Henry Russell, the Boston captain, came another tribute: "Bill Thompson was born in Boston, and we never should have permitted him to get away! We salute a great team and a great captain!"

Bill Thompson was truly an athletic hero. Chicago youths flocked to the C.A.A. to watch him work out with the water-polo team. At victory dinners he was toasted with clear water as the purest exponent of purest sportsmanship. Elected vice-president of the C.A.A. and chairman of its athletic committee, he staged sports benefits, sports festivals, directed a sports carnival for the *Inter-Ocean*, and with his sister, now married to Pelouze, arranged a series of benefit football games with Eastern college teams. He ran the banquets and parties of the C.A.A. with a showman's flair; at one, a Wild West night, he and Gene Pike acted the parts of bunco steerers and raised $1,100 for charity. He organized, directed and announced boxing tournaments, played on all the teams, vanquished all handball opponents, and even won the club billiards championship by defeating his brother Gale and John Drake, owner of the Grand Pacific Hotel.

By 1897 he was an important man in national athletics. When

he was elected a vice-president of the Amateur Athletic Union, the *Evening Post* predicted his nomination as the American candidate for director of athletic events at the Paris Exposition in 1900.

3

Busy with athletics, Bill had little time to worry about politics, although Gene Pike was talking of running for alderman of their Second Ward, or city affairs, although some of his other high-toned friends were joining the Civic Federation, the organization devoted to fighting grafters and thieves in public officialdom. He rarely went to his real-estate office, and when he did he spent as much time chatting with Locke's attractive secretary, Mary Walker Wyse, as he did in examining the latest profit sheets.

Thompson now lived with Gene Pike in a bachelor apartment in the Metropole Hotel, not far from the Levee where the two could enjoy a respite from athletic activities. He was glad for Pike when he won his way into the city council, but sorely disappointed for himself when in the spring of 1899 he lost out to Clarence K. Wooster for the presidency of the Chicago Athletic Association. He immediately set out on a long hunting trip to Montana, Washington and Oregon. Most of the summer was spent in the family's summer estate at Oconomowoc, Wisconsin, where he was vice-commodore of the local yacht club, composed of Chicago millionaires, and where he sailed his boat, the *Myrone*.

When Thompson returned to Chicago, Pike told him the Republicans were seeking a reputable candidate for the other aldermanic job in the Second Ward. The city then had two aldermen elected in alternate years in each of the thirty-five wards. "You'd be great," said Pike. "I can take you to the boys who'll put you in. It'll be in the bag. I'll help you campaign."

"Gene," Thompson replied, "I don't ever want to run in another election of any kind. It's all right when you win, but it's not so good when you lose."

But Pike returned to the idea after Thompson had been named captain of the C.A.A. football team again. On a day late that year he turned the talk to politics while he and Thompson and several of their companions sat around a card table in the club.

"I think Bill should run," he told George Jenney, a member. "He'd be great, don't you think?"

"He's scared!" cried Jenney. "He's afraid to run!" Then Jenney pulled out his wallet and pushed a fifty-dollar bill toward Pike. "This money says Bill Thompson is scared!"

Before Pike could speak, Thompson covered the bill with his big palm. "I'll take this one myself," he bellowed. "George Jenney, you've got yourself a bet."

4 ‖ In the Gray Wolves' Lair

I

TO WIN HIS BET, BILL THOMPSON, THE All-American boy and champion of purity in athletics, was about to flex untried muscles in an arena more rugged than the football field or the water-polo tank.

Chicago's Second Ward was now a rich political prize, eyed longingly by those thoughtful appraisers, Michael (Hinky Dink) Kenna and "Bathhouse John" Coughlin, rulers of the infamous First Ward and privy councilors in the political realm of Carter H. Harrison the Younger. In the eight years since these two precious lawmakers had joined forces the Levee district, once on the edge of the city's business section, had moved its brothels, saloons and gambling houses southward into the Second Ward. What had started as a move to catch the business from the World's Columbian Exposition had developed into a migration of vice, and now, in 1900, it spilled over the limits of the First Ward. On Twenty-second Street, Ike Bloom, known as "King of the Brothels," kept his Freiberg's Hall open twenty-four hours a day. It was a hang-out for thieves, whores, pimps, gunmen and small-time politicians who mingled nightly with visiting business and professional men from out of town or respectable neighborhoods in the city itself. Girls met their customers at Freiberg's, took them to the crib houses or cheap hotels surrounding it. Curiously, during the day the hall was often the scene for official political meetings to which came honorable or semi-honorable officials and candidates. To the

34

north, along Wabash Avenue, and on State and Dearborn streets, were long lines of brothels, concert saloons, gambling dens, barrel houses and shady hotels. Westward were even lower dives. Each night the streets were packed with drunks and roisterers who were quickly set upon by pimps and prostitutes and taken to cheap brothels, or by perverts who lured them to rooming houses patronized by male prostitutes. Here were such vicious dens as the Bucket of Blood, Black May's, the Silver Dollar, the House of All Nations, a place simply called Why Not? and scores of others. In Armour Avenue, the notorious madams were Vic Shaw, who also dealt in opium, French Emma, Zoe Millard, Frankie Wright, side by side with the houses of the white slavers, Roy Jones, Harry (Greasy Thumb) Guzik, and Maurice Van Bever, who abducted farm girls and bewildered immigrants from railroad stations and forced them into lives of prostitution. Through the district were scattered saloons, dance halls, panel houses and hotels that offered sanctuary from the police for the country's criminals. Few policemen entered the western sector of the Levee, except on riot calls. But gunmen, bank robbers, thieves and pickpockets were safe there.

Such an area, with so much vice and crime and illegal activity, needed protectors. It had them in Aldermen Kenna and Coughlin, who had maintained their control over this sordid patch through pro-consuls ever since the district had moved southward. Now The Bath and The Hink wanted urgently to annex this new and immensely richer and more wicked Levee to their original domain.

In this year of Big Bill Thompson's entry into politics, the time seemed propitious for just such a coup. Notorious for years as the grayest of those aldermanic grafters known as the Gray Wolves, Hinky Dink and Bathhouse John had recently redeemed themselves and risen high in the affections of Mayor Harrison by aiding him in a showdown fight with the traction baron, Charles Tyson Yerkes. They had cast the deciding votes which prevented Yerkes from obtaining a long-term streetcar franchise at terms unfavorable to the city. Harrison's victory had saved the citizens about $46,-000,000. It also established his supremacy over a band of West Side Democrats led by Roger Sullivan, Harrison's chief rival for party power. In his jubilant gratitude Harrison called Kenna and Coughlin his "Rocks of Gibraltar" and even hailed them as reformers. But Bathhouse and Hinky Dink wanted more tangible compensation. They would be satisfied with nothing less than the new Levee.

There was a major difficulty. In 1896 the normally Republican Second Ward had elected a Democratic alderman, Charles F. Gunther, a fierce old veteran of the Confederate Navy. A respected businessman who had made a fortune as a candy manufacturer, Gunther had transported the Confederates' Libby Prison stone by stone to Chicago and reconstructed it as a museum filled with Civil War relics. Gunther's reform ideas annoyed the City Hall boodlers and even irked Harrison from time to time, but in the battle with Yerkes and the Sullivan crowd his loyalty to Harrison matched that of Coughlin and Kenna. They could hardly hope to snatch a portion of the Second Ward from a fellow Democrat and strong Harrison supporter. But if the Second Ward should choose another Republican to sit beside Alderman Gene Pike . . .

2

The Second Ward's respectable citizens normally cared little about aldermanic elections. Both the aldermen and the Levee were considered necessary evils, to be ignored as much as possible. These people lived in the silk-stocking precincts, on such tree-lined thoroughfares as Prairie Avenue, "the street of the sifted few," and Grand Boulevard, graced by splendid homes, parkways and churches. This eastern section of the Second Ward was a region of comfortable homes, fine trees, bewhiskered businessmen driven to their offices and stores by liveried coachmen, bustling matrons and handsome children. The Silk Stockings, as the others in the district derisively termed them, lived blocks and worlds apart from those in the western sector, that territory of tenements, slums, factories and warehouses, and the new Levee, screened from the Silk Stockings by a façade of splendid hotels and apartment houses on Michigan Avenue.

Ordinarily the Silk Stockings would have paid but little heed to the aldermanic election of 1900. But on the night of February 1 their attention was drawn forcibly to the Levee. On that raw evening Ada and Minna Everleigh opened their sumptuous Everleigh Club in a refurbished mansion at 2131-2133 South Dearborn Street. It was the most elegant and costly brothel in the world, and typified the daring gaudiness of the Levee. Prices began at fifty dollars, and champagne was twenty dollars a bottle, although money was not mentioned until a guest was ready to depart. The furnishings were magnificent, the cuisine was superb, the girls were the most comely and most gracious ever collected in a house of that kind. Customers were welcomed by the Everleigh sisters themselves. Negro servants accepted their wraps and escorted the guests to the card rooms or the ballroom, where women in evening gowns awaited them and a band played lively tunes. The ballroom was a shimmer of gold leaf and dazzling parquet floors under the glittering chandeliers. Even the grand piano was leafed with gold, and the cuspidors, discreetly hidden by long velvet draperies that framed exotic murals, were gold-plated. Upstairs were gold, silver and copper rooms, ornately decorated in those metals, designed to intrigue any owners of gold, silver and copper mines who happened in. There were also a Persian room, a college room, a Pullman room fitted as a private railway car, a mirrored room covered from floor to ceiling and wall to wall with silvered glass. There were lace-frilly rooms and plain rooms.

This Everleigh Club presented a challenge which the Silk Stockings of the Second Ward could not ignore. Women could not yet vote, but they were free to complain to their husbands of the evil conditions so near to their homes. Often they had endured insults from drunks and hoodlums of the Levee who dared to invade Michigan Avenue and even swaggered insolently along Prairie Avenue or Grand Boulevard. Besides, businessmen of the ward were growing tired of being terrorized by Levee bums. No one thought or suggested that the segregated district be wiped out, but there were many who felt that the excesses should be curbed. The ostentatious grandeur of this newest brothel must not be tol-

erated, said these indignant ones, and the Levee denizens must be
kept within their territory.

3

A cry for reform rang in the Second Ward. As if in answer,
Bill Thompson announced his candidacy for alderman on the day
after the opening of the Everleigh Club. George Gibbs, the ward's
Republican committeeman, scheduled the nominating convention
for February 17 in Freiberg's Hall, and the newspapers, calling
attention to Thompson's fine record as a sportsman and real-estate
executive, concluded he would win the party nomination with no
trouble.

Thompson's announcement gladdened the evil hearts of Bathhouse John Coughlin and Hinky Dink Kenna. With a Republican
victor, their hopes for passage of a redistricting ordinance to give
them the new Levee would be bright. At the First Ward ball on the
night of February 14, they were gay. Coughlin, in his famous suit
of billiard-cloth green, and Hinky Dink, smartly dressed in a silk
evening suit, strolled from box to box, informing the assembled
brothel madams, panderers and saloonkeepers that they did not
expect Alderman Gunther to be re-elected.

When Gunther heard the news, he demanded that Harrison
help him in his campaign. Harrison promised to make speeches,
although he could not promise to control Kenna and Coughlin,
nor to order police action against the Levee. Harrison was often
called a reformer; he was also a political realist, smart and intelligent and as handsome as a matinee idol. He once remarked that
he ruled a mob of rowdies by playing one against the other. Chicago's thirty-five wards were really thirty-five feudal fiefs, some
controlled by aldermen, some by committeemen of both parties,
some by known criminals, a few by men of great respectability.
These ward bosses made their own alliances, waged political wars,
and exacted tribute. A mayor could rule only by maintaining strong
alliances. Kenna and Coughlin had provided Harrison with his margin of victory over Roger Sullivan and Yerkes. He could not afford
now to lose them in any effort to save Gunther.

In a desperate bid for attention and the good will of the Republican Silk Stockings, Gunther announced on February 16 that he was giving his famous Civil War collection to the city. The Garfield Park Board, controlled by Democrats, promptly voted $100,000 to erect a building to house the collection.* On the day of this offer, hailed with gusto by the newspapers, Bill Thompson, awaiting the ward's nominating convention, was dealt a blow that was recorded on the front pages alongside the news of Gunther's gift. Thompson and nineteen other athletes of the Chicago Athletic Association, stated an announcement of the Amateur Athletic Union, were suspended for professionalism. This climaxed a long feud that started when Thompson's enemies in the C.A.A. demanded the ouster of various members of the prize football team for failure to pay dues. The athletes had countered with the claim they had been promised by Thompson and Frank Wentworth, the club's athletic director, that they would not have to pay because they were brought in to play football. Wentworth proferred a long public explanation, denying irregularities, but Thompson dismissed the furor, saying, "The matter is entirely too small to worry about."

Under these conditions, the Republicans filed into Freiberg's Hall on February 17. They were virtually committed to an athlete who had been publicly disgraced the day before, and here they were meeting in one of the lowest dives on the Levee. The crowd was small and unenthusiastic, the proceedings were brief.

After introductory remarks by James B. Bradwell, a former judge, a Major J. J. Healy nominated Thompson for alderman. Committeeman Gibbs and Alderman Pike made short seconding speeches. Then Thompson arose and grinned at his friends. "Fellows," he said, "pay no attention to that stuff you read in the papers. There's nothing to it but a political trick. I aim to be a first-class representative of this fine ward. What the Second Ward needs is decent streets and enough lights at night to protect the citizens from holdup men. I want to pledge myself to work for better condition of the streets. It is time the aldermen of this ward pay some attention to the demands of those who employ them!"

---

* The building never was constructed. A few of Gunther's relics ultimately were given to the Chicago Historical Society.

Gene Pike blushed at this sally. Then he burst into laughter. "See!" he cried. "Bill Thompson calls them the way he sees them! Let's win with Big Bill!"

By acclamation Thompson was nominated. Ike Bloom's flimsily clad waitresses burst into the meeting room, looking for customers. "All the drinks are on Bill Thompson!" cried Pike. Everyone noted happily that Bill Thompson set up twenty-cent whisky, not the usual five-cent beer or ten-cent rotgut other candidates offered.

4

Although this was not a year for electing a mayor, Harrison bore much of the attack on Democratic candidates for the city council. The Municipal Voters' League, organized to drive Gray Wolves from the City Hall, professed high hopes for success. Margaret Haley, fiery spokesman for the reformers and the schoolteachers, went from ward to ward denouncing the iniquities of the Harrison administration. The newspapers excoriated "Harrison's Gang," led by Bathhouse John and Hinky Dink. To show how wicked Chicago was under Harrison's rule, statistics were quoted: 6,400 saloons, 2,000 gambling houses, 900 brothels, and only 3,325 policemen for the 1,700,000 inhabitants. The Commercial Club turned its annual banquet at the Auditorium Hotel into a hymn of hate for Harrison. Its indignant officers charged there was no law enforcement, that gambling, vice and crime flourished, that city business was paralyzed by graft, that politicians were growing rich on ill-gotten money, that Chicago was "a sinkhole of iniquity."

"The Commercial Club millionaires," Harrison replied, "cannot worry me. Any man who thinks I will pay any attention to what is said by anyone in that organization is wasting his time. I'll take my criticism from the people, but not from men who made their millions out of franchises for which they paid the city nothing. The so-called reformers are mostly millionaires who loot the people while they criticize me."

In the Second Ward, Gunther was in distress. He had always gained a measure of support from the Silk Stockings, but now he sensed their hostility. They normally distrusted Democrats, and they considered Bill Thompson one of their own kind. While Gunther lost ground in the wealthy precincts, Bill Thompson vigorously and expensively canvassed the saloon precincts. He went from place to place, buying twenty-cent drinks, shaking hands, slapping backs. He made no speeches, but he visited every one of the 270 saloons in the ward. "I'm spending $175 a day," he told his C.A.A. cronies. "I've worn out two pairs of shoes, and I've gained fourteen pounds. Fellows, politics is really the life!"

Finally Harrison came to Gunther's aid several days before the election. His rotund helper, Robert Emmett Burke, organized a mass meeting and Harrison spoke. Predicting Gunther's re-election, Harrison lashed Bill Thompson with choice scorn. "Tell Willie Boy to go home and play for another ten years," he said. "Then maybe he can come back among men. Why, if anyone was foolish enough to elect him, the first thing Willie Boy would want to do is pass a law against the sale of cigarettes! He'd be just like Alderman 'Deah Boy' Gene Pike. Pike claims he cleaned up this ward. . . . Are you going to send Willie Boy Thompson to the council? Why, if you went down to visit him or Gene Pike you'd have to send in your card by a valet on a silver salver and then wait until they were through chewing gum! We can stand two Willie Boys in the council, but for heaven's sake don't send me a third! Just think of the ordinances they'd pass. 'No real Willie Boy can wear a silk hat and a sack coat at the same time! No dress suit at five-o'clock pink teas! Consider the proprieties!' Why, they'd organize a Willie Boy Union in the council. They would probably pass a resolution that Bathhouse John be excluded because the regulation color is black and white and he wears a green dress suit!"

The speech boomeranged. The Silk Stockings bristled and redoubled their efforts. William Kent, president of the Municipal Voters' League, which had endorsed neither Thompson nor Gunther, now warned the Second Ward that it would have to fight the pressures of the City Hall crowd. The businessmen of the ward announced they were closing their stores to man the polls for Thompson on election day. To Thompson's advantage, Bathhouse

John and Kenna refused to help Gunther, although in the past they were not averse to dispatching hordes of sluggers, chain voters and vote thieves into other wards to aid worthy associates.

On the morning of election day fine carriages rolled up to the Silk Stocking polling places. The businessmen closed their shops as they had promised. And in one of the ward's quietest elections, Willie Boy collected 2,516 votes to 2,113 for Gunther. In the city itself, twenty-two candidates with the M.V.L. endorsement were elected in the thirty-five wards, and Bill Thompson, adjudged a reform candidate, was counted with this number. "I rejoice in the result," exulted George E. (Buzzsaw) Cole, the M.V.L.'s peppery founder. "We can now start a cleanup!"

5

Buzzsaw Cole was too optimistic. Although the M.V.L. had campaigned for a nonpartisan council and had pledged its candidates to vote on nonpartisan principles, the forty-two Republicans announced they intended to organize on strict party lines. It was a declaration of war that forced the twenty-eight feuding Democrats to make peace among themselves. Once again Coughlin and Kenna ran with the Gray Wolves, joined from time to time by several of the nineteen Republicans whom the M.V.L. had not supported and who shuddered at the idea of being thought reformers. Hinky Dink and Bathhouse saw the prospects for their annexation of the lucrative section of the Second Ward grow brighter.

They were encouraged in this devious venture by the fact that Alderman William Hale Thompson, having won his fifty-dollar bet and the election, took only a moderate interest in city government affairs. He was not even present when the Republican caucus leaders appointed him to serve on committees on gas, oil and electric lights, the City Hall, the police stations and the Bridewell city jail. During the summer he spent most of his time on his boats and rarely attended council meetings. He introduced one measure which brought him general commendation. It provided $1,200 to build a playground at Wabash Avenue and Twenty-fourth Street, in the heart of the Negro section. It was the city's first public playground.

From the beginning little Hinky Dink Kenna flattered the new alderman with his attentions. He pretended to ask his advice on weighty matters and often was seen conferring with the flushed young man in a corner of the council chambers. Such parleys disturbed Alderman Charles Alling of the Third Ward, a reform leader, and also caught the attention of the *Tribune:* "It is known that Alderman Kenna favors a redistrict ordinance that will extend the boundaries of the First Ward south into the Second Ward. It is said that Alderman Thompson of the Second Ward will join Kenna in such a scheme."

Alderman Thomas Carey, ordinarily a silent man, was preparing such an ordinance, but Alling told his fellow reformers that the proposal would benefit the Gray Wolves and warned them to make a fight against it. Alling's chance came on the snowy night of December 11. When "Gray Tom" Carey arose and presented his ordinance redefining the city's ward boundaries, extending, among others, the First Ward far enough into the Second to include the flourishing Levee in the Coughlin-Kenna domain, Alling was on his feet.

"Everyone knows that the population of Chicago is disproportionate," he declared. "Everyone knows that redistricting is needed. But this measure is designed to keep all the Democrats in the old wards while it forces the Republicans to run in new wards. The aim of this ordinance is to give control of the city back to the boodlers."

Others in the reform group took up the cry, but not a word came from either Alderman Thompson or Alderman Pike. Mayor Harrison ordered a roll call. He grinned widely at Hinky Dink as Pike and Thompson, first of the "reform" Republicans to be called, voted "Aye." The roll went on and the final tally showed the measure had passed, 43 to 23.

6

There was uproar the next day. "This is a retrogression to the disgraceful days of half a decade ago, when this device was successfully employed in behalf of boodle ordinances," said the *Tribune.* And the *News:* "By their votes on this disgraceful measure, Aldermen Pike and Thompson have prevented their re-election to the council. This is small comfort for the defeat good government has suffered." The *Journal:* "The Gray Wolves rule again. They have eaten the sheep who wore the clothing of reformers!"

Harrison delayed signing the measure until Tom Carey could offer an amendment on December 21. Originally, Coughlin and Kenna had asked only for that part of the Second Ward extending to Twenty-second Street. Now they asked for an additional bit of territory extending south to Thirty-first Street. They got it, with Thompson and Pike again voting "Aye."

So far as Pike and Thompson were concerned, the new ordinance had gerrymandered them out of the Second Ward into the First, for the Metropole Hotel was now in the Coughlin-Kenna ward. Alling, too, suffered, for he was shifted to the Second Ward where, except for those in his immediate neighborhood, he would deal with a new constituency.

Harrison was pleased. With a single blow three irksome aldermen had been felled. "The chief feature of this ordinance is the way it has split up the Willie Boys," he gloated. "It has set Alling, Pike and Thompson fighting among themselves, and it looks as if they'll keep it up."

The Second Ward's businessmen raged. Summoning Thompson and Pike to a mass meeting, they shouted, "Why? Why? Why?" How could these two, they demanded to know, have voted twice for an ordinance that would deny them re-election? "Why did you hand over the business section to Kenna and Coughlin?"

Pike failed to make an explanation, but Thompson, obviously befuddled and embarrassed, offered confused answers. "This nefarious ordinance is designed to keep gangsters in office," he admitted freely to the astounded businessmen. Then why had he voted for it? "We wanted to separate the bad and good parts of the ward," mumbled Bill. "Since we couldn't get adequate police protection in the Levee, we wanted to get the Levee out of the Second Ward. We didn't realize the ordinance would carry all the way to Thirty-first Street!"

As the newspapers howled their derision, Pike and Thompson realized how the wily First Ward aldermen had tricked them. Pike made a superfluous announcement that he would not be a candidate in the spring. But Thompson, growing angrier as his humiliation piled higher, promised to fight. "I'm going to be a candidate for alderman from the First Ward when my present term ends," he threatened. "I'm going out to beat Bathhouse Coughlin. There are men with money who will back me up." To this rash threat, the *News* offered wry comment: "Alderman Thompson's threats are taken lightly in the First Ward. It is pointed out that a man cannot commit political suicide twice."

5 ‖ The "Blond Boss"

THE REMAINDER OF BIG BILL'S ALDER-
manic service was remarkably unimpressive. As the council's only
star athlete, he felt obliged to introduce an ordinance to legalize
boxing bouts, but it was soundly defeated. He was often absent
from the council chamber when important legislation was in the
making and, to the disappointment of the Silk Stockings, he sat
idly by when the boodlers pushed through one infamous ordinance
after another.

The second year of his term was notable not for what he did in
the council but for what happened outside. In athletics, he captained the C.A.A.'s water-polo team to a national championship
and built a thirty-five-foot sloop, the *Yankee*, with which he intended to defend the Royal Canadian Yacht Club trophy won the
summer before in races at Toronto. And he took time to fall in
love. The girl was Mary Walker Wyse, the attractive and efficient
young secretary in his real-estate office. Her friends called her
Maysie. She came from a modest Louisville family and lived at
the southern end of Prairie Avenue, far from the stretch of expensive
homes. Bill's mother, furious at his attentions to Maysie, refused
to announce their engagement or to discuss wedding plans, but Bill
took Maysie to St. Joseph, Michigan, on December 7, 1901, and
they were married by the Reverend H. A. Decker in the Evangelical
Lutheran Church.

Because he wished to keep his marriage a secret, Bill returned to his bachelor apartment in the Metropole Hotel and Maysie to her home. But two weeks later, while the newlyweds packed their bags for a honeymoon in Louisville, the newspapers disclosed the marriage. Cornered as he was leaving, Bill growled, "It has been a great deal of trouble to us to have this announcement made before we planned it. We have been keeping the secret because of my mother's illness."

Politically, as his term drew to an end, he was still talked of as a candidate to run against Bathhouse John Coughlin. Even the *News* showed some enthusiasm: "William Hale Thompson is the only possible opponent who can give Bathhouse John a fight. He is one of the few men who can make votes in the silk-stocking residential district or the slums. He hobnobs with the millionaires who live in the southeastern corner of the new First Ward and he can go into the lodginghouse district and make friends at the rate of a score a minute."

When he and Maysie returned from a honeymoon that extended into Florida, he still had enough friends in the First Ward to be elected chairman of the district's Republican delegation to the Cook County convention in the spring of 1902. One of his new friends was John M. Smyth, the West Side furniture dealer who headed the party's central committee. And one night in Mickey Conlon's saloon on West Madison Street, Smyth introduced Bill to a big, bluff man with bright blue eyes, Congressman William Lorimer, the "Blond Boss" of Republican politics in Illinois.

2

Unlike Thompson, Billy Lorimer had risen in politics the hard way. Born the son of a minister in Manchester, England, he was brought to Chicago by his parents when he was five years old. When his father died seven years later he was forced to quit school. He worked at many jobs—as a newsboy, a bootblack, a painter's helper, a department-store cash boy. After five years in the stockyards, he became a conductor on the Madison Street horsecars. Here he received his first experience in political organizing by helping to form the Street Car Men's Benevolent Association. While he was still in his twenties, he gathered other young men about him in the kitchen of his mother's home and formed the Sixth Ward Young Men's Republican Club.

Lorimer's eager industry commended him to the Republican political bosses. Shortly after he opened a real-estate office, he was appointed superintendent of the city's water main extension division by Mayor John A. Roche. He set up a teaming company and quickly got a contract with the city to supply horse teams for construction projects in the water-main department. He also organized a brick manufacturing company and a contracting firm, both of which prospered through ready contracts from the city.

Unlike other men who worked more efficiently behind the scenes, Lorimer yearned for public office. He made alliances with downstate politicians, devised party strategy, built—most important of all—a network of allegiance in the West Side wards through Christmas donations, political favors, loans to the needy and advice on election days about which were the right men to vote for. Defeated in 1892 for clerk of the Superior Court, he ran successfully for Congress two years later, and went to Washington.

Now there appeared signs of revolt in his organization, and he was back to re-establish his supremacy in Cook County before dealing with insurgents in the rest of Illinois. He was most dangerous when he was hardest pressed. Slow-moving, patient, tricky, he neither smoked nor drank nor swore. Except for a decisive manner in issuing orders, he spoke softly and with kindly calm. Big and dark-blond, he could assume a childlike innocence, with compassionate, drooping eyelids that deceived his foes. "Lorimer," the *Tribune* once stated, "maintains the same placid, benign attitude through praise and abuse. He endures all and bides his time, always observing the doctrine of nonresistance. Then gently and blandly he gets his way."

In Thompson's eyes Billy Lorimer was a demigod. He listened eagerly as the Blond Boss told him, "We need men like you in the party, Bill. We need men of good connections." Lorimer discouraged Thompson from running against Coughlin in the 1902 aldermanic election. "Don't waste your efforts. No one's going to beat Bathhouse. I'll tell you, though. You turn your ward delegates over to me and I'll put you up for county commissioner. That way you can run where there are some Republican votes. Tie to me, Bill."

3

Although Lorimer had little trouble slating Thompson for the county board on the party ticket in May, he was in a desperate situation.

This was a bad year for Republicans in Cook County, for Democrats controlled the county patronage. Lorimer depended in the campaign for his own re-election, and that of the others on his ticket, on state and federal jobs. But the state patronage to be fed to precinct workers was menaced now by the downstate rebellion of Governor Richard Yates against Lorimer. Yates was determined to unseat the Blond Boss from power. Put into office by Lorimer, Yates was threatening to create his own political machine in an alliance with an upstart in Kankakee named Len Small, who had the downstater's customary suspicion of the big-city politicians. William (Billy) Mason, candidate for the United States Senate, was threatening to bolt the Republicans and run as an independent. And an unknown named Allan C. Durburow emerged from obscurity to declare his candidacy against Lorimer in the Sixth District.

There was real danger that Lorimer's ticket could be defeated, that he would lose his own campaign for his Congressional seat, that his political dictatorship would fall. In this situation, Lorimer received some startling but sound counsel from one of his followers, a bucktoothed man in black coat and black string tie. He was Fred Lundin, a smooth-talking fellow who had made money selling patent medicines and professed a humble but deep love for politics. Lundin's advice consisted of three words: "Get a tent!"

"A tent?"

"Yep, a tent. Give them a show, forget about the issues. Give them a good time and you get the votes."

Lorimer got a tent. All through Cook County his tent show traveled, and the citizens piled in. The rabble-rousing meetings under canvas combined the theatrics of a Barnum circus and a revival meeting. The crowds loved every minute of every meeting, and they applauded a new star political performer named William Hale Thompson.

Bill learned political oratory as quickly as he had learned football and water polo. He seemed to be able to sense and exploit the temper of a crowd in a few seconds. His voice was big and bellowing, but he was often too serious. To correct this defect, James Pugh, a pugnacious Welshman associated with Lorimer and Lundin, devised an effective technique. Whenever Thompson appeared on a platform, Pugh, in the front row of spectators, held a brick in his hand and a slab at his feet. At strategic intervals, Pugh struck the slab with the brick, a signal to Thompson to smile. After a few false starts the method was successful. Before the campaign ended, Thompson's delivery was smooth and he and Pugh were good friends.

Once the campaign increased in intensity, Thompson needed no help from Pugh or anyone else. Still furious at the humiliation Coughlin and Kenna had caused him, he lashed out steadily at the Democrats. "We've got crooks in the City Hall because we haven't got the guts to throw them out! Let's start now by throwing them out in the county. Vote Republican this fall. Put Bill Thompson on the county board and I'll show you clean, liberal government!"

Through an interesting coincidence Bill Thompson was able to challenge not only his immediate rivals, but those traditional enemies of his clan, "the Britishers." Chicago's newspapers were then reporting fully the observations of John Foster Fraser, a British journalist, on his visit to the city. In his home paper, the Yorkshire *Post*, Fraser wrote of the brothels he had seen, the gamblers, police veniality and brutality, corruption, bribery and graft. For good measure he also accused Chicago businessmen of overworking and underpaying shopgirls and of failing to clean the streets regularly. "For goodness' sake, don't take Chicago as a typical American city," Fraser warned his British readers. "Take Denver, or Cincinnati, or St. Louis, but don't take that vulgar city, Chicago, which by day is all feverish making money and by night is riotous debauchery!' "

Fraser said less than Thompson was shouting in the Lorimer tent and he said it more discreetly, but Bill's patriotism was conveniently outraged. At each tent rally in the campaign's last two weeks, he gave a two-part speech. First he raked Coughlin, Kenna and Harrison, charging to them more villainy and corruption than Fraser had. Then he took out after Fraser, who "maligned the fair name of our beloved city." He railed against the foreigner who had dared criticize Chicago. He confided to his listeners that he had met Britishers on the Western range: "They were all seedy and untrustworthy! . . . If he wants to write about Chicago, why doesn't he tell about our factories, our workers, our two million citizens, our wonderful stockyards, our trains?"

Thompson's was the only good show in the campaign. The Irish, Swedes, Germans and Italians of the city flocked into Lorimer's tent to hear Bill Thompson excoriate the Democrats and damn the British. On election day they went to the polls to help Big Bill win. Lorimer barely squeaked through in his own district, winning re-election by a paltry plurality of 413 votes. But Thompson, the young newcomer to county politics, was third highest man on the Republican ticket, only a few hundred votes behind Charles S. Deneen, campaigning for re-election as state's attorney, and Henry G. Foreman, seeking re-election as county board president.

Lorimer was delighted. Thompson's triumph helped him forget his own narrow escape and the defeat of all but six men on his ticket. He spoke to his friends about running Bill Thompson for mayor, a suggestion echoed by the *News*. Bill accepted the tribute modestly. "I have no political ambitions, at least not so far as the mayoralty is concerned. I have been a member of the city council and have just been elected to another office. In my opinion, however, the time is ripe for a Republican victory in the spring. This is a young man's age and if a clean, liberal, bright young man of broad ideas and a desire to give Chicago a business administration is given the nomination in the spring, he can be elected. While I am not a candidate, I am more than anxious to do my part toward supporting and aiding such a man."

4

Only a week later it appeared that Bill Thompson might have difficulty supporting and aiding anyone. On the morning of November 14, 1902, Chicago's newspaper readers were served a juicy bit of scandal. A Mrs. Josephine Moffitt had brought action for separate maintenance against Thompson's friend, William Pike. She claimed she had lived with Pike as his wife, but his defense was that he had met her in Frank Wing's brothel and that her relationship to him was of a professional nature. What was more, said Pike's lawyer, Alfred S. Trude, he would produce other young men who had frequented Wing's with Pike to verify the details.

But when the case came to trial, all the young men fled except one. He was Big Bill Thompson, bringing his ideals of true-blue sportsmanship to the aid of his friend.

In a packed courtroom, the new county commissioner testified that on a day back in 1898 he and some companions had gone to the Levee. First they visited Gladys Forbes's establishment. Thompson called it a restaurant, although police records listed it among the dozens of Levee brothels. Later the gay party went to Frank Wing's, where Willie Pike met Mrs. Moffitt. The meeting led to firmer friendship, and months later he learned, declared Thompson, that Willie and Mrs. Moffitt had set up housekeeping.

"Were there other parties like this?" asked Trude.

"Well, yes. One other time we were celebrating a football win. We were in a restaurant. No ladies were invited, but about midnight they rushed in——"

Women in the audience let loose with mocking laughter. Judge William Gifford threatened to clear the courtroom.

"Then what did these females do?" Trude asked.

"These females, as you call them——" Thompson began. He shifted in his chair. "I really don't know. All the gentlemen went home. They were supposed to."

"Did the gentlemen take the females with them?"

Thompson admitted he had seen Pike get into a carriage with Mrs. Moffitt, and Trude asked, "Were there any manifestations of affection?"

"Yes," replied Thompson. "I was glad to get away. I was disgusted."

Thompson insisted he had left immediately. "All I know is that the girl asked him to go with her. She was no lady."

"Oh," said Judge Gifford. "Up to that time you thought she was?"

"Not necessarily. I was sure she was no lady after that."

"Just what was it that disgusted you?" asked Trude.

"She was encouraging the young man to go home with her. That disgusted me."

"Did you know any of the other young ladies at the party?"

"Aah . . . not well. There was Myrtle Goodrich and Freckled Sal and Sheeny Cora and Baby Jo."

"Was Baby Jo really Mrs. Moffitt?"

"No, she was another one, another lady."

Thompson was dismissed. Trude had won his point. He went on to obtain a ruling that Mrs. Moffitt was not Pike's common-law wife. She was denied her plea for separate maintenance, Judge Gifford ruling, "Mrs. Moffitt's morality is on a par with the defendant's."

5

Hurriedly Bill Thompson left the city after his testimony. He had reasons, he told his associates, beyond his shame at being forced to admit he had patronized Levee brothels. There were his investments in Oregon mines and California timberlands. His Nebraska ranch had to be visited.

He stayed away for nearly two months and when he returned he bought a new house for Maysie on Twenty-first Street off Michigan Avenue. To his surprise, he was warmly welcomed by his fellow county commissioners. The courtroom incident was forgotten except by those who enjoyed their quiet chuckle at the memory of Bill's uncomfortable wriggling in the witness chair. Another who remembered was Billy Lorimer. He liked a man who stood up for his friends, whatever the consequences. "We ought to help that young fellow," he told his cronies.

6 ‖ Seventy-Nine Ballots and Twenty-Two Days

I

THE BLOND BOSS NOW NEEDED ALL
the help he could get, both from sagacious veterans and earnest new-
comers in politics. New rebellions and angry strife stirred his party's
ranks.

For two full decades Lorimer had been the man responsible for
the Republicans' growth to power in the state. More than any
other single leader, he was able to bring together the feuding leaders
in the Chicago wards and downstate Congressional districts for
the periodic struggles with their common foe, the Democrats.
These local leaders, strong and independent, had their own organizations in their districts, and they could usually deliver the vote
for any selected candidate, especially in a party nominating convention or a primary. Most of them were fixers, those middlemen
in government who obtained jobs for the faithful, contracts for
the contributors of campaign funds and their leading supporters,
special favors for constituents who voted as they were told. Any
citizen, of course, was entitled to deal directly with the duly elected
or appointed public officials, but he usually discovered he secured
quicker results through his local political boss as long as he repaid
the boon with his vote.

Some party princelings, few in number, exercised their powers
in the public interest. Many others shared in graft, protected vice
and gambling in their bailiwicks, suspended the laws when their
favorites were in trouble, and bossed the elected officials. To con-

trol a state and tap its resources, these local lords needed the organization and leadership Lorimer provided. He could dramatize election issues. He knew where the fattest contracts lay, how the best jobs could be grabbed. He knew the intricacies of bipartisan arrangements with the Democrats that enabled him to salvage jobs and minor privileges in lean years, thereby enabling the local leaders to survive even when they lost an election. He knew when to fight, when to retreat and when to make peace.

Although the Republican chieftains had prospered and risen to high office under Lorimer's guidance, they gradually were discovering that they had surrendered some of their power. Lorimer dictated terms for the patronage and contracts they had won by their united efforts. Worse yet, he insisted on choosing his candidates for public office and making them, if victorious, directly responsible to him. At the behest of his good and true friend, Charles Tyson Yerkes, the Chicago traction magnate, Lorimer had forced through the state legislature a law giving Yerkes the right to seek a ninety-nine-year streetcar franchise in Chicago. When this measure, which aroused the city, was defeated in the city council, some followers of Lorimer who suffered great public abuse in the fiasco complained they had been paid not nearly enough for their votes in Yerkes' behalf.

Lorimer's miserable showing in the 1902 Cook County elections whetted the eagerness of the party rebels to shake him from his seat of power. For a few months they planned and plotted. Their chief aim was to prevent Lorimer from choosing a man to be the party candidate for governor in 1904.

2

Lorimer was prepared to fight his factional foes. Before any other group could name its candidate, Lorimer announced his: Frank O. Lowden, a former teacher of Latin in Minnesota, a lawyer, an experimental farmer in Oregon, Illinois, a colonel in the Spanish-American War, a man without a record in politics. His father-in-law was George Pullman, the rich railroad-car builder, but Lorimer shrugged off any idea that this connection would be unfavorable.

Lowden's only political liability, so far as the professional politicians could see, was his Phi Beta Kappa key.

Lorimer's support of Lowden brought two reactions. One was a renewal of newspaper attacks on the Blond Boss, calling on "honest Republicans" to eliminate him from politics. The other was an open challenge from a strong group of rivals who offered State's Attorney Charles S. Deneen as an opponent for Lowden.

Deneen's candidacy was an ironic climax. Lorimer had shaped Deneen's political life to a point where he could now feel powerful enough to oppose the wishes of the Blond Boss. A stern-visaged man, Deneen had come to Chicago after graduating from McKendree College in downstate Lebanon, where his father, Samuel, was a teacher of Latin and medieval history. Studying law by day and teaching night school in the slum areas of the near West Side, Deneen entered politics through a meeting with J. N. (Doc) Jamieson, a Lorimer lieutenant. Lorimer advised him to settle in the town of Englewood so that when this outlying section would be incorporated into Chicago he would be an old resident and a ward boss. This happened in 1892, the same year Deneen was elected to the state legislature at Lorimer's behest. Lorimer also had helped elect him state's attorney in 1896 and again in 1900. In his two terms Deneen had established a good record as a prosecutor. Not only did he send criminals to jail or the gallows, but he also secured convictions against eleven bankers for fraud. And he collected for himself $243,000, a perfectly legal bonanza since his office then operated on a plan by which a percentage of fees was turned over to him.

Deneen now aligned himself with such North Side wily ones as fat Fred Busse and Edward J. Brundage, smooth politicos, both former Lorimerites. He organized his wards and precincts ably, and in the first skirmish with the Lorimerites won an impressive victory. He was able to force through his slate of candidates at the party's county convention, basing his power on the recent primary in which Lorimer's men had been beaten. When the slate of county commissioners was drawn up, Bill Thompson's name was one of the missing. Lorimer, his mustache drooping, told reporters, "We are shut out, but we are not complaining. We are perfectly satisfied. We know who the Judases are. At the state convention we will nominate our entire slate, from Colonel Lowden on down. The Judases will hang themselves."

3

In thirty days of the sweltering summer of 1904 Bill Thompson learned new lessons in the ways and crossways of politics.

Lorimer and his followers came to the important nominating convention in Springfield with several advantages. Friendly with the "Washington crowd" of Illinois politicians led by Senators Shelby M. Cullom and Albert J. Hopkins, Lorimer still had his hands in the patronage barrel. By promising to shift his delegates to Governor Yates if a deadlock developed, he secured Yates's agreement to appoint Congressman Joseph (Uncle Joe) Cannon, the wily speaker of the House of Representatives, as convention chairman. Lorimer had favors and privileges to trade with downstate bosses. Deneen had the support of the newspapers and public opinion.

Thompson was given the task of directing the showmanship of the Lorimer delegates. On May 12 their train rolled into Springfield and they emerged, five hundred experts in the arts of convention warfare. They formed ranks behind a brass band, and Thompson, wearing a derby hat and a red WIN WITH LOWDEN banner across his massive chest, marched them to the state capitol and there led them in songs and cheers. "That," sniffed the *News*, "is as close as the Lorimer crowd will ever get to the state capitol!"

Soon the Deneen men marched into the city, another five hundred, stomping along in perfect order. They stopped in front of the Leland Hotel where their orators harangued them, some calling Lowden "the machine candidate" and others "the great unknown."

All that morning more politicians and their followers swarmed into Springfield. Besides Deneen, Governor Yates and Lowden, there were other hopefuls, planning to benefit from deals if a deadlock developed; they included Lawrence Y. Sherman, former speaker of the House of Representatives, Attorney General H. J. Hamlin and Congressman Vespasian Warner. Each had his dele-

gates, bands and marchers, and to add to the clamor set up by these
and the supporters of Deneen and Lowden, Governor Yates sent
two bands and a fancy drill team.

As the 1,449 delegates prepared to march to the state arsenal
for the convention's opening, Springfield was jammed with more
than 5,000 additional visitors, shouting, sweating and sticky. All
hotels and rooming houses were filled. Cots were set up in public
buildings, stores and even in bowling alleys and poolrooms. The
walls of the Leland Hotel, headquarters for both the Deneen and
Lowden factions, blazed with political banners and its lobby was
enveloped in clouds of blue cigar smoke. Outside the hotel, where
Thompson sought to marshal his marchers for the parade to the
arsenal, there was nothing but disorder. Yates men swept by
carrying a huge oil painting of the governor and jangling cowbells,
jeering at the Lowden men as they shoved them back to the curb.
Then came the precise Deneen men, wearing derby hats and carrying new brooms. "Sweep Illinois clean with Charles Deneen!"
they yelled.

Finally Lorimer and Doc Jamieson joined Thompson, followed
by men carrying boxes of red carnations which were distributed to
the crowd. Other men came up with placards: LOWDEN FOR GOVER-
NOR! "Put these under your coats!" cried Thompson as the placards were passed to the marchers. "In the hall, when I give the
signal, pull 'em out and holler." The band struck up "There'll
be a Hot Time in the Old Town Tonight!" Tugging at his mustache, Lorimer nodded. "Lowden men! Forward march!" boomed
Big Bill.

4

In the arsenal there was frenzy and pandemonium. Women
in gay colors lined the gallery, shrieking at the sight below. Men
fought for seats, and the place shook with shouts and the music
of the bands and reeked with the smell of cigars, whisky and the
heat of nearly 8,000 persons packed into space for 6,000. The Yates
forces had hung an enormous banner from the girders above, to
be unfurled when Yates was nominated, but a broken rope had

dropped it prematurely. Now men crawled about on the girders to fasten similar banners for their candidates, and four of them drooped above the sweating delegates and the scores of shouting visitors in the galleries.

After an hour of turmoil Joe Cannon banged for order with a gavel cut from a cannon ramrod. "Order! Order!" shrilled Uncle Joe, but he was a long time getting it. His friendship with Lorimer was well known, and the supporters of Deneen, Warner and Sherman jeered him while the Lowden and Yates delegations yelled louder, trying to drown them out. For twenty minutes more this battle of sound persisted. The women in the galleries cheered, screamed, waved their hats and flags and tossed flowers upon the delegates' heads. Whenever the clamor promised to subside, the rival Cook County delegations started it up again.

Quiet was gained for a few moments, but the noise started more fiercely than before when Lorimer and Cullom strode upon the stage arm in arm. With this gesture, Lorimer was serving defiant notice that he had the senator's support in any plan. Cullom was verifying the heated rumors that he had obtained pledges from Yates and Warner to join in a "Stop Deneen!" movement. "No deal!" howled the Deneen delegation. "No deal with Lorimer! Throw him out! Down with Lorimer!"

5

Toward midnight—after a day of nominating speeches, noisy demonstrations and hot and excited mass meetings in the streets— Lorimer met with Lowden in a private Pullman car in the city's railroad yards. With the Blond Boss were Jamieson, Thompson and Graeme Stewart, a rich wholesale grocer interested in Lowden's candidacy. To them Lorimer explained the strategy by which he planned to secure Lowden's nomination. Yates, said he, would remain firm until Deneen was out of the running. Then Len Small of Kankakee would break away from Yates and start the landslide to Lowden. "It's in the bag," said Lorimer confidently.

But he was wrong. On the first ballot on the morning of Friday, May 13, Yates showed surprising strength. A great cry arose from his supporters as the clerk called the totals: Yates, 507⅔ votes; Deneen, 386⅔; Lowden, 354⅔; Hamlin, 121; Sherman, 87; Warner, 45.

Suddenly Yates was the man to beat. Lorimer fought to delay a second ballot, but the delegates clamored for it, and Bill Thompson, standing on a chair to exhort the Lowden forces to shout louder, could not smother their cry. On the second ballot the result was almost the same. Lorimer paled as the Yates men forced a third, then a fourth. Something definitely had gone askew in Lorimer's plans. His deals and schemes were bringing none of the results he had anticipated.

For eight hours in the stifling hall the session went on and on. Yates's forces, eager for the kill, refused to quit. Their opponents dared not lose a vote. Furious maneuverings and trading on the floor failed to bring any change in the tally. On each roll call the demonstrations grew more violent. No one would give or retreat. Someone had managed to hang from the girders the biggest banner of all—for Vespasian Warner—but no one thought it funny as Warner's delegation, smallest of all, cheered this feat. The crowd was evil and angry, unwilling to compromise or quit.

At the end of the day, the balloting showed slight change. Cannon, unable to get order, arbitrarily called for adjournment, angrily threatening to bar all visitors from the next day's proceedings.

6

It was clear the convention was deadlocked, hopelessly and helplessly.

That night bellboys carried liquor, cigars and steaks to conference rooms in the Leland and the St. Nicholas hotels, while Yates's strategists huddled in the statehouse. At a meeting in Lowden's private car, Lorimer predicted a long session. "Small won't come in with us until Yates's vote is reduced," he said. "From now on, every vote is important. We can't make wholesale deals. We'll have to get a delegate at a time, even if we have to kidnap or steal him. Our friends'll try it too." To Thompson he said, "Bill, you have to keep our boys in line. They've got to be here every minute. Don't let them talk to the other fellows if you can stop it. Tell them to be careful of what they eat and drink."

On the next morning delegates brought sandwiches and soda pop along with their whisky. Again the day produced clamor and wild action, but no great changes in the balloting. Someone tore down the Warner banner, and then others climbed to the girders and ripped down all the banners. Fist fights broke out on the floor every five minutes. Women fainted and women shrieked. "Thompson and Lorimer worked like beavers among the delegates," recorded a *Tribune* reporter. But all they were able to accomplish was a switch of Rock Island's twenty-one votes from Yates to Lowden. At the end of the nineteenth ballot, Yates still led with 481, far short of the 752 needed to nominate. Lowden had 420, and Deneen trailed with 383.

Lorimer, later that day, sent Uncle Joe Cannon to Yates to offer him the post of ambassador to Mexico if he would withdraw and turn his delegates over to Lowden. Yates refused, and called in the reporters to inform them of his refusal. "What did you say?" they asked him. "Sacred Jehoshaphat!" he replied. "I expressed indignation!" And Lorimer's efforts to break into the ranks of the lesser candidates met with equal lack of success.

On the convention's eighth day Cannon made a supreme attempt to end the rowdyism. He handed his gavel to little Virginia Maltby of Chicago, who sweetly whacked for order. Springfield ladies went among the delegates passing out candy kisses. Uncle Joe berated the delegates for not behaving like Republicans. They howled him down. It was Friday, May 20. After the fifty-eighth ballot, Cannon shrugged and entertained a motion to adjourn for ten days. It was carried uproariously.

7

In the ten-day interim, the Lowdenites held many parleys in Chicago. Lorimer commanded them to hold firm. Len Small would still make good his pledge to take his Kankakee delegation to Lowden when Yates's forces broke. Colonel Isaac Ellwood, the barbed-wire king from De Kalb, also was wavering. Once these two left Yates, Lorimer predicted, others would join the Lowden band wagon.

Back to Springfield the Lowden men rode in a special train of eight cars. On the steps of the state capitol they had their photographs taken, as they raised their placards: LOWDEN FOREVER! They wrapped Lowden slogans around their derbies, passed out cigars with "Win with Lowden!" on the bands, wore carnations in their lapels, and waved American flags as they strode through the streets.

On the morning of May 31 the convention was called to order. "I want order!" howled Uncle Joe. "Do you want to stay here till the day of doom?"

Lorimer was sure of victory. He had made his deals. He knew where the votes were. His delegates were the noisiest and most confident in the hall. Yet by June 1, after sixty-eight ballots, Yates still led with 465 votes, Lowden had 401 and Deneen 393. In desperation Lorimer demanded that Small take his delegation to Lowden.

Small hesitated. Yates had promised him a place on the ticket as state treasurer. When he told this to Lorimer, the Blond Boss bristled and said, "We'll give you the same thing."

Small pondered longer. He could not afford to make a mistake. He was still a small-time politician, a power only in Kankakee and the surrounding area. He had been a schoolteacher and a court clerk until Governor John Tanner, Lorimer's man, had made him a trustee of the Eastern Illinois Hospital for the Insane. Later he was elected president and used the hospital patronage to build his political machine. He had risked his political future when he joined Yates's rebellion against the big-city politicians. He was in a good position now, for he could make peace with Lorimer on highly favorable terms, and without greatly antagonizing Yates. He also wished to maneuver himself into a position to deal with Deneen, if such a course seemed wise.

When, on June 2, Lowden drew within 121 of the 752 needed

for the nomination, Lorimer again summoned Small. This was the right time to switch, he told the ambitious little man.

"All right," replied Small. "I'll take my delegation to Lowden for one ballot. After that, I can't promise. We'll go for Lowden tomorrow."

8

Very late that night Governor Yates called a meeting in the statehouse. Present were all the other candidates and their advisers —except Lorimer and Lowden. After reviewing the proceedings of the day—mobs charging through the aisles, banners torn from rafters, men's coats ripped, fights and noise—Yates noted that the vote on the seventy-eighth ballot stood exactly as it had been on the seventieth: Yates, 373; Deneen, 355½; Lowden, 631.

"Gentlemen," said Yates, "we've got to do something about that Washington crowd. Today they used their plug-uglies. They'll use more tomorrow. Either Billy Lorimer is going to pick the candidate, or we are. Are you with me?"

Warily, Deneen asked for more details. Yates offered to withdraw and throw his votes to Deneen. He urged Sherman to do likewise, offering to back him for lieutenant governor. "I want a few of my people on the ticket and I want some jobs," he told Deneen.

"What about Len Small?" asked Deneen.

"It's Mr. Small I'm thinking of. He'll take Kankakee County to Lowden for one ballot. And he'll tell his friends in other counties to go for Deneen. But he'll do it only if he gets on the ticket for state treasurer."

"Can you deliver?" asked Deneen.

"I can deliver. I'll go before the convention tomorrow to announce my withdrawal. Then we'll be finished once and for all with that bastard from Washington."

It was past midnight when Yates went to the Leland Hotel to deliver a message he would trust to no one else. He went to Room

150, dark and seemingly empty. In the shadows sat Len Small. The two men conferred in whispers. The deal was closed.

9

Despite newspaper stories that Lowden's nomination was expected, there was a strong air of confidence among the Deneen men on the following morning.

It was soon made evident why they exuded this confidence. When order was established, Sherman announced his withdrawal. "I urge my delegates to support Charles S. Deneen," he said. Hamlin and Warner followed.

Then Governor Yates arose. "I am withdrawing from this race in the interests of the great Republican party," he cried. "I release my loyal delegates and urge them to do all they can for the candidacy of——"

"Frank O. Lowden!" called Bill Thompson from the front row.

"Frank O. Lowden!" chorused the Lorimer men.

"Charles S. Deneen!" yelled the red-faced governor. "Charles S. Deneen!"

The rival factions yelled the names of their champions across the aisles. Finally Cannon began the roll call. "Adams County!"

"Adams County, first in Illinois, casts one vote for Governor Yates and nineteen for Charles S. Deneen."

"Clark County!"

"Clark County casts fourteen votes for Charles S. Deneen!"

This was in Cannon's home district, and he was furious. He ordered the delegation polled. Fourteen men rose to be counted, defying the political boss.

When Kankakee was called, delegates fought with one another. Some refused to go along with Small's promise to Lorimer now that it was clear Deneen would win the nomination. But Edward G. Curtis, the Small lieutenant, whipped them into line. "Kankakee County casts fourteen votes for Frank O. Lowden!"

There were cheers and boos. The roll call went on. Thompson, casting the Lorimer faction's votes for Lowden, went down with his friends. At three o'clock in the afternoon Deneen was the

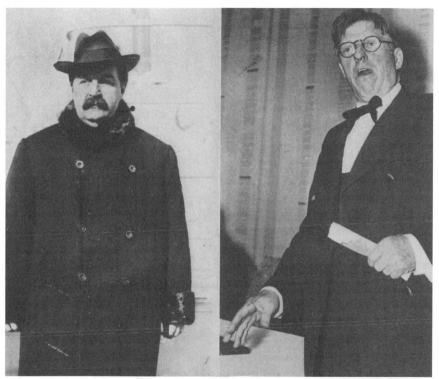

Senator Billy Lorimer   Fred Poor Swede Lundin

BIG BILL'S MENTORS

Charles E. Merriam   Charles S. Deneen

William E. Dever   John H. Lyle

A Few of Big Bill's Foes

Republican nominee for governor, the first Chicagoan ever to be nominated. Lowden arose to make the selection unanimous; Lorimer smoothed his mustache; Bill Thompson sat in glum despair.

The rest was anticlimactic. Sherman was nominated for lieutenant governor, Len Small for state treasurer. Then the convention adjourned. It had been the longest state political convention in history. In its twenty-two days, seventy-nine ballots had been cast. It had dealt Billy Lorimer and his band of ambitious men a mighty blow, and it had split the Illinois Republicans into two factions whose enmities, except for rare peace gestures, would prevail for the rest of Bill Thompson's career.

7 ||| A Man to Go Places

I

WHEN GOVERNOR YATES AND DE-
neen set out to exterminate Lorimerism, Bill Thompson was quickly
made aware of an old and inflexible political law. Week by week
Lorimer was shorn of his patronage in the state and in Cook County;
those to whom he had parceled out jobs in county offices, in the
Sanitary District, in Chicago's state-controlled parks and in state
bureaus were thrown out and replaced by the faithful in the Yates-
Deneen faction. Even Theodore Roosevelt, campaigning for Presidential election, made it clear that federal appointments recommended by Lorimer would not be renewed when the terms ended.
"It is difficult to realize what has happened," commented the *Tribune*. "Lorimer thought he is bigger than the government. Now he's
through. Colonel Lowden is merely the Ogle County farmer. . . .
This is a great day!"

Deneen, campaigning against the Democratic candidate, Lawrence B. Stringer, stumped the state still vowing to demolish all
traces of Lorimerism. He made no overtures to the Lorimerites,
for he was certain that Teddy Roosevelt would be re-elected by
such a majority that even without Lorimer's aid and even with an
attempt by the Blond Boss to double-cross him he could ride to
victory. He was right. Roosevelt won handily, and Deneen captured Illinois by the impressive margin of 228,000 votes.

Now Deneen had his turn to build a strong machine. He made

careful appointments, rejecting suggestions by Yates and Small several times and immediately incurring their displeasure. He was confronted with a balky legislature whose bipartisan deals for individual gains disturbed him and forced him to upbraid some who had supported him in the 1904 convention. Yates and Small grumbled and complained to each other, but were far from an open break with their hardheaded governor.

In Chicago Deneen began to construct a loyal organization by shrewdly ladling gubernatorial patronage wherever he sensed possible allies and withholding jobs from wards still under allegiance to Lorimer. He was aiming for more power, now that Mayor Carter Harrison the Younger had declared he would not run in the next mayoral campaign. With this popular Democrat out of the race, Deneen hoped to install his own man in the City Hall.

2

Aware of Deneen's intentions, Lorimer, who still retained his hold on many Republicans in seventeen of the city's thirty-five wards, proposed at first that Bill Thompson be his mayoral candidate in the 1905 campaign.

But Bill, for the time being, had had enough of active politics. Since the disaster at the Springfield convention, he remained close to Lorimer, but he also concentrated on his athletic-club activities. He had spent the summer at Oconomowoc and had twice entered yacht races, the first over the 332-mile route from Chicago to Mackinac in the *Mistral* and the second in the Chicago Lipton Cup race with his *New Illinois*. Both times he had been defeated in close contests. While Lorimer urged him as a candidate against anyone Deneen proposed, Thompson was busy organizing the Illinois Athletic Club and getting subscriptions for a five-hundred-thousand-dollar building to be built near the Chicago Athletic Club. Elected president of the new club, he staged a sports show for the benefit of the Children's Memorial Hospital, an event attended by society folk and described by the newspapers as a "leviathan affair."

When Thompson declined to run, Lorimer picked Graeme Stewart, the wholesale grocer who had fought alongside him in the lost Lowden cause. But Stewart, with few jobs to offer and less money, carried on a desultory campaign. Deneen's man, John Maynard Harlan, a former alderman who often fought the council's Gray Wolves, defeated him easily, and Lorimer's only solace—and threat —was that his seventeen wards had gone for Stewart.

To oppose Harlan the Democrats nominated Circuit Judge Edward F. Dunne, a firm advocate of municipal ownership of the streetcar lines and a rigidly honest man who always proposed that his epitaph read: "Here lies the body of Edward F. Dunne. He died a poor man but he was the father of municipal ownership and thirteen children. May he rest in peace!"

In a campaign that raged with bitterness Lorimer and his group did nothing to help Harlan. In the First Ward, where Thompson was the party committeeman, Hinky Dink Kenna and Bathhouse John Coughlin carried on their customary activities of registering thousands of bums, drunks and floaters, but no word of protest came from Thompson. In every Lorimer-controlled ward there were no rallies, no enthusiastic meetings for the Republican candidate. On election night Thompson and a friend dared to visit the Harlan headquarters and ask James Reddick, central committee chairman, "How are the Lorimer wards going?" "What Reddick replied," a *Tribune* reporter wrote later, "cannot be printed."

Lorimer had gained revenge for Deneen's earlier triumphs. Dunne defeated Harlan by 30,000, and the fewest Harlan votes were in the seventeen wards still loyal to the Blond Boss.

3

Throughout Dunne's term Lorimer and Thompson were outcasts from the high officialdom of Republican politics. In May, when President Roosevelt was guest of honor at a banquet in the Auditorium Hotel, neither was among the 650 prominent Republicans invited. Governor Deneen, having vowed publicly that Lorimer's defection in the mayoralty race would never be forgiven nor forgotten, denied all state jobs to Lorimer's wards and promised he would soon seize full control there. He placed the First Ward, Thompson's bailiwick where Hinky Dink Kenna had been re-elected with 6,006 votes to 656 for all three of his foes, on the top of his purge list.

But Thompson was unworried. Lorimer assured him that such dreary phases were part of being in politics, that Deneen could make a mistake in judgment or action to give them a chance for retaliation. Thompson listened carefully to Lorimer's counsel, but he was not averse to making friends with individual Deneenites or, more precisely, ex-Deneenites. One such man was portly Fred Busse, who had stood high in the Deneen ranks at the 1904 convention but whom Deneen, once elected, had neglected to reward properly. Busse and Thompson often played cards together in the new Illinois Athletic Club. They drank well at these poker sessions, Thompson preferring bourbon with wine chasers. With them at such games sat James Pease, a West Side Lorimer man who had gone over to Deneen at the convention; Jim Pugh, the little Welshman who had helped Bill learn to orate more effectively; and Gene Pike, his inveterate companion.

While Mayor Dunne wrestled with such irksome civic problems as municipal ownership, a teamsters' strike and the renewed clamor of reformers who insisted vice and gambling were worse than ever despite police raids, Thompson shied away from political activity. Now he was the sportsman, taking part in regattas, sailing his boats in races, organizing new sports festivals for his Illinois Athletic Club. He had no business worries, for his brother-in-law, William Burkhardt, and his general manager, John F. Miller, were carrying on his real-estate business in a four-room suite of offices in the First National Building, erecting new buildings to lease to small manufacturing companies, collecting rents on dozens of flats owned by Thompson.

He was so content with his lot that when Lorimer, late in 1906, suggested he be the party's candidate for the city's first four-year mayoral term he shrugged. "I think Fred Busse's your man, Mr. Lorimer," suggested Thompson.

4

Fred Busse was ready for peace and an alliance with the Blond Boss. He had much to commend his candidacy, in the eyes of Billy Lorimer. He had grown rich in the coal-and-ice business. He was a politician experienced in the rigors and rough tactics of the craft. He was a good friend of Charles Tyson Yerkes. And he was allied closely with the only gang of gamblers and saloonkeepers that was not owned by the Democrats. His good companions included Tom Burke, who bossed the North Side underworld from his saloon at Clark and Division streets, and Christian (Barney) Bertsche, a two-gun hoodlum who kept order in Burke's territory and longed to organize a protection and pay-off system for all the city's gamblers.

An advocate of the wide-open town and the Sunday saloon, Busse offered a jovial change from the confusion of Dunne's well-meaning but erratic administration. He won with promises of excessive liberality and in his triumph he found reason to be grateful to Bill Thompson of the First Ward. Although Hinky Dink Kenna won, of course, with a massive vote, Dunne's total in this solidly Democratic district was only 751, the smallest ever given a Democrat. One reason for the absurdly low figure was that Kenna and Coughlin had feuded with Dunne, but Thompson, who had labored well for his rotund poker companion, claimed some of the credit. At a victory dinner on the eve of his inauguration, Busse glowed and gave Bill Thompson a private key to his office in the City Hall.

5

Within a few months the erstwhile poker pals were snarling at each other.

It began shortly after Busse had settled his massive bulk into the mayor's chair. Barney Bertsche, the mayor's boyhood friend, opened a saloon next to the City Hall, where he entertained the new mayor as his best customer. Wielding a brace of guns, he toured the First Ward, proclaiming loudly that Busse had authorized him to organize all the gamblers, brothel keepers and saloon owners in a syndicate.

Loud-talking Bertsche soon ran into trouble, engaging in two gun battles, killing a detective in one and wounding two policemen in the second before his activities were halted.

Then a gambling war broke out in the First Ward. Mont Tennes, a wily gambler associated with Bathhouse John and Hinky Dink, turned from his busy efforts to organize a nationwide racing-news service to repel invasions like Bertsche's from the North Side. Tom Burke's gambling houses were bombed, and in retaliation bombs were exploded in the house of John Condon, one of Tennes' associates, in a Tennes handbook on Clark Street, and in Tennes' office in Forest Park, where he hoped to set up a central station for distributing racehorse results by wire. Bombs also were hurled into the house of James Pease, Bill Thompson's friend who had been elected Cook County sheriff.

When Busse, shaken by the warfare, arranged a peace with Tennes that amounted to downright surrender, there was no outcry from Thompson. But two months later Busse, embarking on a purity drive, raided the Illinois Athletic Club. Arrested were ten men, including a former state senator and two members of Busse's own cabinet. All were charged with gambling, but dismissed in court.

"The mayor," raged Thompson, when he heard of the raid, "should have had enough confidence in me to call me in if he was having complaints about the club. Instead, he treats respectable men like common criminals. Fred Busse is unfit to be mayor of this city." With this defy, he announced he was returning the key Busse had given him.

"Ha!" snorted Busse when he heard of this. "What a fourflusher! Bill knew that key wouldn't unlock anything. That was to the temporary city hall. I gave it to him when I knew we'd be moving to our new building."

6

Thompson was in no mood to continue his squabble with Busse. He was busy training a crew for the 1908 Mackinac race, determined to win in his new yacht, the *Valmore*, then building in New London, Connecticut. All winter he trained his crew—Gene Pike, George

Pease, R. H. McCormick, Jr., Dwight Lawrence and Dr. A. N. Dickinson—at the Illinois Athletic Club. In the spring he took his sailors east, where they joined Thompson's professional crew of seven to sail the *Valmore* to Chicago. Thirty-five yachts bearing the colors of the Chicago and Columbia yacht clubs met the *Valmore* in Lake Michigan, and thousands of Chicagoans along the beaches cheered as the flotilla sped grandly past them. "It is doubtful," wrote John G. DeLong, yachting editor of the *Tribune*, "if Octavius Caesar received a warmer welcome upon his return from the Battle of Actium than William Hale Thompson was accorded yesterday." A week later Thompson captained the *Valmore* to victory in the Mackinac race over a 332-mile course. He set no new record as he had hoped to do. Not until 1910, when he won for the third time, did Thompson set a record of 31 hours, 24 minutes, 6 seconds.

While he was yacht racing, Big Bill lost his committeemanship of the First Ward to State Senator Francis P. Brady. He also was under attack by a group of critics in his Illinois Athletic Club who claimed he was using the organization as his private club, handing out privileges and contracts to his personal friends. But this was only a minor loss of prestige. To Billy Lorimer he was still a young man of political promise, and was needed again.

It was time, decreed Lorimer, to make plans for defeating Deneen, coming up for re-election. Deneen's stubbornness and passion for reform had alienated others than Busse. Len Small and Yates now were openly among the disaffected and Lorimer welcomed their allegiance. They plotted and schemed, and Lorimer assigned Thompson to address crowds at meetings and at all rallies. Again Big Bill served his teacher well. He organized parades, made speeches, and generally whooped things up for the Blond Boss and his Congressional choices, Frank O. Lowden and Fred Lundin. To thwart Deneen, Lorimer arranged one of his tricky bipartisan deals with Roger Sullivan, the boss of the Democrats. He promised to support Adlai E. Stevenson,* Sullivan's candidate for governor, if Sullivan would swing votes to his Congressional favorites and to his pet project, a bond issue for an Illinois link in the Lakes-to-Gulf waterway.

---

* Vice-President under Grover Cleveland; grandfather of Democratic Presidential candidate in 1952.

The Lorimer victory in November was sweet but incomplete. Lorimer, Lowden and Lundin won their congressional campaign. Lorimerites were returned to the state legislature and to Cook County offices. The waterway bond issue was approved. William Howard Taft won the Presidency, amassing in Illinois some 185,000 votes more than his Democratic rival, William Jennings Bryan. But Governor Deneen also won, though by a comparatively scant margin of 25,000 votes.

7

Lorimer was hungry for more power and prestige. Now his goal was the United States Senate.

At that time federal senators were elected by the state legislatures. In the November election the Lorimer men had snared enough seats to prevent any candidate the Blond Boss disapproved of from winning. The Deneenites gave their support to Albert J. Hopkins, the dour political ruler of Aurora, but could produce only 91 of the 108 votes needed for election. The Democrats were in the minority so that their candidate, Lawrence B. Stringer, had no chance.

For nearly five months the Deneenites, calling themselves "The Band of Hope," cast their 91 votes day after day for Hopkins. Lorimer, absenting himself from his duties in Washington, bustled around Springfield, making deals and maneuvering among Democrats and supporters of Hopkins' six Republican opponents. Then in May 1909 Lorimer announced his own candidacy. He received one vote on the eighty-sixth ballot on May 16. Ten days later he had the necessary 108 when 53 Democrats joined 55 Republicans in his behalf.

The vote created a sensation. Lorimer set out for the Senate, once more the Blond Boss of Illinois politics. Deneenites were hastily thrown out of federal jobs. Speculation grew that Fred Busse had gained the ill favor of Lorimer and that the next mayor of Chicago surely would be Big Bill Thompson. He was cruising in the Caribbean when the excitement developed, but when he returned, Thompson insisted on talking on all subjects except politics. He discoursed on the wonders of the Panama Canal, the progress of his real-estate business, Jim Pugh's plan to build a three-deck pier into Lake Michigan at the mouth of the Chicago River. "I will do all I can to build Chicago," he declared. "I will support good men for office. But I do not plan to run for office myself. I am finished with active politics."

8

Thompson's vow might have been kept except for the suspicions of James Keeley, the ebullient managing editor of the *Tribune*. Skeptical about the reasons for the switching of the 53 Democratic votes to Lorimer, Keeley assigned his shrewdest reporters to the Lorimer case.

Nearly a year later, on April 30, 1910, Keeley had his story, and he spread it over the front page of his newspaper. It was the confession of State Representative Charles A. White that he had been paid $1,900 to vote for Lorimer. Within a week came another confession, from Representative H. J. C. Beckemeyer, that he received $1,000. Then a third, and a fourth, and the admission from other members that a $100,000 slush fund had been raised to elect Lorimer to the Senate.

The outcry was loud. In September a Senate committee started its investigation. "Who furnished the dust?" demanded the *Tribune* every day. "Who furnished the dust to bribe the legislators?" By December the inquiry was finished and a report issued, clearing Lorimer. In the following March, after long and acrimonious debate, the Senate voted to permit Lorimer to keep his seat. The vote was 46 to 40.

But a cloud still hovered over Lorimer's heavy head, and he and his friends were determined to dispel it. Chief among the supporters was Big Bill Thompson, who abandoned his yacht racing and leaped into the fray.

Lorimer, he cried, was the victim of a foul plot. As his personal antagonist in the battle Thompson chose Robert R. McCormick of the *Tribune* family. Ironically, McCormick had been an admirer of

Thompson's in Big Bill's heyday as captain of the Chicago Athletic Club water-polo team. Like other Chicago youths McCormick went often to the club tank to watch Thompson work out. His admiration had dimmed when, at one practice session, Thompson stepped to the end of the diving board, poised for an instant, then turned to call to a friend, "Jesus Christ, was I drunk last night!" before knifing into the water. Yet, except in the 1904 convention, McCormick had never fought Thompson. As a member of the city council McCormick, like Thompson, favored a bigger and better Chicago. As president of the Sanitary District, McCormick had directed the deepening of the Illinois channel, a project Thompson and Lorimer favored, and the *Tribune* had been enthusiastic about Jim Pugh's three-decked pier. McCormick had not started the Lorimer exposé, but as the new treasurer of the Tribune Company and a family representative in the business, he accepted responsibility for it. On him Big Bill poured out his invective.

"Bob McCormick represents the trust press that would crush the life out of Chicago," Thompson told his friends. "He will smear any man that gets in his way. I know him! He's a Deneen pipsqueak and a tool of the public utilities. I'm gonna smash Bob McCormick!"

To raise funds for the defense of Lorimer's good name, Thompson helped to organize the Blaine Club, named for Maine's late Senator James G. Blaine. Lorimer was president, Thompson vice-president and David L. Frank secretary-treasurer. "We'll fight Bob McCormick up and down the state of Illinois," vowed Thompson. "We'll bust the trust press. The people will speak!" The price of each member's articulation was ten dollars.

Lorimer returned from Washington to tour the state. With Lorimer's cronies, Billy Cook, Gus Nohe and Ernest Magerstadt, Thompson formed a singing quartet. They began each meeting with a hoarse, off-key rendition of "Illinois," after which Thompson invariably introduced Lorimer as "the ablest senator and finest American this country ever will know!" Sneered the *Tribune:* "Senator Lorimer is trying to make a case for himself with his Never-sweat Male Quartet. He is getting no place. Let them sing 'Illinois!' Let Illinois weep!"

9

Late in 1911, Lorimer, still pleading innocence, joined with Thompson, Lundin and other factional leaders to draw up a slate for the 1912 elections. For governor they picked Len Small, and Thompson was recommended for the Cook County Board of Review, an important body which adjudicated tax disputes and gave its members much political influence. At Lundin's suggestion the Blaine League was changed to the Lincoln Protective League. "No one knows Blaine out here. Everybody knows Abe Lincoln," he said. Almost from the start the hostile newspapers—except the *Inter-Ocean*, now owned by Yerkes, and the *Journal*, determinedly neutral—called the organization the "Lorimer-Lincoln League."

Stung to action, the *Tribune's* Robert McCormick led the anti-Lorimer Republicans. He organized a Committee of One Hundred, comprising leading business and professional men, and announced that money would be raised to beat the "Jackpot Candidates." When Thompson's enemies in the Chicago Yacht Club charged him with trying to convert it into a political organization for Lorimer, Bill knew where to place the blame. "Bob McCormick can't run the Yacht Club! All I want is efficiency and McCormick knows nothing about that! If I am re-elected president I will choose my staff on the basis of efficiency. We must expand. This club must either grow or die! Politics has nothing to do with my plans."

In the primary campaign Thompson's rival was Matthew Mills, a wealthy coaldealer, whom he promptly denounced as "the candidate of the coal men and the trust press." Having already assailed McCormick of the *Tribune*, Thompson stole another leaf from Lorimer's political textbook and attacked Victor F. Lawson, publisher of the *News*. He charged that Lawson had paid only $17.32 in taxes on his $1,500,000 residence on Lake Shore Drive. In vain did Lawson and the *News* explain that Lawson had overpaid his taxes the year before and the smaller sum represented an adjustment. Thompson mailed thousands of copies of pictures of Lawson's home beside a ramshackle cottage, each labeled $17.32.

For all the shouting, the Lorimer hopefuls were defeated decisively. Thompson ran ahead of other Lorimerites in Cook County, but even he was 15,000 behind Mills. "Lorimer was the issue," said the *News*, "and the issue has been decided." The *Tribune* chortled: "There is nothing left but the ruins and the odor."

10

But the end, decisive and tragic, was not in this defeat alone.

While the legislature opened a separate hearing into the Lorimer bribery case, Clarence S. Funk, a leading churchman and president of the International Harvester Company, had told Herman H. Kohlsaat, publisher of the *Record-Herald*, that Edward N. Hines, president of one of Chicago's biggest lumber companies, had asked him to contribute $10,000 to the $100,000 jack pot for Lorimer.

"That explains Lorimer's vote for a high lumber tariff!" shouted Kohlsaat.

Two weeks later, in April 1911, his newspaper printed a report of this conversation. An outcry arose for a new Senate inquiry. "What lumber company built Lorimer's senatorial chair?" the *Tribune* cried. "Who furnished the sawdust to bribe the legislators?"

In June the investigation started anew. It lasted nearly a year, and again a committee exonerated Lorimer. But this time the Senate rejected the committee's recommendation. Even Lorimer's old friend, Shelby Cullom, voted against him, and on July 14, 1912, despite a six-hour speech by Lorimer, he was ordered ousted from the Senate by a vote of 55 to 28.

"Truth wins! Justice is done!" exulted the *Tribune*.

11

Shaggy and sad-eyed, Lorimer stole out of Washington with his wife and quietly went to their summer home in McHenry County. But soon they received a telephone call from Bill Thompson. "C'mon to Chicago, Senator. Your friends want to show you how they feel!"

At Union Station, when the Blond Boss and his wife stepped from their train, a band blared, men and women cheered and waved flags, some shouting, "To hell with the *Tribune!*" and some "Down with Kohlsaat!" In front of the throng stood Big Bill, waving his huge arms over his head and yelling, "Three Cheers for Senator Lorimer!"

With Mrs. Lorimer on his arm and his cronies all around him, Lorimer, tears streaming from his eyes, walked to the long line of cars. Before he stepped into one, Thompson signaled to Jim Pugh, who unfurled a huge American flag and handed it to Thompson. The crowd yelled again as Big Bill draped the flag over Lorimer's shoulders.

After a parade through the downtown streets in flag-decked automobiles, the crowd streamed into Orchestra Hall, where hundreds more had waited for over an hour, stamping and waving their banners. When Lorimer entered on Thompson's arm, the audience stood and cheered for fifteen minutes.

"We have come here tonight," shouted Bill Thompson, "not to meet an unseated United States senator, but to meet a martyr. He is a living example of the fact that a trust press controls the city and this nation, that a man who will not bend a knee to its dictates can be driven from political life or public life!

"The honored and honorable man you are going to meet is not going to take this lying down. And I want you to tell him—and tell him loud—are WE going to take it lying down?"

"No! No! Give it to 'em, Bill! You tell 'em, Bill!"

"Are we going to fight?" Thompson chanted.

"Yes, we're going to fight!"

"You bet we're going to fight. We'll never stop fighting! We're going to fight and win!"

Bill spread his hands to quiet the yelling, then raised them, palms upturned, toward the box where Mrs. Lorimer sat. "And we'll meet someone else," he cried. "A sweet little lady who, through it all, has known the truth and has been steadfast and understanding. How bravely she has suffered! No one, knowing her, could ever doubt that her husband is all we know him to be—a loyal, fine, courageous, outstanding American! I give you Mrs. Lorimer."

Mrs. Lorimer began to weep. So did some of the women in the audience. Some screamed in anger at the persecutors of the Lorimers. The crowd went wild and Thompson beamed on it through misty eyes.

Others had their say. Father John O'Callaghan, pastor of St. Mary's Church, declared, "We know Senator Lorimer is a fine man. We know that powerful interests have poisoned public sentiment against him. We know that the *Chicago Tribune* is the greatest criminal in Illinois, a moral leper, unfit for association with decent people."

But none who spoke stirred the crowd as Bill Thompson had done. And none was more aware of this than Lorimer's good friend, Congressman Fred Lundin. It had been a fine meeting, Lundin reflected. But the cold political fact had to be faced: Billy Lorimer was finished.

"Y'know," Lorimer said to a friend seated next to him, "I think we've got a man to go places with. He may not be too much on brains, but he gets through to the people. I think maybe we can do something with Bill Thompson."

8 ||| Enter the "Poor Swede"

I

IN THE MELLOW AUTUMN OF 1912 THE cry of the Bull Moose echoed through the land. Waving the banner of the Progressives and rampaging against the trusts and special interests, Teddy Roosevelt set out to drive from office his onetime friend, President Taft. "We stand at Armageddon and we battle for the Lord!" cried Roosevelt, and to him flocked Republicans and independents by the many thousands.

Chicago was the center of the Midwestern revolt against Republican orthodoxy and Big Money. Hungry liberals joined with sons of millionaires to fight for Roosevelt. Imitation Rough Riders galloped through the streets of the city, cheering their hero. Lillian Russell led brigades of pretty girls into the Loop to sell kisses and Bull Moose certificates to raise campaign funds. Women swooned at mass meetings addressed by the bellicose Teddy. Such was the fervor of the Roosevelt supporters that at the height of the campaign waggish Democrats, whose presidential candidate was Woodrow Wilson, the Princeton professor, sent agents among the Loop crowds to distribute handbills reading: "At high noon tomorrow off Grant Park, Theodore Roosevelt will walk on the waters of Lake Michigan."

From the start of Roosevelt's campaign, the Illinois Republicans were split. Governor Deneen, opposed by former Mayor Dunne in the race for governor, supported Taft. McCormick, who had backed Deneen in the famous convention of 1904, now led his Committee of One Hundred into the fight on the side of Roosevelt and the Progressives. Deneen was denounced by Roosevelt as a double-crosser, and the "trust press" assailed the governor as it had once assailed Billy Lorimer.

The November election left the Republican Party in a shambles. Roosevelt's vote enabled Wilson to win over Taft. Deneen fell before Dunne. With Deneen most of the state and county Republican candidates went to defeat. Beset by losses and factionalism, the Republican party in Illinois needed someone to compose the dissident elements.

One man was prepared to try. Congressman Fred Lundin, with all the other hapless Lorimerites, had been inactive in the campaign. Neither Deneen nor McCormick had asked for advice or vote-getting help, and Lundin, Thompson and the other Lorimer loyalists stood on the side lines of the struggle between the regular Republicans and the Bull Moosers. Lundin now saw that the party needed reorganization. Without patronage Deneen was no longer a major figure, although his lieutenants assumed the powers of Republican officialdom and remained in control of party machinery. The once-magic name of Lorimer could not be used by Lundin, despite its sentimental appeal in West Side wards.

What was required, Lundin decided, was a new political personality, well-liked and bright-appearing and popular; a man whom he could mold and guide and control. Such a man might well be placed into a public office whose wires Lundin could pull to his and the party's advantage. Lundin was sure of his man, had been sure since the stirring Lorimer meeting in Orchestra Hall. He told a few close friends that he would work efficiently, patiently and persistently for Big Bill Thompson to become the next mayor of Chicago, although that election was more than two years in the future. From that foundation he would build and build a new machine, said Lundin. But he would remain quietly in the background.

2

In this dismal period in Republican fortunes, such an ambition seemed incredible. But Lundin considered himself ably qualified by experience, a shrewd political sense, a talent for organization and a flair for dramatic showmanship.

His boyhood, like that of his political master, had been spent in jobs on the city's streets. Brought by his parents from Sweden shortly after the Great Fire of 1871 when he was twelve, Lundin worked as a bootblack and a newsboy near Quincy No. 9, a saloon frequented by politicians. Later he was a clerk in a clothing store, but soon quit to peddle pills among immigrants in the Swedish district on the city's Northwest Side. He was only twenty when it occurred to him that he could make more money by concocting his own medicines and tonics. He sold his watch and as much clothing as he could spare to secure enough dollars to buy a horse and wagon. In the kitchen of his parents' home he distilled, using an old family recipe, a drink from juniper berries. Soon he was out among his neighbors, hawking his Juniper Ade as a temperance drink, although every purchaser knew how fine the liquid tasted when spiked with gin.

By 1893 Lundin's Juniper Ade was known to thousands of Chicagoans. So was its inventor, for in driving through the streets and setting up his stand, he wore an outlandish costume few could forget. His long black frock coat was tight at the waist and it flared around his thighs. On his head was a black plainsman's hat. He wore a black Windsor tie and a black, low-cut waistcoat, ornamented with an enormous gold watch chain. His round eyes hid behind amber spectacles. When, in a burst of oratory, he swept his broad-brimmed hat from his head, a home-shorn shock of wheat-blond hair tumbled over his forehead. His rickety wagon was decorated in gaudy style and equipped with kerosene torches. Before he made his flamboyant sales talk to the crowds that quickly assembled, two Negro boys strummed guitars and sang popular songs of the day. The music was his signal.

"Step right up, folks!" Lundin cried. "It's all free. It costs you nothing to hear these sweet singers of the South, direct from New York's matchless Academy of Music! They sang there for the nabobs of Fifth Avenue! They are offered here for the first time as an open-air attraction under the auspices of that wholesome, delicious, incomparable, refreshing, foaming but non-alcoholic beverage—Juniper Ade! Juniper Ade, my friends, that human boon! Delightful and refreshing to young and old! Recommended by all doctors, too."

Before Lundin embarked on his full sales talk there followed an impassioned discourse on the troubles all immigrants encountered in the New World. "We are saddened, my good friends, but there is joy and delight for us, too. Our hearts are hungry, my friends, and thirsty, too—thirsty! Thirsty for the old home drinks our mothers used to brew! Remember the pitcher that stood by the well? Remember how you used to go to it when you were tired and dusty, and how its magic coolness made new life surge through your veins? That wonderful drink, that life-giving drink, that invigorating drink is with us tonight! That historic libation of our forefathers—the old home beverage—Juniper Ade. It's cheap! It's tasty! Add a teaspoonful to a gallon of water! Add anything else you like! It's good! Step up, folks, step right up!"

Such oratorical powers soon came to the attention of Henry L. Hertz, a Lorimer leader among German and Scandinavian immigrants. Late in 1893, Hertz appointed Lundin one of his precinct captains. A few months after Lundin joined the Hertz organization, he won new popularity. On Christmas Eve a roistering laborer named Swan Nelson was killed by two policemen when he ended his holiday revelry by smashing up a saloon. There were indignant demands from the Scandinavian communities that the policemen, Joseph Moran and Thomas Healy, be prosecuted for murder. Lundin and F. A. Lindstran, publisher of a Swedish newspaper, led the campaign, addressing crowds in Swedish churches and lodge halls, demanding justice. Through their efforts Luther Laflin Mills, a leading criminal attorney, was named special prosecutor and he brought about the conviction of the policemen for manslaughter.

The grateful Swedish community heralded Lundin as its champion, and its leaders proposed that Lundin run for office. Hertz brought Lundin before the moguls at party headquarters, who gaped at the outlandish garb he still wore. "Never mind," advised Hertz, "he's not much on looks, but he has a cunning brain." Billing himself in his campaign as the Poor Swede, Lundin was elected in 1895 to the state senate, where he established a strict record of loyalty to Lorimer and a dislike of newspapers, whose Springfield representatives insisted on poking fun at his strange sartorial habits. In the big Lorimer victory of 1908 he had gone to Congress with his chief and Lowden. He shared a room in the Washington Y.M.C.A. with Lorimer and served loyally as a cog in the well-greased machine run by Uncle Joe Cannon. His one defection was his rabid campaign for an old-age pension law, waging a futile fight despite Cannon's warnings that Republicans frowned on such radical legislation. Defeated in 1910, he was inactive politically until Lorimer's downfall brought him out to defend his mentor. Meanwhile, his business enterprises had multiplied. Now he owned a factory where patent medicines were manufactured, a warehouse, an interest in an insurance firm, a company that made steel doors, and a prosperous mail-order business. He was rich and he wanted the taste of real power.

3

Methodically, Lundin labored to build his new organization on the ruins of Lorimerism and the weakness of Deneen.

First he called a series of meetings in the precincts where he had always been most popular. They were held each week, whether anyone attended or not. Often he and his nephew, Virtus Rohm, and a close crony, Percy B. Coffin, were the only ones at the meeting. When the voters refused to come to him, he went to them, invading the neighborhood saloons, where he laid a twenty-dollar bill on the bar and, after ordering drinks for all, began a spiel not unlike his orations in behalf of Juniper Ade. After each speech he distributed pledge cards for customers to sign in support of the candidacy of William Hale Thompson for mayor. Sometimes only two men signed the cards, promising to work for Thompson. Sometimes a dozen, sometimes two dozen were mesmerized by Lundin's words and free drinks. From each signer Lundin learned his capabilities in electioneering, his political aspirations and his standing in his neighborhood. This information was entered on a card in his office, and the card carefully filed for future use.

All through 1913, the card-index file grew. Lundin soon had

the names of hundreds of men who would work in the precincts for his budding organization. He shifted and sifted, interviewed men by the dozens, selecting the ambitious and the alert, naming keymen in each district to ring doorbells and hand out more pledge cards. He emphasized to these workers the importance of knowing exactly how many votes each could command. "If you promise 141 votes I don't want 131 votes and I don't want 151," he told them. "I want 141." On each card was a space for a notation of what kind of job the precinct captain wanted in case of victory. Each card was blue, for Lundin considered blue his lucky color.

To make certain that Thompson received good advice at all times, Lundin enlisted the aid of James Pugh, the Welshman who had become friendly with Big Bill in the Lorimer campaign of 1902. Pugh's nickname was "Dynamite Jim" and he was boisterous and colorful. He doted on diamonds, drove fast automobiles and fast speedboats. He had once paid $2,000 for a bulldog. He was politically ambitious, and he could afford to spend money for his political favorites, since he was a partner with Lundin in a chain of small department stores and owned properties along the lake front.

While Lundin worked endlessly in the precincts, Pugh joyfully assumed his share of the assignment. To keep Thompson close to him, he invited him to join in the project of building a new hydroplane, *Disturber III*, with which he hoped to win the American motorboat races. In the locker rooms of the Chicago Yacht Club Pugh invariably turned the talk to politics whenever Thompson was with him. Sometimes they were joined by George F. Harding, a millionaire sportsman and former alderman of the Second Ward, who was more austere than Pugh but shared his fondness for Big Bill.

In August, after his *Disturber III* won the race, Pugh was chosen by the American Motor Boat Association to represent the United States in the British International Trophy contest to be held off Cowes, the Isle of Wight. Pugh accepted and invited Thompson to accompany him. The pair caroused in New York so vigorously that they almost missed the ship on which they had booked passage. In the last-minute rush special gasoline Pugh had purchased for his craft had to be left behind. This was an unfortunate mishap, for the English petrol failed to mix properly in the carburetors of the *Disturber III*. While Bill Thompson lolled on the deck of the official committee yacht *Erin,* a bottle of Old Antique near by, Pugh floundered on the course with his expensive boat. On the first day the *Disturber III* finished seventh, on the second it was fifth, on the third it caught fire, but managed to finish, although far behind the winner, E. Mackay Edgar's *Maple Leaf IV*.

Pugh and Thompson took the defeat in good spirits. At a dinner Bill arose to praise British sportsmanship. He spoke kind words for Sir Thomas Lipton, chairman of the race committee, and invited all the contestants to come to Chicago. "I promise we'll give you a real Chicago welcome and Chicago hospitality."

Then the pair hurried back to Chicago, as abruptly as they had come.

4

His campaign progressing favorably, Fred Lundin felt strong enough to invite the established ward bosses to join him. The former Lorimer men, with no other place to go, quickly fell into line, giving the Poor Swede a valuable hold on the West Side. On the South Side there was Harding and a bright lawyer named Samuel A. Ettelson, whose firm represented Samuel Insull, the British-born successor to Charles Tyson Yerkes as the most important utilities magnate in the state. Edward J. Brundage, having assumed command of the North Side after the sudden death of former Mayor Busse, shifted his allegiance from the faltering Deneen to Lundin. To Lundin's further advantage, Teddy Roosevelt, launching an attack on President Wilson, called on his Bull Moosers to unite again with Republicans; some strategic segments of the dissidents came into Lundin's fold, although many who had hated Lorimer scorned the new boss.

Other developments pleased Lundin. For the first time in the mayoralty elections, women were to vote; Lundin was sure he knew best how to present his virile protégé to robust advantage when the right time came. Among the Democrats there was dissension, with Carter Harrison the Younger, having returned to the City Hall in 1911, heading one faction and the ambitious Roger Sullivan scheming in the other to prevent Harrison's re-election. Reform elements cried out constantly that Harrison take out after the Levee, noisier and bolder than ever. A candidate who hoped to win in 1915, mused Lundin, would have to be good-looking to attract the ladies, pleasing to the varied elements in his new organization, and a man who would speak firmly for reform and purity in politics.

5

Lundin's plans for shaping Bill Thompson into such a figure almost went awry in the summer of 1914. At his annual picnic in Kolze's Electric Park, Billy Lorimer emerged from the political shadows. Not only had he lost his fight in the Senate, but the Illinois state bank examiner had closed his La Salle Street Trust and Savings Bank and Lorimer and fourteen associates were awaiting trial on charges of embezzlement. But on this August day, hottest of the year, Lorimer had other matters to speak of.

"My friends and neighbors," he told his sweating adherents, "you have been loyal to me through trying times. I have stood up for your rights and I have been unfairly punished by vicious men. I promise you that I will never stop fighting. And to help me in the fight I bring to you a good friend of all, a loyal American, a man who knows how to fight and never quits—William Hale Thompson, the next mayor of Chicago!"

Dripping with perspiration, Bill responded. "If I become candidate for mayor, it will be to fight the crooked trust press that has tried to ruin the name of an honest and honorable man and will go on to ruin all unless it is stopped. But it is not for me but for the people to choose. I leave it to you, my friends! If you and the other good people of Chicago sign my petitions 100,000 strong, then Bill Thompson will be your candidate for mayor!"

With cheers, the crowd flocked to registration booths to sign pledge cards. Prizes of ten dollars were offered to each man and woman who brought in the most signatures. The band played

"Illinois," and Bill Thompson, in his shirtsleeves, led the crowd in the musical tribute to Lorimer.

Bill was pleased with his performance, but Fred Lundin snorted with rage. For almost two years he had worked hard and almost alone, building a political band that bore no taint of Lorimerism. In a single speech Thompson had nearly undone these efforts. Lundin explained angrily to Thompson that it would be more difficult than ever to attract balky Progressives and Deneenites who already suspected that Lundin's real aim was to revive the rule of the Blond Boss. "From now on," said Lundin, "you don't make speeches unless I know about them—and write them for you. We can't take chances."

"You know best, Congressman" was Thompson's meek response.

9 | "Bill Thompson Is the Man for Me!"

I

IN NOVEMBER THE MAYORAL BATTLE started to take shape.

Among the Democrats there was the expectation that the major rivals in the primary would be Carter Harrison and Roger Sullivan, with round-faced Robert M. Sweitzer, the popular Cook County clerk, as a possible compromise candidate. Among the Republicans hardly a day passed without mention of some new aspirant, this judge or that distinguished attorney, this civic leader or that esteemed ex-federal official. But rarely was there mention of William Hale Thompson.

Yet Fred Lundin was prepared for this moment. On November 11 he summoned 800 precinct leaders to the grand ballroom of the Hotel Sherman. They came equipped with flags and placards: WILLIAM HALE THOMPSON, CHICAGO'S NEXT MAYOR! They cheered speeches by Percy Coffin, Jim Pugh, spade-bearded Dr. John Dill Robertson, Lundin's politically minded physician. Then Poor Swede himself, wearing his funeral garb but smiling a bucktoothed smile, announced that 110,000 pledges had been collected for Thompson and would be displayed at a mass meeting to touch off his campaign on December 22. "And now," Lundin yelled, "I give you Chicago's next mayor, Commodore Bill Thompson."

In a blue business suit, his neck encased in a high, tight collar, Thompson licked his lips and waved his hands to still the clamor that Lundin's assigned cheerleaders raised. "All right, folks," he said. "I see you're with me. Let's save some of that fight for the opposition!"

89

Lundin nodded, and Thompson began his formal speech. "Let the people rule! That's going to be my platform. Let the people rule! You, my good friends, are going to be the bosses of Chicago if I become your mayor. And with you bossing the job, I am going to clean up the dirt of the rotten administration in power!" Smiling at the women in the front rows, Thompson cried, "You ladies! You know what goes on. You've been proving that and doing a fine job of it! I tell you I am going to clean up Chicago and I mean it! I know you can't run the risk of walking on the sidewalks of Chicago without being insulted, or worse. If I am elected mayor, I will protect the fair womanhood of Chicago!"

He went on to promise lower streetcar fares and better streetcars, improved garbage collections and bigger schools. "What is life worth if we do not do the best we can for our children? What do you think of a mayor who plays politics with the public schools? I tell you I will give the schools a business administration. I promise you I will put a mother on the board of education."

The women screeched and waved their placards. "Now go out and get more pledge cards!" yelled Big Bill. "Tell your neighbors and friends what I stand for. Bill Thompson will fight for you. He'll fight the bosses, even the Republican bosses who try to keep him from becoming the people's candidate! Help me throw out the rascals and build a new and better Chicago!"

2

Thompson was right about opposition to his candidacy from the Republican high command still headed by Deneen. When Lundin showed his pledge cards, they scoffed. "Bogus! You've got to have an organization, and we have it."

It appeared they did. For all his careful work, Lundin had only five sure votes on the Republican Central Committee that customarily gave its important blessing to an official party candidate. When one of them, Thomas J. Healy, tried to pass a motion that the committee withhold endorsement from any primary candidate, Deneen called this "a trick to thwart the will of the majority." In the vote Healy's motion lost, 29 to 4; he himself quickly abandoned Lundin and cast his ballot against his own motion. But the majority could not agree on a candidate. It was too early, said some, and besides, the Thompson-Lundin threat was ineffectual and would obviously come to nothing.

So the Deneenites played for time, attempting to persuade the Progressives to agree with them on the candidacy of Judge Harry Olson of the Municipal Court. And Thompson, carefully guided by Lundin, spoke on and on, and opened campaign headquarters in the Union Hotel on Randolph Street, with Gene Pike as his campaign manager. In a bold move he also established a campaign office in the heart of Deneen's territory on the South Side. This attracted attention to Thompson, with the *Journal*, an old Deneen foe, announcing its support for Big Bill.

Thompson's activities aroused public curiosity. On December 22 the curious ones and the loyal ones had a chance to see and hear the daring young man. Into the Auditorium they came by the hundreds, leaving little room for the Lundin workers. The theater was festooned with bunting and just off the stage was a huge Christmas tree, loaded with ornaments and thousands of pledge cards. Around the base of the tree were thousands more, wrapped in tinsel. In the confusion, dozens of men and women tore down bunting and decorations to have something to wave whenever the Lundin cheerleaders gave the command. To add to the din, a number of Civil War veterans, wearing their blue uniforms in tribute to Thompson's father, had to fight their way into the hall. Many of Lundin's own precinct workers, carrying placards and sleigh bells, were trapped in the lobby, with them the professional singers Lundin had hired to help lead the new Thompson campaign songs. Finally Mrs. Page Waller Eaton, chairman of women's activities, obtained order. She presented Madame Diana Bonnar of the Century Opera Company, who led the singing of the official Thompson-for-Mayor song composed by a Mrs. Frank Catlin:

> "We want a great and fearless mayor!
> Thompson's the man! Thompson's the man!
> One who is on the square.
> While the thugs are plying, the grafters trying,

We want a cleaner city
Where the good can thrive and shine.
No more picking pockets!
No more graft skyrockets!
This must go out! They're put to rout!
Bill Thompson's the man for me!
There's a man in the heart of this old town
With a heart that is big and free.
He'll pull the crooks and grafters down.
Bill Thompson is the man for me!"

Then Big Bill strode in from the wings, led by Dr. William Reid, a Lundin-Lorimer veteran. Reid proffered Chicago's Christmas present, pledge books containing, he said, no less than 176,000 names. Thompson doffed his plainsman's hat and waved it above his head while the crowd, sparked by the cheerleaders, howled for a full nineteen minutes.

"Why are you here?" Bill roared, his voice almost cracking with strain. "I'll tell you why you are here! Because you want an un-bossed mayor to represent you in the City Hall. And what do these so-called Republicans on the county committee want? Those wild-eyed mavericks want to hand-pick their candidate. Why? So they can boss him! What does Bill Thompson say about this? I say, give the people their God-given right to vote as their conscience directs. I say, let every candidate go into an open primary with no strings attached. Is that fair?"

Roars of approval echoed through the theater.

"You bet your bottom nickel that's fair. That's why these four-flushing, make-believe Republicans don't want it. Our campaign is essentially local. In assuming leadership, I deem it right and proper to procure a recognized Republican nomination. If I get that nomination in the Republican party, I will wage a vigorous campaign. Let the people rule! That's our slogan!"

He attacked the Democrats for the poor streetcar facilities. "We've had enough of this broken-down service! You elect Bill Thompson and I'll take them and change those streetcars!" And he charged the Democrats with criminal alliances. "I will clean out all faithless police officers. I will divorce the department from politics. No policeman will be sent to a cabbage patch if he offends some politician, not while Bill Thompson is your mayor." He spoke out for development of the lake front, for more playgrounds, for new business, for new factories. "Build with Bill Thompson and you'll have bigger and better pay rolls, more jobs, more money for workingmen and women of Chicago, more food for mothers and children. My friends, get busy and help elect Bill Thompson mayor! Let's clean out the crooks and grafters and knockers! Go out and tell your friends you're going to build a new Chicago with your friend and theirs, Bill Thompson!"

3

Thompson's maiden oration as an official primary candidate perked up the editorial writers. He had indeed made a fighting speech, admitted the *News*, adding, "This will not set well with party leaders." The *Tribune* warned that the size and enthusiasm of the crowd was an indication to the party regulars that a candidate needed to be chosen soon to oppose Thompson. The *American*, William Randolph Hearst's newspaper, sneered, "Thompson talks big, but he is a man without political experience. His attack on the county committee was a mistake. He sounds like a man who will make plenty of them." The *Journal*, of course, was captivated: "Thompson demonstrated he is the kind of fighting candidate the Republicans need."

The Democrats were soon faced with a choice between Harrison and Sweitzer, the latter offered as Roger Sullivan's man. Harrison had intended to quit politics, but now he bristled and declared he would not hand over control of the party to Sullivan. "I'm not going to turn Chicago back to the gangs and let them open the Levee." At a mass meeting of his followers on New Year's Day, Harrison declared officially he would run. "The decision in this campaign will rest with womanhood. In fact, it already has. My wife finally decided to let me run."

Still the Deneenites had not named a candidate. Thompson took full advantage of the lull by roaring ahead with his campaign.

Women formed "Ships of State" clubs, and lawyers, janitors and hod carriers organized special Thompson-for-Mayor groups. George Harding, popular in the Second Ward's Negro sections because of many benefactions during his aldermanic terms, took Thompson to meetings there. Every afternoon and night Thompson made a speech in some part of the city. Women's clubs passed resolutions hailing him as "woman's best friend." Society groups formed "New Thought" clubs for him. Boosters Lundin had never dreamed of came to Thompson's cause; they sent poems, speeches, monogrammed handkerchiefs, songs to the Union Hotel headquarters. A troop of Civil War veterans marched in to present Big Bill with the sword his father carried with Admiral Farragut. A firemen's committee fetched a fire marshal's command trumpet, which they insisted had been used by Stephen Gale, Thompson's grandfather. Flags of every nation and of the country's yacht clubs were brought by special delegations to deck the office walls. At the Congress Hotel, John Burke, the chief clerk, invented the Thompson Tango and offered to teach it free. "No waste of energy, no complications, no posing, and no waste of time," explained Burke. "A straight run with no hesitation."

4

Finally, in mid-January, the Deneenites officially announced the candidacy of Judge Olson.

This time, through Lundin's adroit maneuvering, enough members on the central committee abstained from voting so that Olson failed to receive an official endorsement. But many Progressives, including Jane Addams, the founder of Hull House, backed him with speeches and advice and called on voters to elect him so that vice and crime and evil living conditions could be eradicated.

From the *Tribune* Thompson received accidental and unexpected help. Since the start of the war in Europe, the newspaper had been skeptical of atrocity stories and anti-German dispatches issued by the British foreign office. In the middle of the primary it published an exposé of such propaganda written by Robert J. Thompson, former American consul in Germany. Each day the stories appeared under big headlines: THOMPSON SAYS BRITISH DIPLOMACY STARTED THE WAR! and THOMPSON DENOUNCES BRITISH ATROCITY PROPAGANDA! and THOMPSON SAYS GERMANS FIGHT FAIRLY AND BRAVELY!

Lundin was quick to capitalize on this unexpected boon. In Chicago the largest foreign bloc was composed of more than 600,000 Germans and Austrians, one of the biggest German-speaking groups in any American city. Few could read English. Lundin enlarged the *Tribune's* headlines and sent dodgers by the thousands floating through the German neighborhoods, giving them the quick impression that it was his Thompson who made these charges against the British. Invitations to speak came from dozens of German clubs, and the German-American Alliance made Thompson an honorary member.

For the rest of the campaign Thompson electioneered eighteen hours a day, seven days a week. He grinned and made sweet promises at women's teas. He bellowed at ward meetings and held up the lure of good jobs for willing workers. He traveled everywhere in the Second Ward, where he was well known not only to his wealthy friends but to the Negroes, to whom he cried, "I'll give your people the best opportunities you've ever had if you elect me!" Three days before the election, even the *Tribune* conceded he was an expert campaigner. "He has great physical vitality and a fighting spirit," stated Henry M. Hyde, its special writer. "There is nothing about him which would suggest a student. Good or bad, there will always be something doing if William Hale Thompson is elected mayor. His old-fashioned boom talk is loosely expressed and not carefully thought out, but his listeners like it!"

Olson's campaign was dignified and mild, for Deneen was certain Lundin's man could not possibly win. A few days before election he was the victim of a political roorback. Thousands of leaflets were dropped into mailboxes charging that because Judge Olson's wife was a Catholic he would deliberately destroy the public-school system. Judge Olson replied, "That's a lie!" but his answer came too late.

On a cold primary day the thousands of men and women whom Lundin had coached and persuaded for two years helped Thompson slide narrowly to victory. By only 3,591 votes he defeated Judge

Olson, and in the Second Ward he had found his miraculous margin of victory. There he had carried the ward by a plurality of over 6,000, more than enough to chop away at Olson's leads elsewhere in the city.

5

There was, despite the triumph, little elation in the Thompson ranks.

Sweitzer's defeat of Harrison by nearly 80,000 votes showed that 287,000 Democrats had voted, while the Republicans and Progressives together totaled only 171,000. As running mates, Thompson had acquired two Progressives, Charles H. Sergel for city treasurer and John Siman for city clerk. But Harold L. Ickes, the doughty Progressive leader, promptly announced that his party would not support either Thompson or Sweitzer, but would pick its own candidate. Sweitzer, said the experts, would have an easy time of it, with special appeal in German wards and united support from the Democrats.

As for Bill Thompson, the strapping Republican winner, he collapsed from the work of electioneering. He was so ill that he could not even celebrate his victory. Jim Pugh issued a bulletin for the reporters, informing them he was suffering from "rheumatism, a sore throat, a cold and a near physical breakdown."

Thompson's illness worried Lundin. After nearly three years of toil and the investment of cash and his own political future, Lundin had a listless candidate on his hands. With the election only a month away, Thompson had to continue to play the part of a virile, good-natured, fighting hero. Instead, he was cross, dispirited and discouraged. He had little appetite for the battle ahead, which he saw as a hopeless struggle. Jim Pugh could not raise his drooping spirits, nor could George Harding's words of encouragement, nor Gene Pike's incessant analysis of the returns.

Determined not to lose out on his investment, Lundin bundled Thompson to Pugh's country home near St. Joseph, Michigan. There he began a psychological process of building up his protégé as he would a petulant child. He applied unguents and restoratives—

Flanked by Alderman John Richert (left) and Charlie Fitzmorris, Big Bill marches in 1916 Preparedness Day parade.

Al Capone—whose heyday came in Big Bill's third term.

thick steaks, whisky toddies, rich flattery, confidential whispers of good tidings that the newspapers did not print. He called Thompson "Mistah Mayuh" and recalled in exquisite detail all the splendid compliments reported to him whenever Bill had addressed a meeting.

Such treatment seemed to cheer Thompson, but Lundin was by no means confident of beating Sweitzer or even giving him a good fight. He confided to his secretary, Leslie (Ike) Volz, that much needed to be done in the next thirty days. After all, he still did not have a united party behind Big Bill. Stubborn Deneenites and Progressives were ruining his plans. Judge Olson, still angry over the scurrilous pamphlets, refused the usual pledge of party loyalty. "They committed atrocities on me," he muttered. "They introduced the religious issue and aimed it at my wife. Any man who would do that is not fit to hold public office." Deneen and his chief aide, Roy O. West, issued perfunctory statements of party fealty, but Deneen declared he was too ill to take an active part in the campaign, and West said his business affairs would keep him out of Chicago well past election day. The Progressives still threatened to run a candidate, a move that would easily elect Sweitzer. The Swedish voters were irate because of the unfair charges against Olson, and the Germans expressed enthusiasm for Sweitzer.

Some cheerful sounds were heard in all this dissonance. The Illinois Republican Women's League endorsed Big Bill. Some of the Harrison Democrats, notably "Hot Stove Jimmy" Quinn and James McInerncy, Harrison's city prosecutor, were reported willing to desert the party temporarily to help Thompson with money and votes.

But Lundin realized that he needed, most of all, the experienced Republican ward leaders of the Deneen camp. He had his precinct captains, selected over the few years since he decided to make Thompson mayor; the old Lorimer men, mostly discredited or powerless; rich men who were personal friends of Thompson, Harding on the South Side and the slippery Brundage on the North Side. These were not enough. The precinct workers needed command. Veteran ward chiefs knew how to organize parades, hold rallies, lure voters to meetings where Thompson could stir them with his emotional oratory. Lundin needed to be sure of men who knew how to watch the polls in their wards and, more important, get Republican voters to them on election day. Most citizens rarely did these things for themselves, no matter how much steam was generated in a campaign. Too many women who had screamed for Thompson at meetings stayed home on primary day. Lundin had to pull all these separate forces together. To do so, he pulled a brilliant bluff.

6

Over Bill Thompson's signature, Poor Swede sent letters to the Republican and Progressive committeemen in the city's thirty-five wards. "I am appointing you as one of four men to take charge of my campaign in your ward," it read in part. "One of the four will be a prominent businessman, one will be a close personal friend of mine. Each of you may appoint a woman of your choice to complete the committee in your ward."

It was a bold, smart move. It recognized the women as a new force in politics. It demanded a working alliance of Progressives and Republicans. And it carried a threat. The committeemen thus addressed could clearly see what would happen if Thompson formed such ward committees. His "close personal friend" would become the new ward boss. The committeemen had gone hungry for patronage through the long Harrison regime. It seemed unlikely that Thompson could win, but he had surprised them all in the primary and he might do it again. If he did win, any committeeman who failed to support him would have no share in the jobs and privileges. That would mean political extinction, except perhaps for a few Progressives, whose followers possessed a crusading spirit. Most of the committeemen had no choice.

Soon their telegrams poured in on Thompson. The Cook County Central Committee assembled and formally endorsed him. Even Deneen, prodded by these job-hungry politicians, roused himself to make a speech. "Mr. Thompson comes from one of our oldest and best-known families," he mumbled. "He has character, energy, knowledge and experience. He should be elected mayor of Chicago." David Matchett, Deneen's chairman of the county committee, was especially fervent: "We hail you as a great and inspiring leader for our city and our party. We are with you to certain victory." Even Judge Olson announced he would back Thompson. The Progressive leaders, dismayed by the trend, withdrew plans for running their own man. A few die-hards switched to Seymour Stedman, the Socialist, but most of the others swung to Thompson.

The telegrams and protestations of full support lifted Thompson at last from his lethargy. Lundin's letters had helped to close the rifts in the party, as big chiefs and little czars ended their squabbles and vied with one another in the scramble to climb on Thompson's band wagon. Thompson was grateful. He sat with his cronies at Pugh's summer home, drinking and talking big. "We're in the saddle," he roared, "and we're going to ride!" And the skinny fellow who had done it all doffed his ridiculous frock coat, tucked his black Windsor tie into his shirt front, happily mixed bourbon toddies for his protégé, and pondered the future.

10 ||| Mayor Big Bill

1

BOB SWEITZER, RESTING AFTER THE
primary in Hot Springs, Arkansas, bubbled with confidence.

The Democrats had polled almost twice the combined vote
of the Republicans and Progressives. They had the money and they
had the jobs. The newspapers seemed willing to support genial
Bob against Thompson. Not even the threats that disgruntled Harrison men would be inactive disturbed Sweitzer or Roger Sullivan
or the party's strategist, George E. Brennan. Besides skilled Democratic electioneers, Sweitzer's aggregation of supporters included
such noted Harrison-haters as John McGillen and Billy Skidmore,
bondsmen de luxe for Chicago hoodlums; John F. O'Malley, once
the leader of the notorious Market Street gang and now boss of the
North Side; Barney Grogan, West Side saloonkeeper and political
fixer; Big Jim O'Leary, gambling czar of the Stock Yards district,
offering odds of five to one on his man and covering every bet he
could find.

Things looked good, said beaming Bob as he prepared to return
to Chicago. Maybe some of the newspapers would frown on a
few of those in his camp, but they would have to admit that Bob
Sweitzer was a man with a good reputation—"the man with a million friends."

Lundin had no intention of attacking "the man with a million
friends." He chose another target for Thompson—Roger Sullivan.

Not only could Sullivan be denounced as a boss, but his role in the infamous Ogden Gas scandal could be recalled. Back in 1895 Sullivan, head man in the city council, had forced passage of an ordinance giving his Ogden Gas Company—which existed only on paper—the right to build and maintain gas lines and electric-power conduits in Chicago's streets for fifty years. When the newspapers screamed that the ordinance was an outright fraud designed to sandbag the People's Gas Light and Coke Company into buying Sullivan's firm, Sullivan actually started an Ogden Gas Company. Soon, however, he sold it to People's Gas Light and Coke, as predicted. Sullivan was no longer connected with any gas companies, but Lundin meant to have Big Bill bring up Ogden Gas—and, more important, the existing high gas rates.

"We'll blame Sullivan for the high prices," Lundin advised Thompson. "Every man and woman who pays a gas bill is going to listen. They'll vote against Sweitzer to get at Sullivan. We'll never let them forget that Bob Sweitzer is the creature of Sullivan and the gas trust."

In his Union Hotel rooms, Lundin prepared the speeches he wanted Thompson to make. Few were aware of the role he played, and he preferred it that way, grinning broadly when a reporter referred to him as "a man of mystery." But behind the scenes Lundin planned. He schemed, organized, held secret conferences, reached out to his precinct captains and ward workers through his telephone network. Occasionally he slipped out of the hotel on missions he refused to tell even Ike Volz about. From everywhere he received complete reports on strength and weaknesses, of men who wanted to leave the Democrats and join the Republicans, of men who dared to proffer their services to Sweitzer.

Thompson, fully recovered from his illness and eager to leap at Sweitzer, had to be restrained and counseled against wild statements. When Sweitzer returned from his rest, he said enough to set Thompson bristling with anger. "Just who is this Bill Thompson? Who ever heard of Bill Thompson doing anything worth while? Who ever heard of him doing anything? Oh, I had him looked up. I find he is the man who plays with sailboats. Nothing wrong with that. He's a millionaire and he can afford it. Outside of that, he's nothing but a water-carnival promoter and he helped to promote the discredited Lorimer-Lincoln League. He's a playboy. He is a rich man's son whose estate is managed by an agent. Bill Thompson never earned a dime in his life. He doesn't know how!"

Big Bill swore and made ready to reply in kind. But Lundin held him off. "He's trying to make you mad. Now you take Jess Willard. When he goes out there to fight Jack Johnson, he's going to fight according to plan. He's not going to let Johnson make him mad. If he's smart he'll stick to his plan, unless he sees an opening that's too good to miss. Let's stick to Sullivan and the gas trust. Every woman will look at her gas bill and vote for you. Make Sweitzer fight the way you want him to."

Given his theme and his lines, Thompson did nobly as he met the reporters when he returned from Pugh's summer home. "Boys, the real issue is the gas trust! It gets its profits by gouging unfair prices from the little fellow. The scandal of Ogden Gas is still reeking. Now, I know Bob Sweitzer, he's a pretty good fellow. But he's the servant of Roger Sullivan. The question in this election is: 'Do the people want to turn over the government to Roger Sullivan and the utilities?' Ask a man with a family to look at his outrageous gas bill and give you an answer. Ask any mother who must take the food from the mouths of her children to feed the greedy coffers of the gas trust. Take a look at your own bills and tell me if you want Roger Sullivan to run Chicago!"

Lundin nodded when he read the newspaper reports of this statement. Things were starting well. Thompson would be a good actor in this drama if he followed orders. Meanwhile there was other work to be done, and Lundin, shifting here and there in the Union Hotel headquarters, supervised it. Virtus Rohm, a relative, worked on the telephone switchboard. Ike Volz saw the visitors and the suppliants.

Once, returning to the hotel, Lundin was met by a reporter. "What do you think of the race, Congressman?" the reporter asked. "I hear you are supporting Thompson."

Lundin grinned and shrugged. "He would be a good man, of

course, but I'm not anything in this campaign, just a poor Swede, insignificant and unimportant. I don't even read the newspapers."

3

If Thompson called him Sullivan's errand boy, Sweitzer thought he knew whose errand boy Big Bill was. "He's a nothing, a political unknown," he told a roaring mass meeting in Cohan's Grand Theater. "He's an errand boy for the discredited Billy Lorimer. Why has Lorimer put Thompson into the campaign for mayor? Why does he sneak about, pretending he's no longer in politics? I'll tell you. Lorimer knows he can't go before the people. So he puts up his chore boy, Thompson.

"What does Bill Thompson have to offer? He's a promoter of water carnivals. He says he'll build a great city. But he never worked at anything a day in his life. He says he's against crime and vice, but I wonder if he was against crime and vice when he was spending his time in the red-light district with Billy Pike? You can look up the court record on that! What kind of a man is Bill Thompson? He once fought what he called the crooked trust press. Now he's against something he calls the gas trust. What happened to his fight against the trust press? Bill Thompson, have you changed your mind? Maybe those honest Republicans and Progressives who've been fooled into supporting you will change their minds about you, Mr. Thompson!"

The battle was joined now and not even Lundin wished to restrain Thompson. Big Bill dutifully raised the ghost of Ogden Gas, lambasting Roger Sullivan and sneering at Sweitzer as "Boss Sullivan's boy, waiting to run the errands of the gas trust." But he talked about other things, too.

In residential wards with heavy reform and feminine votes: "I'll appoint a mother to the board of education! Who knows better than a mother what is good for children?"

In neighborhoods with saloons: "I see no harm in a friendly little drink in a friendly corner saloon."

In Negro wards: "I'll give your people jobs. And if any of you want to shoot craps go ahead and do it. When I'm mayor the police will have something better to do than break up a little friendly crap game."

To men out of work because of German submarine warfare and the British blockade: "I'll get jobs for you when I'm mayor! We'll build this great city up. We'll have a waterway going from the tip of Lake Michigan to the Gulf of Mexico! We'll have new wide streets, new buildings, new factories, new pay rolls. We'll have full prosperity and a full dinner pail! Go tell your friends that!"

In the Silk Stocking districts: "I'll clean up this city and drive out the crooks! I'll make Chicago the cleanest city in the world!"

"Thompson tries to be all things to all manner of people," gibed William Randolph Hearst's *American*, backing Sweitzer. "In the Polish wards he's anti-German. In the German wards it's '*Unser Wilhelm für Bürgermeister.*' There he sounds like Kaiser Bill himself. In the Irish wards he damns the King of England."

Thompson's sole newspaper supporter, the *Journal*, printed a front-page editorial in reply. "There is in this city," wrote Publisher John C. Eastman, "a political miasma so deadly that no public man can breathe its fumes for any length of time and survive. It is the noisome, noxious and fatal friendship of William Randolph Hearst. Hearst's Hooligan Howlers are supporting Sweitzer in this campaign, and that should be enough for all decent people. The Hearst polecat press is fighting for Sweitzer and that alone will defeat him. With all his popularity, Sweitzer cannot stand up under the burden of Hearst support. William Hale Thompson is certain to be elected the next mayor of Chicago!"

4

Fred Lundin worked more feverishly to make sure that he was.

Having glimpsed Thompson at meetings, he was pleased with his protégé's oratorical efforts. Big Bill was a born campaigner. He swung easily into his speeches, grinning, grimacing, smacking fist into palm, waving his arms. He speared out hecklers in the audience and wagged accusing fingers at them while he bawled replies in his whisky baritone. He never failed to make at least one reference to the American flag, one to George Washington, and one to glorious American womanhood. He moved his crowds to cheers and to tears, to roars of laughter and roars of anger. He was a complete showman, learning fast and improvising with surprising skill. He relished every sound that came from his audiences.

Lundin, tireless, keeping always to the background, worked on every level of the campaign, from intriguing with Democrats to declare publicly their support of Thompson to organizing rallies and instigating demonstrations. He formed dozens of specialized groups for his candidate. In addition to the Ships of State and New Thought Clubs, there were Mothers for Thompson, Republican Women for Thompson, Democratic Women for Thompson, Teachers for Thompson, a Showmen's William Hale Thompson Club to supply entertainment at meetings and a William Hale Thompson Baseball Boosters Club. There were Thompson organizations for every profession and all crafts, and in every nationality and racial group in town.

Sweitzer, seeking to match Thompson's reputation as an athlete, told the voters that he once had played with the Chicago Spaldings, a semipro baseball team, and a Sweitzer team was formed to defeat riffraff nines in the various wards. Lundin swiftly retaliated. He staged nightly athletic contests in the Coliseum where gymnasts, track stars, weight lifters and high jumpers performed, all wearing shirts with Thompson's name on the chest. "Perhaps," sniffed the *News*, "Thompson and Sweitzer will fight it out in the ring the night before election!" In the stockyards a Cowboys for Thompson Club invited Big Bill to attend a fancy roping contest and he showed up wearing a new ten-gallon Stetson, had his photograph taken atop a horse, and yelled, "This is the best day of my life! It's good to be back in the saddle again. Boys, with you behind me I'm going to ride into the City Hall. We're going to put the old B T brand on the Democrats!"

While Thompson talked, Fred Lundin was quietly rounding up some of the more useful Democratic mavericks. His secret trips from Union Hotel headquarters were beginning to produce results. Ten days before the election, Charles C. Fitzmorris, secretary to Mayor Harrison, declared his renunciation of Sweitzer and his support of Thompson, and other Harrison officials followed him. The action stunned the Sweitzer men. They were aware of Harrison's hatred of Roger Sullivan, but had been sure he would never countenance a bolt by his City Hall followers. What was worse, Fitzmorris was acting secretary of the Democratic Central Committee. He possessed the only authentic list of registered Democrats. Equipped with such a list, Thompsonites could accurately challenge Democratic voters in every ward. The moving of colonizers from one ward to another on election day, a technique popular with both parties over the years, would not work for Sweitzer in this crucial election.

The Sullivan-Sweitzer organization still controlled many jobs through aldermen, committeemen and county officers. They put pressure on other potential rebels, threatening to deprive them of patronage. But the revolt could not be stopped. George R. Schilling, head of Harrison's board of local improvements, joined Fitzmorris and staged an anti-Sullivan mass meeting of "loyal Democrats." Governor Dunne, from Springfield, issued a statement: "I have known William Hale Thompson for many years and I know him to be a man of clean personal character." Richard Folsom, law partner of Democratic Senator J. Hamilton Lewis, took up the insurgents' cause and openly endorsed Thompson.

That for which Lundin had long hoped and worked had come to pass. The strategy of making Sullivan the villain and Sweitzer his errand boy had proved a success. Now he directed Thompson to concentrate his attack on his mayoral opponent. And Thompson gleefully obeyed. "Here is a man, this Bob Sweitzer, who is repudiated by his own party! He is good enough for Boss Sullivan, but not for decent Democrats. Who'll be boss if Bob Sweitzer is elected? He's got nobody left but Boss Sullivan and his discredited hacks. The Sweitzer gang is composed of the most unscrupulous, most unspeakable and evil men who ever attempted to steal an election. They're raising a million-dollar slush fund to buy votes on election day!"

Jim Pugh also was raising a slush fund, but with less success. Businessmen listened to his argument that a Thompson win would start the trend toward Republican victories throughout the country, then brushed him off with comparatively modest contributions. They were not impressed with Thompson's chances. Finally Big Bill himself had to borrow $50,000 from Pugh, on his personal note, as his contribution toward the campaign.

As his drive for votes entered its final week, Thompson made a final gesture of combat against the Gas Trust. He filed with the Illinois Utilities Commission a petition to reduce the city's gas rates by thirty per cent. He promised to take this fight into the courts if he should fail to win a reduction, and his followers in the wards joyfully told their listeners that Big Bill was going to save Chicago's gas customers $60,000,000.

5

Long before he was sure of Fitzmorris' aid and that of other Democrats, Lundin had often lectured to Thompson, Pugh, Pike and Harding in the Union Hotel headquarters about the need for a rough campaign at the right moment. "In order to elect a Republican mayor in Democratic Chicago," he told them, "we'll have to stir up the public so much that you'll have a fight every fifteen minutes at Clark and Randolph!"

The time for rough campaigning was at hand. Into the mail went thousands of pamphlets detailing Sweitzer's Catholic affiliations and his high rank in the Knights of Columbus. A new organization sprang up called the Guardians of Liberty, and its members spread stories in strongly Protestant neighborhoods that if Sweitzer won the Pope would be the real ruler of Chicago. "How long will you stand for a school board dominated by Catholics?" whispered these scoundrels. And the Democrats issued their own pamphlets in the Catholic neighborhoods, asserting that every Masonic lodge hall in Chicago was a political headquarters for Thompson.

First to bring up publicly the ominous new issue was Sweitzer. "In his desperate effort to win votes," he declared, "Mr. Thompson has sought to prejudice some people against me by introducing the religious issue. This is nothing new for the scurrilous Thompson crowd. Have you forgotten what he did to his fellow Republican,

Judge Olson? I call on all decent people to condemn these dastardly activities of Mr. Thompson and his supporters!"

Thompson denied everything. "I deplore the raising of the religious question," he said. "It was raised by a formal statement from the headquarters of my opponent. I say that the man or candidate who will deliberately plan a campaign move that injects this subject into politics breathes treachery to America and denies the letter and spirit of our federal and state constitutions and is unfit to be elevated to an American office!"

The hatemongers continued their work in a fertile field. In neighborhoods where the city's half-million Germans lived Sweitzer men distributed handbills bearing portraits of Kaiser Wilhelm and Austria's Emperor Franz Joseph. Beneath the pictures were pleas that votes for Sweitzer would aid the Fatherland and the German soldiers on the battlefronts in the war in Europe. Lundin reprinted the handbills and flooded the German-hating Polish and Bohemian districts with them, decrying the appeal of "Sweitzer, the German candidate." In every ward fights broke out at meetings. Tough young men from the German districts invaded Polish neighborhoods and battled other tough young men. Some ministers denounced the unloosing of these furies, but many others took sides. "The vicious bitterness of this campaign has never been equaled," wrote the *Tribune's* Henry Hyde. "Perhaps it is because people, forced to remain neutral about a war in Europe that is so close to many of them, have now turned loose all the hatreds that war and its propaganda have engendered."

6

In the Loop, as Lundin had predicted, tempers flared even higher. Each day there were meetings in theaters along Clark Street, across from the City Hall. Each day Thompson held a rally in one theater while Sweitzer held his in the theater next door. Their respective rooters, carrying banners, jangling cowbells and whirring sirens, packed the streets and then the theaters, either to cheer their hero or hoot their enemy. They cursed one another, started fights, trampled bystanders. Mayor Harrison ordered special squads of police into the area, but the policemen, too, had their political feelings, and the newspapers warned of the danger of riot.

On the Friday before the election, Marion Drake, a feminist who had tried in vain to defeat Bathhouse John Coughlin in the First Ward, announced a noon meeting of her "Can't Stand Thompson" club in Cohan's Grand Theater. Although she herself was for Seymour Stedman, the Socialist candidate, Miss Drake had been lent the use of the theater by the Sweitzer forces, whose regular meeting place it was. She declared the meeting open to every party, and invited all candidates to speak.

Hundreds of Miss Drake's followers marched on the Grand for her rally. They arrived to find the theater filled with Thompson rooters yelling, "All for Chicago and all for Big Bill!" The girls fought their way in and sat in the aisles. When Miss Drake yelled for order, she was drowned in a wave of howling and stamping. "The finger of scorn will be pointed at us women if we help elect a man who is backed by Lorimer and the greedy, hungry forces of the underworld," she screeched. "Thompson means Lorimerism!" Few beyond the stage heard her.

Miss Drake presented Stedman but he was yelled down. She introduced John H. Hill, the dour Prohibitionist candidate, and a contingent of women in the front row leaped up to shrill:

> "Let us rescue all Chicago
> From the awful curse of drink.
> Let us save the helpless drunkard
> Who is struggling on the brink."

"That's right!" bellowed Hill. "We will sing Chicago dry, talk it dry, then vote it dry!"

The startled Thompsonites permitted him a few words, then started their jeering and catcalls again.

Sweitzer stepped out to speak, while a few brave partisans chorused: "Ice cream, soda water, ginger ale and pop! Sweitzer, Sweitzer, always on top!" Good-naturedly, Sweitzer began, "This is like a football game . . ."

He got no farther. The theater roared with sound. Outside,

a crowd of 5,000 pushed at the theater doors, shouted threats and taunted the police guards. A woman who yelled, "We want Big Bill!" was pummeled and it took seven policemen to rescue her. As tension mounted, someone turned in a fire alarm for the theater. Trucks with sirens screaming bore down on the crowd outside, and mounted police tried to clear the way. Scores were knocked down and trampled. An unnamed fireman was the day's hero. He burst into the theater just as the hundreds inside began to surge toward the doors. He quietly informed those nearest him that they were violating the fire laws and would have to leave. These men and women filed out in orderly fashion and the others soon followed. But outside the theater the Thompsonites surged into the pro-Sweitzer crowd and fighting broke out. The rival partisans pounded one another while firemen fought to get space for their hose lines and equipment and police swung their clubs, bawled commands, and sought to disperse the crowd. "The scenes of disorder were unparalleled in political history," reported the *News*. "This was the sensational climax of the campaign. It might have been a terrible tragedy."

7

That very night Lundin put into action another plan he had conceived early in the campaign.

Shortly after his victory in the primaries, Sweitzer had affirmed his loyalty to the principles of the local Democrats. "I'll be a good soldier," he declared. Lundin clipped a newspaper report of this statement and filed it for future use. Then he suggested to Jim Pugh that handsome photographs of Thompson be taken, showing him to his best advantage as a robust man with a smiling, forceful mouth, a strong jaw, bright and piercing eyes with a plainsman's crinkles at the temples—a virile, wholesome, fighting portrait. "When the right time comes," said Lundin to his partner of mail-order days, "we'll shoot copies of this picture over the city, thousands of 'em for thousands of windows."

Now was the time. Lundin had ordered thousands of labels on which was printed: IF YOU WANT TO DEFEAT THE GOOD SOLDIER OF

THE GAS BOSS, HANG THIS IN YOUR WINDOW AND VOTE FOR WILLIAM
HALE THOMPSON. The labels had been affixed to the pictures and the
pictures placed in tubes, ready for mailing. Now they went out,
to every registered Republican and to selected Democrats on Charlie Fitzmorris' list. Two days later Lundin and Volz rode about the
city in Lundin's automobile. In every block there blazed scores of
pictures of Big Bill. Lundin grinned and said, "Well, that's going
to help!"

8

Over the pre-election week end there were more speeches, more
promises, and more pandemonium.

Saturday was the traditional day for final street parades and the
crowds began to gather early on State Street. At noon Thompson
held a meeting in the Cort Theater but found it packed with Sweitzer rooters led by Barney Grogan, furious because his saloon license
had been revoked that morning by Mayor Harrison. When Thompson stepped forward to speak he was greeted with groans and jeers.
Then he was pelted with vegetables. Wiping a tomato from his
shirt, he called for his helpers to bring out a huge blackboard. With
a grin, he wrote on it: "All Republicans, all Progressives, and 100,-
000 anti-Sweitzer Democrats are going to vote for William Hale
Thompson for mayor." This was his speech, and, leering at Grogan,
he walked off the stage and out of the theater.

All afternoon the Thompsonites paraded behind floats that displayed him as a friend of the Germans, the Poles, the Swedes and
the Irish, the defender of American mothers, the savior of gas-users.
Twelve bands and dozens of marching clubs tramped down State
Street, while on the curbs Sweitzer gangs shouted, "G'wan, you
lousy Protestants! Down with the A.P.A.'s!" E. C. Racey, the
parade marshal, rode up and down the length of the procession on
a prancing horse. A calliope tooted incessantly behind a contingent
of elephants and camels.

When Racey turned the parade into Randolph Street toward
the Union Hotel where Thompson was to review it, men wielding
staves and sticks sprang from buildings and alleys. Howling and

clubbing, the hoodlums stopped the marchers and set the bands scurrying to the sidewalks. They bore down on a group of women who had been chanting "Everybody for Bill Thompson!" and drove them into the crowds on the curbs. As the thugs began to pull apart the floats and overturn cars, screams and cries echoed through the narrow street. A detachment of mounted police finally arrived. The raiders fled into the alleys, the parade re-formed, and Thompson stood in the hotel window waving his sombrero as the marchers moved past.

Sweitzer's parade lasted much longer, continuing far into the night. His floats were as colorful, his marching cohorts carried red flares, and from time to time Roman candles were sent into the night air. "Sweitzer, Sweitzer, the Irish Kaiser!" chanted the Thompsonites along the route of march. Two rival gangs clashed at one corner and were carted to jail. For six solid hours State Street was filled with Democratic lights and noise. Sweitzer seemed to have won the battle of the parades.

9

For their windup speeches, Sweitzer addressed a confident group of West Side leaders, and Thompson went to the Pekin Theater in the Negro district. That afternoon Jess Willard had defeated the Negro heavyweight boxing champion, Jack Johnson, in Havana, and Thompson made allusion to it. "Only a good cowboy like Willard could beat a good man like Johnson," he told his audience. "Tomorrow the cowboy will be on your side. Remember this: Bill Thompson is going to win for you at the polls. Get out and make it a big one!"

As the last meeting ended, Chicagoans agreed that they had witnessed one of the fiercest and most spectacular campaigns in the city's history. There were few who cared to forecast victory for Thompson. The straw polls conducted by the newspapers showed him to be gaining, but still running behind Sweitzer. Analysts conceded the effectiveness of Big Bill's campaign personality, but could find no evidence of a Thompson organization able to produce results at the polls. Some experts hedged, saying that the woman's vote, for the first time a factor in a Chicago mayoral election, was unpredictable. And they added that feminine participation in the campaign had not quite developed the refining and elevating influence which women had been expected to exert.

The *Tribune*, which cared little for either Sweitzer or Thompson, suggested that Chicago would survive its most vicious campaign on record. "Whichever candidate is elected, we do not believe there will be a loose and disorderly city. Probably there will be greater latitude and a letup on certain restraints, but we do not believe that we are headed for the bowwows."

Citizens with money in their pockets raised the gambling odds on Sweitzer to eight to one. A syndicate of First Ward gamblers was reported to have placed $500,000 on the Democratic candidate, with Andy Craig, an old-timer in the district, boasting that he had wagered $45,000 of his own funds. There were the usual official predictions. Thompson's was supplied by Lundin, who had been checking and rechecking with his representatives in every precinct. "I predict," intoned the Republican candidate, "that 240,000 of the 284,000 registered women voters will vote—165,000 for me. I look for a total vote of 690,000, of which I will receive 390,000, Sweitzer 250,000, Stedman and Hill the rest."

This done, Thompson left the rest to the voters. In an unusually quiet election day, considering the wildness of the campaign, a record outpouring of citizens went to the polls. Thompson voted early, then posed for the inevitable photographs. "It looks like the cowboys are going to win," he told the reporters. "Jess Willard was a cowboy, and I've had some experience at that." Casting his ballot, Sweitzer theorized that the heavy voting meant a Democratic landslide. Asked if he voted for Thompson, Mayor Harrison replied, "No, I just held my nose and voted the straight Democratic ticket, although I hated to do it."

By four o'clock that afternoon of April 6, Lundin and Thompson, flanked by other stalwarts, were in the Hotel La Salle, where they had rented a suite of rooms to await the returns. The first results, from six scattered precincts, gave Sweitzer 638 and Thompson 1,408. Three hours later, after a steak dinner and a stiff round of Lundin's whisky toddies, the news was less cheerful. Sweitzer was pushing ahead. In the First Ward he had a lead of 3,570 votes. But then the Second and Third Wards came in, and Thompson lifted his whisky glass in a toast to his sterling friend, George F. Harding. In the Second, 15,409 for Thompson, 6,359 for Sweitzer; in the Third, 15,232 for Thompson, 7,769 for Sweitzer!

By eight o'clock, it was clear that an incredible triumph was unfolding for Thompson. An hour later Jim Pugh picked up a ringing telephone. When he jammed down the receiver a minute later, he shrieked, "Bill Thompson, you old sonofabitch! You've done it! Sweitzer's conceded. You're the mayor!"

While Gene Pike yelled, "Hoorah for Bill!" and Jim Pugh danced crazily about the room crying, "Bill, you're the greatest sonofabitch Chicago ever saw!" and others shouted, "You'll be President someday!" and some pounded Thompson's back and others gripped his hands, Fred Lundin sat quietly in a corner, his big teeth set in a grin. At just the proper moment, he arose. "Mistuh Mayuh," he said calmly, "permit me to offer my deepest and most sincere congratulations."

Thompson wrung Lundin's hand and cried, "Fred, you're a wizard! You did it all, and I'm not ever going to forget this!"

10

When the final returns were in and the observers made their comments, Thompson found new reasons to marvel at Lundin's political sagacity.

Lundin had predicted a total vote of 690,000. Thompson, he estimated, would get 390,000 and Sweitzer 250,000. The actual result was 669,309 ballots cast, with 390,691 for Thompson and 251,502 for Sweitzer. Small wonder that Thompson gasped. "You're uncanny, Fred!" he cried. Lundin smiled and had his answer: "Bill, we built an organization and the organization came up with the votes like we planned."

Lundin had been right in every maneuver, every element of strategy. He had advised Thompson to talk about the Gas Trust and a full dinner pail for workers; in wards where such groups lived the Thompson score was high. He had urged him to play to the lady voters and promise to install a mother on the Board of Education; Big Bill had snared sixty-three per cent of the women's vote. He had urged him to capitalize on the angry resentments of minority groups and immigrants; in these districts Thompson had submerged Sweitzer. In a succinct and accurate analysis the *Tribune* concluded: "Mr. Thompson appeared on the impatient voters' horizon bulging and shining like a full dinner pail and ringing like a dinner gong."

Now Big Bill stood before a broader horizon. His plurality of nearly 140,000 votes was the largest that had ever been given in Chicago to any Republican. William McKinley had been helped along to the White House in 1896 with a margin of only 96,000. The size of the vote was the biggest that had ever been recorded in an American municipal election. The Democrats, so strong and mighty a week before, were shattered, and political observers read into Thompson's astounding triumph portents for the next year's Presidential election.

All this drew to Big Bill, now accepting cheers and plaudits and uttering promise after promise, a flurry of national attention. It was what he reveled in, and it was attention that, through good years and bad years, he would never lose.

The Reign

11 ||| Reformer and Rascal

HIS YEARS OF RULE AND MISRULE started with a promise and a parade.

On the happy morning after his triumph, sitting grandly in an overstuffed chair in his Hotel La Salle suite, he met the reporters. "The crooks had better move out of Chicago before I am inaugurated! This town will be cleared of criminals so completely before the new administration is in power many weeks that the whole world will for once understand that Chicago is a safe place to come to!"

And he would do this, cried Big Bill Thompson, because he alone had the will and the right. "I am free of boss hindrance!" he declared, waving a fresh cigar as he glared belligerently about. "I want it clearly understood that in no manner whatsoever is this to be a political machine-building administration. I am my own man!"

The reporters took it down, this and much more, as Thompson pinched a pair of horn-rimmed spectacles to his nose and read a statement written by Lundin. Other newsmen, meanwhile, had journeyed out to call on Mrs. Thompson. "I knew he'd win!" she told them. "I think it's wonderful! We women supported him strong, didn't we? He'll give Chicago a fine administration."

On the day of his inauguration Big Bill stood on the reviewing stand outside City Hall, while 70,000 marchers streamed along La Salle Street shouting, "Big Bill and Prosperity!" This was Fred Lundin's big show for his man, a four-hour Prosperity Parade twelve miles long with not only the marching army of pay-rollers, precinct captains, schoolteachers, union members and plain citizens, but with 350 floats, 6,000 autos, fire engines, ambulances, police patrol wagons. The marchers waved huge banners: BIG BILL IS OUT TO FIGHT FOR RIGHT, SO CROOKS BEWARE AND TAKE YOUR FLIGHT! and PROSPERITY, BORN IN CHICAGO APRIL 26, 1915. TO LIVE MANY YEARS and CHICAGO, THROW AWAY YOUR MOURNING GOWN, PROSPERITY AND THOMPSON HAVE COME TO TOWN! When an I.A.C. float glided by, one of those aboard hurled a football at Big Bill and he deftly picked it out of the air while the crowd, remembering his gridiron days, chanted: "Yea! Yea! Captain Bill!" A delegation of students from the Art Institute displayed a banner: G.O.P. SPELLS ART, and an automobile filled with gray-haired men sported one reading FRIENDS OF THE GRANDFATHER, COMRADES OF THE FATHER, SUPPORTERS OF THE SON, and a float sponsored by a corn-removing company exhibited a man, his bare foot in a nurse's lap, throwing samples of the wondrous product to outstretched hands. Charles Wheeler, the *Tribune's* political expert, took a last look, then went to his office to write: "No mayor ever entered the city hall with such a backing, such apparently universal good will and sincere spirit of co-operation. If he doesn't make good he will be the most despised mayor of the whole lot." Said the newspaper's editorialist: "The hurrah has been had. Now let's see what was the occasion for it."

That night, in the crowded council chamber, Carter Harrison shook Mayor Thompson's hand, saying, "Make yourself at home." And Big Bill had more promises. Again he vowed to drive out the crooks. He would also solve the city's ancient transportation problems. He would secure from Springfield home rule over public utilities. He would reduce gas bills. "My greatest desire," he said in a voice that throbbed hoarsely, "is that no shadow of corruption, dishonesty, wrongdoing shall cloud any of the varied and multitudinous activities of the city government during my term of office."

2

For a time this surface glow stayed bright.

As his new police chief Big Bill appointed Charles C. Healey, a dour man with a good record as traffic supervisor. "Drive every

crook out of Chicago!" sang the mayor. "It's up to you. Do it and
do it now! Let's have every crook out of here in sixty days!"

Solemnly, as if he really believed it could be done, Healey responded. "I shall do the job. I will close every vicious poolroom
in Chicago. They are the breeding places of murders, holdups and

violent crimes." Within hours Chief Healey's deputy, Herman Schuettler, assembled fifty raiders. They swarmed into poolrooms, rounding up known hoodlums and police characters. Each arrest was hailed by Big Bill as another step in ridding the city of its worst criminals. A few weeks after the raids began he told members of the Chicago Athletic Club that he and Healey had received anonymous threats on their lives because of their war on crime. "They demand," Bill told the sportsmen, "that we call off the police. My answer is this—Bill Thompson is an ex-cowboy. He has mixed and lived with the gunmen of the West and he knows how to be quick on the trigger. And if these crooks don't get Bill Thompson as quick as a flash then they're taking an awful chance!" There were, of course, many cheers.

In other places and in other speeches Big Bill stressed the sweetness-and-light aspects of his intentions. At a banquet of the Chicago Methodist Social Union he promised to institute a city-wide program of athletics: "Athletics are great because a boy in them has to stop smoking cigarettes and eating pie." At the South Park Methodist Church he promised to start a drive to provide more recreation centers for boys: "We can have pool tables in them and that way we can beat the pool-hall evil because the boys can play pool in these recreation centers." He spoke in other churches, always remembering to tell about the telegram he said he had received only that morning from his cowboy friends in Cheyenne. " 'Bill,' they wired me when they heard I was going to speak in a church, 'we always thought you were on the square, but keep out of that sky-pilot stuff!' "

3

Reading the reports of all the promises, listening to Big Bill as he vowed to end all unemployment and all poverty, the *Tribune's* Bert Leston Taylor, BLT of the "Line O' Type or Two" column, made wry, brief comment: "In six months we'll know if it's Big Bill or Big Bull."

Another newspaperman, more august and more serious, had no doubt what it would be. Shortly after his election Thompson asked

Victor Lawson, owner of the *News*, if he would visit him at the Hotel La Salle. Lawson took his editor, Charles H. Dennis, along. In his suite Big Bill, surrounded by cronies, grew expansive and exhorted Lawson to stand behind him in his efforts to improve Chicago. "I'm gonna be a good mayor," Big Bill repeated, while his friends glared at Lawson, then beamed at Thompson. Lawson listened to all Bill had to say. As he got up to leave, he stared for a moment at him. "Mr. Thompson," he said, "everything you do as mayor that is beneficial to Chicago will meet with the approval of the *Daily News*. I should be lacking in frankness, however, if I did not say to you now that I have no confidence in either you or your chief supporters."

4

By June, however, even the most skeptical among Big Bill's critics had kind words for him. His dramatic settlement of a strike involving 11,000 streetcar motormen, conductors and maintenance men that tied up the city's transportation with violence and bloodshed drew more national attention to Big Bill and won him all Chicago's good will.

Strike threats had rumbled through the early days of the new regime. The workers, represented by bluff William D. Mahon, president of the Amalgamated Association of Electric and Street Railway Employees, wanted a wage increase and shorter working hours. The companies, whose spokesmen were L. A. Busby, president of the Chicago Surface Lines, and Britton I. Budd, president of the Chicago Elevated Railways, called the union demands for a wage boost of twenty-eight cents an hour "ruinous." In the first week of June, as the strike danger increased, Big Bill summoned Mahon and his underlings—William Quinlan, of the streetcar men's union, and John J. Bruce, of the elevated men's group—and the company officials to conferences. For a few days he was able to delay the actual walkouts, but on June 14 his efforts at peacemaking failed. For the first time in a generation, the newspapers announced: "CAR MEN STRIKE!"

By vans, trucks, automobiles, buggies and jitneys Chicago's riders made their way to the Loop stores and offices, to factories and plants. Guided by maps in the newspapers, thousands flocked to the steam railway stations. When the companies hired strikebreakers to run the streetcars, crowds of strikers halted the vehicles, threw out the scabs and sometimes overturned the cars.

At first Thompson sought to end the strike by force. He ordered Chief Healey to issue 500,000 additional rounds of ammunition to his men and prepared an ordinance granting him the right to hire several hundred more policemen for such emergencies. But he abandoned this second plan after the aldermen passed an ordinance fathered by John Kennedy, one of the two Socialists in the council, barring the employment of strikebreakers on the streetcars. Instead the councilmen empowered Thompson to name a special committee to seek a settlement.

On the night of June 16, Big Bill gathered with his committee in his City Hall office. He conferred with them for an hour or more, then announced to waiting reporters that he was summoning the union and company leaders. "Let's get their feet under one table," he was quoted, "and see if there is not some way in which this deplorable paralysis of the city's activities can be averted."

Busby, Budd and Henry A. Blair, another company official, came from the Chicago Club. Mahon, whose bags were packed for a return to his home town of Detroit, Michigan, arrived, and so did Quinlan and Bruce. They ranged themselves on opposite sides of a big conference table, glaring at one another. Near by were the aldermen, John A. Richert, Willis O. Nance, Henry D. Capitain, James H. Lawley, W. J. Healy. And Jim Pugh, smiling and bouncy, was in the office too, in a seat near Thompson.

Hour after hour passed without result. Both groups snapped angry words about the hiring of strikebreakers, the union's wage demands and the company's claims. There was especially bitter wrangling over the selection of one or more public figures to help arbitrate the controversial issues that had caused the strike. "You don't want arbitration!" yelled Mahon to Busby. "You have bluffed all the way through. You have proposed men you knew would be rejected!"

From time to time Thompson and Pugh left the room to tell the

THE "LOCK-IN" AS A REMEDY FOR THE "LOCK-OUT."

reporters of the lack of progress. "I am not going to let them leave," Thompson said suddenly, "until they make peace. I am determined no one should get out until we get somewhere!" He sent for five-dozen sandwiches and coffee. During a lapse in the parley he filled the tub in his lavatory with water and put in a small model of a sailboat, making bets with some of the men on whether they could sail it from one end of the tub to the other.

Shortly before dawn Busby, striding about the room and heading for a closet where he had hung his coat, suddenly turned to Mahon.

"You're wrong about our plan for arbitration. We do want it. We'll prove it. Here! We offer you Mayor Thompson as arbitrator!"

Mahon and his men conferred, then cried, "We'll do it! We'll take Mayor Thompson!"

In a few hours the newspapers announced the end of the strike, and early-morning workers near the City Hall gathered in the streets and yelled "Hooray for Big Bill!" That night, with the streetcars running again and the elevated cars trundling on their tracks, Karl Eitel invited Big Bill and his whole cabinet to the grand opening of his Bismarck Gardens, and when the mayor and his wife entered all the celebrants stood and cheered: "Hooray for our mayor!" Even the cautious *Tribune* said: "He had the power and he had the sand." BLT echoed the sentiment: "Send Big Bill to Yurrup instead of any peace evangels. He appears to have the sand."

5

All this, of course, was to Fred Lundin's liking. Behind the noble façade Lundin was quietly, efficiently and ruthlessly building his machine, the one he hoped would propel Big Bill into positions far more important and powerful than the one he now held.

He played his craft wisely and shrewdly, this Poor Swede. A few days after his election Big Bill had handed to Lundin the city pay roll. "Here it is," he said. "You play with it." Each name was entered on a card by Lundin's Ike Volz and helpers in the Union Hotel headquarters. The cards were shuffled about in accordance with party affiliation, service to Thompson and the Lundin organization, rank and influence. Not for some months would all this be disclosed, angrily and furiously, by Big Bill's enemies, but Lundin was handling all patronage now. He never went to the City Hall; he sent Volz with messages about whom to hire and whom to fire. He appointed for Thompson a Committee on Literature, Publicity and Printing, with such stalwarts as Percy B. Coffin, the mercurial boss of the Civil Service Commission; the Ward brothers, Harry and Charlie, masters of the fiery phrase; William F. Mulvihill, Edward H. Wright, a Negro leader in the Second Ward, and Volz. This committee would, Lundin hoped, write all of Big Bill's messages, speeches and public statements; and it did this, by and large, often attempting to undo damage wrought by extemporaneous comments blurted by Thompson.

The favorable reaction to Mayor Thompson's handling of the streetcar strike—in the summer he actually worked diligently as referee, finally securing a settlement agreeable to both sides—prompted Lundin to advance his timetable. In July he started a Presidential boomlet for his protégé. He persuaded Thompson to dispose of $1,670,000 of stockholdings in the big gas and electric companies—"We'll build you as an enemy of the trusts." Even more remarkably, he got Thompson to stop drinking—"We'll sell you as a decent man with decent habits." He wangled interviews with friendly political reporters, in which they sounded out Thompson on his chances for becoming a "dark-horse" candidate for the Republican Presidential nomination. At such times Big Bill, after swiping broadly at President Wilson and the Democrats, earnestly declared, "I will be a candidate, if the younger element of the Republican party wills it."

Another dramatic, eye-catching event was needed, Lundin decided, to bring Thompson into national view. Sensing that the forces supporting dry laws were growing larger—large enough, perhaps, to influence the choice of a Presidential candidate—Lundin made an important decision and influenced Big Bill to abide by it. On October 4, much to the surprised dismay of many who considered Thompson an advocate of the wide-open town, Bill sent a message to the city council, just before departing with his wife and an entourage of followers for the San Francisco Exposition.

"I have recently received communications from citizens of Chicago," the message began, "that liquor is sold in this city on Sunday in violation of the state law. I referred these communications to the corporation counsel for an opinion. He advises me that the state law provides that any tippling house or place where liquor is sold or given away upon the first day of the week, commonly called Sunday, shall be fined not exceeding $200." He was further advised, said the mayor, that the city ordinance permitting some of the city's 7,000 such establishments to remain open on Sundays did not nullify the state law.

The closing order came on a Tuesday. It was to go into effect by midnight of the following Saturday. And between those days the excited city was in a fine fury while drys and wets lined up, the first with hosannas and hallelujahs, the second with angry shouts and charges of betrayal.

"Well done, thou good and faithful servant!" intoned the Reverend Leslie F. Potter of St. Simon's Church. "I knew it was coming sometime," remarked Hinky Dink Kenna in his crowded Workingmen's Exchange, "so I guess the only thing to do is get loaded Saturday if you're gonna try to last till Monday morning." Billy Sunday praised Thompson for his "grit and backbone" and hailed the coming of "a new epoch in Chicago's marvelous history—I can imagine the howl when the news reached Hell, and I am sure the devil is in bed with pneumonia!" James (Hot Stove Jimmy) Quinn, leader of the Twenty-first Ward, mourned, "It will interfere with the social life of many of our citizens of foreign birth and descent who are accustomed to make Sunday their great day for the amenities of a healthy life." The Reverend Philip Yarrow, an inveterate reformer: "This is a big step toward making Chicago a city beautiful, with happy, contented people." And Joe Spogot, manager of the popular Bismarck Gardens: "It's a joke, ain't it? That order's O.K. for New York, but not for a town like Chi!" Anna Gordon, president of the Women's Christian Temperance Union, heading a delegation of two hundred aboard the White Ribbon Special for a convention in Seattle, paused to cry, "We thank you, Mayor Thompson, we thank you!" and to gloat over the W.C.T.U.'s prime foe in rhyme:

> "John Barleycorn, you have been the curse of man,
> You stole his very soul!
> You fiend, deny it if you can!
> Now every nation on the globe
> Has raised the battle cry,
> John Barleycorn, good-by!"

The poetic spokesman for the wets was that aldermanic bard, Bathhouse John Coughlin, whose lament read:

> Saloons to close on Sundays is the order of the mayor,
> Prohibition soon will be statewide, 'tis winning everywhere.
> 'Twill not be long, now mark my word, until this town
>   goes dry,
> Then I will quit this mundane sphere for mansions in the sky.
> I never dreamed that such a day would ever come to pass,
> When you and I would be deprived of friendship's social
>   glass.
> But now that Sunday's bars are barred, this poet wants to fly
> To Greenland's icy mountains or mansions in the sky.

But the bitterest plaint issued from the United Societies for Local Self-Government, comprising most of the city's saloon owners, whose secretary was an aggressive young Bohemian-born firebrand, Anton J. Cermak.

Angrily Cermak produced a pledge with Thompson's signature. In the document, signed two weeks before the mayoral election, Big Bill had promised to oppose all Sunday blue laws. He had agreed that the Illinois Sunday closing law was obsolete and should not be enforced by the administration. "He signed that pledge, Thompson did, in his own home on Sheridan Road, with Gene Pike standing there beside us," said Cermak. "He promised he would support us in getting the right to sell liquor after three o'clock in the morning, and now look what he does! He's an anarchist! He's depriving the workingman of his pleasures on his one day off!"

Obliged to reply, Big Bill said blandly that he simply did not remember signing such a pledge. To reporters who boarded his train at Belleville, Wisconsin, he expressed his surprise at the frenzy. "What's everyone so excited about? All I've done is what my corporation counsel says I have to do according to the law. Heavens, I'm no reformer!" Presidential hopes? "This has nothing at all to do with all this talk about my being a candidate." He dropped a vague hint, instead, that by taking this action he had thwarted the efforts of his enemies, principally Charles Deneen, to get him indicted by the Cook County grand jury for not enforcing the Sunday closing law. "And I've now done my duty!" he trumpeted.

7

Back home the dry forces continued to celebrate. Under the Reverend Mr. Yarrow's direction, a Dry Chicago parade was organized, one similar in many ways to the hoopla parades of which Lundin was a master planner. On the Saturday before the fateful midnight, 12,000 drys straggled down Michigan Boulevard, carrying the inevitable banners. Some warned: BOOZE BRUTALIZES, OSTRA-CIZES, ORPHANIZES, ZEROIZES, AND EXTERMINIZES! Others advised, BOOZERS ARE LOSERS! And many heralded the eventual demise of John Barleycorn.

Hot Stove Jimmy Quinn, disgustedly watching the marchers, muttered, "Our liberal city is being run by pale little preachers from cloisters and seminaries and by uplifters." A man on a streetcar expressed admiration for Thompson and was quickly pitched into the street by three irate citizens. In saloon windows signs read: "Don't forget to stock up, tomorrow's Sunday!" His muse giddy again, Bathhouse John counseled:

> "Take a little bottle home for Sunday,
> Don't forget to take it home, I pray.
> You will need it ere the dawn of Monday,
> Take it home and plant it in the hay!"

The Sunday editions of all newspapers carried directories of places saloonless townsfolk might visit, the *Tribune* heading its list of churches, concert halls, museums, theaters, libraries and parks "Entertainment for a Dry Sunday."

Cermak organized a massive parade of the wets, some 40,000 angry men and women, ranging from stolid beer drinkers who resented the ruling on personal grounds to saloonkeepers with a financial stake in Cermak's cause. An invitation was sent to Thompson to review this procession, but he snorted, "I refuse. They're all anarchists!"

Dry Sunday passed with no great turmoil. Only twenty-eight saloons were discovered violating the law, and Chief Healey's enforcement squads handed them warnings instead of warrants. In his soft-drink parlor on Chestnut Street in his "Deestrict" old Cap Streeter, the eccentric who claimed ownership of land east of Michigan Avenue, continued to sell beer, for he considered himself outside the city's laws. It was a fatal error for the stubborn man. When police raided the place Ma Streeter shot and wounded one of them, setting off a series of legal steps that eventually forced the Streeters from the territory they so long and fiercely had insisted was their very own.

Big Bill returned on October 19 to a gala reception at the Grand Central Station and, of course, another parade. At the depot he was acclaimed as "The Man of the People" and "The Man Who Put the Sun in Sunday." Then the crowd swarmed into Cohan's Grand Opera House. Arthur McCoid, the chairman, hailed Big Bill as "the logical candidate for President of these United States." "He is," yelled McCoid, "the leader of Chicago, the leader of Illinois, the man of the hour in the United States." The audience rose, waved its banners and then burst into "The Star-Spangled Banner." Thompson spoke briefly, with righteous dignity. "I did my duty, that's all," he orated. "This is no move for Thompson. This is a movement for law enforcement. When they say they want to block Thompson they are counting their chickens before they are hatched. They are not opposing Thompson. They are opposing an army!" And he sat down again, to blush modestly when the Reverend J. B. Brushingham declared, "You are the first violinist in the orchestral harmony of civic redemption and progress. You are the leader. Let me tell you, William Hale Thompson, that a sober, law-abiding people may insist that you be the leader of the nation!"

8

But the rosy Presidential bubble was quickly pricked.

Cermak had been the first. His disclosure of the signed pledge to co-operate with his saloonkeepers brought ridicule on Big Bill from influential forces outside Chicago. The *New York Times*, chortling over the Reverend Mr. Brushingham's words that "set the candidate to music," counted him out of the running even in the dark-horse class. "It is a sorrow," its editorial stated, "to lose Big Bill Thompson so early. He promised to be the Comic Candidate, who is never wanting in the early stages of a campaign."

Soon complaints arose from the reformers that some saloons and cabarets were being passed over by Chief Healey's raiders. With a great display of ire, Big Bill ordered licenses of such establishments revoked. Then, when the reformers' indignation had cooled, the licenses were quietly restored. Sometimes these restorations were made on Big Bill's own whim. More often he yielded to pressures from such adherents as Albert A. Michaelson, his aldermanic floor leader, or William Burkhardt, his brother-in-law who served as Deputy Commissioner of Public Works, or Oscar de Priest, alderman from the Second Ward and the first Negro alderman in the city's history. And there were strong reports—and vivid evidence—that certain favored denizens of the darkened Levee were operating again. Big Jim Colosimo, the king of panders, was one of these. His Wabash Avenue resort had been shut down in the summer of 1914 in Carter Harrison's big assault on the Levee, but now it was roaring again, not as an open house of assignation, but as a meeting place for prostitutes who picked up customers there and took them to flats owned by Colosimo. Big Jim had his good friends in the City Hall. Already he was the acknowledged overlord of prostitution in what remained of the old South Side Levee and he carried on with a minimum of police interference.

To these complaints others were quickly and vociferously added. Alderman Charles E. Merriam, the vigorous political-science professor at the University of Chicago and leader of the city council's reform bloc, raised a cry against the wrecking of the civil service system. Merriam demanded that Percy Coffin be fired, along with the other members of the Civil Service Commission, George E. Nye and Joseph Geary. Alderman A. A. Buck, who joined the attack, called Coffin a "swashbuckling buccaneer who is scuttling our civil service ship in this city of laws."

Evidence supported Buck and Merriam. In the first four months of Thompson's term nearly 10,000 temporary employees were spread over the pay rolls, all deriving their positions from political affiliations. Owners of horse teams hired by the city were compelled to pay three to five dollars for each team and to join the William Hale Thompson Republican Club, which already had a war chest of over $100,000 originally designed to help Big Bill get the Presidential nomination. Day laborers, including saloonkeepers who appeared on the salary lists as boiler inspectors and sewer inspectors, were assessed three dollars a month and obliged to attend ward meetings.

The councilmen, spurred by Merriam and inflamed by Alderman Otto Kerner, chairman of the judiciary committee, who called Coffin, Nye and Geary "victims of moral leprosy" and "libelous banditti" voted 44-20 to ask Thompson to fire the commissioners. But he refused. "Those fellows in the council who are against me are all a bunch of crooks," he said, "and that Merriam from Chicago University is the biggest crook of them all!"

By November trouble developed among Thompson's closest leaders. Ed Brundage had already been forced out of the inner conferences and denied patronage. Pugh, Pike and Harding were required to give way to Fred Lundin, and they drew together as Lundin played a lone game with Big Bill. Lundin never appeared at the City Hall. Thompson met him every day in a room in the Great Northern Hotel or in a suite in the Hotel Sherman that came to be called City Hall No. 2. On week ends Thompson always drove up to Lundin's farm on Lake Villa, near Antioch. Sometimes Harding, Pike and Pugh were invited, but most often they were not, and when they later met Bill in his office, they found that important decisions had already been made.

Jim Pugh, who was having business troubles with Lundin, soon discovered just how powerful a hold Lundin had on Thompson. On Pugh's suggestion Thompson had chosen a reputable lawyer, Richard B. Folsom, the Democrat who had helped in the election, as his corporation counsel. At once Lundin had demanded that he give jobs to worthy precinct workers and legal hacks, but Folsom refused. He appealed for assistance to Pugh, but when Pugh asked Thompson to demand that Lundin cease this pressure, Thompson curtly turned him down. Folsom resigned, and Thompson chose to succeed him Samuel Ettelson, the lawyer so closely affiliated with Samuel Insull, the utilities magnate.

"A disgrace! An insult!" Alderman Merriam described Ettelson's appointment. "He has been a corporation lobbyist for years. He is associated with Insull's law firm. He will manipulate the mayor as Sam Insull wants him to." Few of the other aldermen agreed, especially after Ettelson's record as a state legislator and generally public-minded citizen was presented to them. Despite his confirmation, however, many remembered Thompson's blarings against the Big Interests and the Gas Trust in his mayoral campaign and wondered how right Merriam might be.

Much of the enthusiasm Thompson had stirred in labor ranks by his handling of the streetcar strike dimmed toward the end of the year. In a strike of some 40,000 members of the Amalgamated Clothing Workers of America, led by Sidney Hillman, there was rioting and fighting. Several persons were killed and many were clubbed by Chief Healey's police. Among the strike supporters were Mrs. Ruth Hanna McCormick, wife of Medill McCormick, co-owner of the *Tribune*, Ellen Gates Starr of Hull House and Frances Crane Lillie, daughter of Richard T. Crane, the multimillionaire industrialist. But when delegations came to protest the brutality and to ask him to act as arbitrator, Thompson refused to see them. He called them agitators and radicals and once he sent word that he was too busy with plans for picking a Miss Chicago in a beauty contest. By December 15, when the strike finally ended, Thompson stood accused of sanctioning brutality toward working people.

9

A few hours before the eve of 1916 the reporters trooped into Big Bill's office.

Despite the growing resentment in the city council, the evaporation of the Presidential hope, the cries of his accusers, the lost and abandoned promises, he was jovial. He handed out copies of his first annual report, yelling, "Just read it and see what we're going to do!"

The reporters read. Chicago, asserted the mayor, needed dream-
ers. "To understand its potentialities is to build dreams for its
future, not to be gratified by what has been done, not to be satisfied
with what we are doing, but to picture it as it shall be some day!"
And on that some day, said the mayor, "Chicago will be the greatest
city in the world!"

The charges? Civil service laxity? Labor oppression? Crooks?
Colosimo? "Lies, all lies!" he cried. "Those fellows making those
charges are my enemies. But what the hell, boys, in a few hours it's
going to be 1916, a new year, time to start all over again! Why, I
wish 'em all a Happy New Year, that's all I got to say!"

12 ‖ "Liars! Hypocrites! Fourflushers! Bunk! Bunk! Bunk!"

I

THE LAST CHAMPAGNE TOASTS WERE drunk, the last words of cheer sounded. Now Big Bill and Fred Lundin were ready to strike back at those who had dared to cry out against them. Their big opportunity came in the February aldermanic elections, when half the council was to be chosen. Now the rebels and the reformers and the scoffers, said Big Bill, would feel the fury of his wrath.

He listed nine aldermen up for re-election as his quarry: Nathaniel A. Stern, Willis O. Nance, John N. Kimball, Frank H. Ray, John Kjellander, Frank J. Link, George Pretzel, Oliver J. Watson, M. L. Dempsey. All, at one time or another, had opposed ordinances and measures proposed by the Thompson group. All sided with Alderman Charles Merriam, who guided them and became their spokesman, although he was not up for re-election. They called themselves "The Honest Nine." Thompson called them "The Bunco Nine" and "The Hungry Nine."

Now Merriam brought many of the whispered charges into the smoky Chicago air. "The mayor's real enemies," he declared in his opening statement, "are not the decent aldermen whom he is vociferously assailing, but his false friends who are attempting to use the administration for their own ends. The evil genius of the mayor is Fred Lundin, who distributes the jobs and favors, performs the work no real mayor should delegate and destroys the foundations of the administration with his daily mining and sapping."

136

Others indicted Lundin as the prime culprit. The Municipal Voters' League, watchdog of local politics, labeled him "The Mayor's Mephisto," and the nine aldermen, in a manifesto, declared that Lundin was "a cunning public enemy who has taken from a slothful mayor the work and power of his office, leaving the titleholder free to orate and parade and boast of deeds never done and dream vain dreams of higher political preferment." The Civil Service Reform League, horrified by Lundin's powers of patronage, accused Thompson and his mentor of trying to build a Chicago Tammany.

Thompson responded characteristically. First came a dignified statement: "Fred Lundin is one of the most honorable as well as one of the most practical men I have ever met in my whole life." Then followed: "Liars! Hypocrites! Fourflushers! Bunk! Bunk! Bunk!" As for Merriam: "I despise Merriam more than I despise any living man. I say to you, Merriam, that you have a black heart and a white liver!" Those who opposed him, cried Bill, were in the pay of the whisky bosses, the traction bosses, the political bosses and the "four-flushing reformers." He drew on the Bible for one of his speeches, telling his audience about David and Goliath. "I am the David in this fight, the people's David, and you can take it from me, I'm going to smash them right square in the face from now on, all of them!"

Merriam persisted, growing bolder by the day. Decrying the crime wave then sweeping through the city, much to Big Bill's discomfiture, Merriam declared: "The vice and crime trusts are advancing their lines as they have not dared to do in years." His charge was based on solid fact. Such places as Colosimo's, the infamous Bucket of Blood, The Arsonia, The Athenia and Freiberg's dance hall, where young whores posed as dancing teachers, were besieged nightly by prospective vice customers. Girls picked them up there and took them to "call flats." Major M. C. L. Funkhouser, whom Harrison had appointed head of the Morals Division in the fight against the Levee, estimated the city had nearly 30,000 such rooms. "Why, in some of them," said the horrified major, "it costs five dollars just to sit down and talk for three minutes!" As for crime itself, said Merriam, in the first eight months of Thompson's regime the number of criminal complaints had been greater by fifty per cent than in 1914. "The police?" he cried. "The police department is just a big sewing circle!"

"Lies, all lies!" blustered Big Bill. The crime trusts were against him, he insisted. "As a matter of fact, I have heard from a responsible source that the crime trusts are out to get me. My life is in danger and so is Chief Healey's, and we are getting special bodyguards." Until the end of the hectic campaign Big Bill was accompanied by six police sergeants in plain clothes.

2

As if to pinpoint the charges of corruption in the Thompson ranks, a scandal developed amid the oratorical hubbub. As scandals went then and would go in Big Bill's years, it was infinitesimal. But it did contribute a phrase that would be brought up again and again in his reign.

Resigning suddenly as Superintendent of Social Surveys, Mrs. Page Waller Eaton complained that her superior, Mrs. Louise Osborn Rowe, Commissioner of Public Welfare, had compelled her to kick back nearly $600 in salary. "She told me," related Mrs. Eaton angrily, "that Billy needed the money for Maysie Thompson's sister. Maysie's sister, Mrs. Margaret Mivalez, is a widow, you know. Mrs. Rowe said the campaign had cost Billy so much that he had to cash in his securities." She refused to yield any part of her pay at first but did so a few days later when Mrs. Rowe summoned her again. This time, said Mrs. Eaton, she was told, "Maysie says you've got to come across."

Mrs. Rowe claimed the story was a lie, and so did Mrs. Thompson and so did Mrs. Mivalez. But the phrase stuck—"Maysie says you've got to come across"—and BLT, the *Tribune's* columnist, suggested that the Thompsonites use it as a theme song then and forever. A flurry of demands that the story be investigated came to nothing, with Thompson calling Mrs. Rowe "that brave little woman" and Percy Coffin quarreling with the aldermen over who had the right to probe Mrs. Eaton's charges, and Lundin declaring, "I don't know the woman and I have nothing to do with all this. All I want to do is to elect Republicans and have prosperity."

Just before passing into obscurity, Mrs. Eaton, having added her bit to the city's political lore, summed up what obviously was the feeling of many who had been Big Bill's supporters. When the request for part of her salary was made, she said, she was aghast that he would condone such activities. "I shuddered then to think that I had once told an audience in the campaign, 'Before God, I tell you I know in my heart that I never will have to apologize for Bill Thompson.' But now the truth has been carried home to me. The idol of a people half mad with hero worship was made of clay, after all."

3

On the evening before the election both sides offered the usual confident predictions. "Why, Bill Thompson," asked the aldermanic nine in a final statement, "are you trying to drive us out of the council? Do you want a rubber-stamp council? Do you want to be a dictator? Do you think the people want only Gray Wolves in the City Hall? Why don't you stop spouting so much bunk?"

Thompson refused to reply directly, but indirectly he defied all his shouting accusers by approving the reopening of a number of Levee dives, including the notorious Cadillac Café, Polack Ben's resort on Twenty-second Street, and Freddie Buxbaum's saloon, one of the city's vilest places, on the ground floor of the Marlboro Hotel, a brothel at State and Twenty-second streets. Bristling at this boldness, Merriam made a final thrust, and a prophetic one. "This carnival of crime, the reopening of the red-light district, the assault on civil service, the levying of assessments on officials and people with whom the city does business—all are disgraces. These and a long train of other and greater scandals will be bound to follow the abdication of the mayor's power in favor of the unseen boss, whose sinister activities are frustrating the hopes of Chicago for a real administration of city affairs."

In the election only two of the Honest Nine, Stern and Ray, were defeated. The Municipal Voters' League called the triumph "a stinging rebuke" for Big Bill. Thompson replied, "The fight has just started against the petty, jealous guerrillas who are intent on

HE LET THE WRONG ONE IN.

continuing to fight for spite and political reasons." And the *Tribune*, deriding him as "Bill the Immense," declared with characteristic finality: "He is, in the only words which can do the subject justice, the bunk."

4

Soon there were new troubles.

In mid-March, 3,000 women gathered in the Auditorium to protest against Thompson's misrule. Mrs. Joseph T. Bowen, a leader among society women interested in good government, presided over a meeting in which representatives of the Chicago Woman's Club, the Municipal Voters' League, the Civil Service Reform Association, Hull House and other civic groups each discussed one aspect of the over-all problem. They drew up a platform demanding, among many things, that Thompson divorce the school system from politics, bar the sale of liquor in dance halls, abolish cabarets, keep his hands off the civil service lists, build new police stations and stop loading the Municipal Tuberculosis Sanitarium with political pay-rollers.

"They're knockers," growled Thompson. "Take that Municipal Tuberculosis Sanitarium, for instance. Why, that Doc Sachs is a terrible superintendent. He's the worst appointment I ever made!"

Dr. Sachs—Theodore B. Sachs, a mild, earnest man—had been head of the big sanitarium since Fred Busse's day. He had come from Russia to Chicago as a youth, attending the University of Illinois Medical School while working as a stock clerk for a clothing company. For years he had toiled in the city's ghetto, treating hundreds free or for small fees.

When Thompson had been elected, he retained Dr. Sachs as chief of the sanitarium. But he soon found cause to regret his action. Dr. Sachs, it developed, had the quaint idea that the sanitarium should not become a dumping ground for Thompson pay-rollers. Thompson and his servile health commissioner, Dr. John Dill Robertson, the Lorimerite now an active leader in the William Hale Thompson Republican Club, applied pressure constantly, yet the doughty Dr. Sachs refused to yield.

But after Thompson made his low evaluation, however, Dr. Sachs submitted his letter of resignation. He was quitting, he wrote, because he refused to permit the sanitarium to become a "political football." He had waged a war to prevent Thompson and Dr. Robertson from firing civil service employees and replacing them with sixty-day temporary appointees. Now, he admitted sadly, he could fight no longer. "I am taking this step because I do not believe in political management of hospitals, sanitaria or similar institutions."

Gleefully Thompson put Dr. Robertson in charge of the huge institution until a permanent superintendent could be appointed. With the typical guile of a political doctor, Robertson purported to find all sorts of extravagances in the hospital, even claiming that Dr. Sachs had provided erroneous figures on the number of cases treated and cured. Such a report, made to the city council, brought an anti-Thompsonite, Alderman A. A. McCormick, to his feet, crying, "Let me remind you, gentlemen, that this same Dr. Robertson who now says Sachs won't do is the same Dr. Robertson who advised Senator Lorimer to back the Duket cure for consumption some time ago, a fraud that was responsible for the death of some of our people!"

Unperturbed, Dr. Robertson carried on for Big Bill. On the basis of a quick ruling by the Civil Service Commission that civil service laws did not apply to the sanitarium, he dismissed dozens of permanent employees and replaced them with pay-rollers. The newspapers promptly dubbed him "The Job King" as he found positions for friends of Jim Pugh, for friends of Percy Coffin, for all worthy vote getters for Big Bill Thompson. The sanitarium's business manager admitted he gave no applicant any consideration unless a note from Dr. Robertson was shown. "If they don't have the note," he said frankly, "they've got to call up the doc."

Each day new resignations from the institution's doctors were accepted. A group of six staff physicians quit, declaring: "No self-respecting residence staff would tolerate the interference which would result from this system." Doctors in and out of the sanitarium who refused to co-operate with Dr. Robertson were demoted. Dr. Walter W. Armstrong, head of the City Food Bureau, was fired, then restored to the post of supervising health officer, a job paying $1,200 less a year. Later Dr. Armstrong was ordered to help campaign for Thompson's ticket in the April primaries, the directive coming from Dr. Clarence W. Leigh, a Thompson patronage dispenser in Dr. Armstrong's ward. The harassed doctor did campaign but was dismissed anyway.

Thompson himself continued his barrage against Dr. Sachs, who had quietly retired to a private sanitarium he had established in Naperville. "Dr. Sachs has not only not been a first-class man from the physicians' standpoint," charged Bill, "but he has been unduly extravagant. He wanted to make the Municipal Sanitarium the

Sachs Sanitarium. Well, we won't have it that way, whether he likes it or not."

In the midst of all the yelling Dr. Sachs killed himself by swallowing poison. Beside his body sprawled in the library of his Naperville sanitarium was a note. After expressing his love for the Municipal Sanitarium and its patients, he had written: "Unscrupulous politicians should be thwarted. The institution should remain as it was built, unsoiled by graft and politics, the heritage of the people. In the course of time every man and woman will know how Dr. Sachs loved Chicago and how he has given his life to it. My death has little to do with the present controversy. I would not dignify it. I am simply weary. With love to all."

Even this tragedy did not soften Thompson's attack. He was sorry Dr. Sachs was dead, he avowed, " . . . but that isn't my fault." At a meeting in Cohan's Grand Opera House he repeated that the appointment was still the worst he had ever made. He assailed his foes—the various bosses and the anti-Thompson Republicans—for making the Sachs case an issue. "My family," he boomed, "had to do with the upbuilding of Chicago for three generations. Yet I know I express the opinion of every man and woman in this vast audience when I declare that any man once elected to an office of public power who won't be a cringing coward, an abject slave to corporate interests and to the newspaper trust of this city must resign himself to the volumes of vilification which will be heaped on his head. Maybe they will destroy me"—at this the audience shrilled "No! No! No!"—"but I will never surrender!"

5

In that troublesome summer of 1916 Big Bill had a new name to add to his list of those he insisted sought to destroy him, the name of Maclay Hoyne, an iron-jawed Irishman whose family also had much to do with the building of Chicago. One of Hoyne's ancestors was an original incorporator of Chicago as a village; another had served as mayor. Maclay Hoyne was now completing his first term as state's attorney of Cook County. Blunt and outspoken, filled with seeming passion for routing evil, he had established a good record by smashing arson trusts, wire-tapping combines, fake spiritualist rings. In the drive on the Levee in 1914, he had aided Carter Harrison, whose protégé he was.

Now he took out after Thompson, aiming specifically at the Police Department. He charged that Chief Healey was inefficient and ineffectual in fighting crime. He deplored the recent appointment of Nicholas Hunt, a dandified fellow with slick white hair and expensive clothes, as chief of detectives, calling special attention to Hunt's resignation from the force in 1912 after it was disclosed that during his term as inspector in the Hyde Park district brothels, blind-pig saloons and low dives operated unmolested. When Healey and Hunt announced a shakeup of the force, Hoyne scoffed. "The crooks of Chicago apparently are still in control." Three newly made captains had taken money from vicemongers, asserted Hoyne, and their promotions "have been bought and paid for."

While Hoyne flailed away and began to collect evidence against Healey, Thompson was occupied with the vital matter of gaining for Frank O. Lowden the governorship in the November election. Lowden still felt he would never win because of his relationship to George M. Pullman, the railroad magnate. But he was willing to listen to Big Bill and Lundin.

He brought to a luncheon in the Chicago Athletic Club the G.O.P. chairmen from 96 of the 101 downstate counties, prepared to hear what Thompson had to say. "We're with the colonel all the way," Thompson assured them. "We'll win for him and you'll win for him downstate." This said—and with Lowden's assurance that he would support Thompson for higher office when that move was to be made—Thompson and Lundin relaxed for a few weeks at the Lowden beach home in Florida, then returned late in the summer to launch the campaign.

When they arrived they learned that Hoyne, preparing to run for another term as state's attorney, was far ahead of them. Week by week he exposed new failures in Thompson's Police Department. In an audacious raid he invaded the headquarters of the Sportsmen's Club of America, Jim Pugh's organization which had done much for Big Bill in the 1915 election. The club, said Hoyne, was being used by Thompson as a collection agency for graft from gamblers, saloonkeepers and vicemongers. Letters sent to these worthies, inviting them to take out life memberships for $100, carried Big Bill's name; among the members were Mont Tennes, "king of the bookies"; Tennes' lawyer, Henry Seligman, who doubled as lawyer for the club; Jimmy Mondi, a lieutenant of Big Jim Colosimo's; Big Jim himself; and various manufacturers of slot machines which, though illegal, were to be found in hundreds of saloons.

Then, on October 10, Hoyne's raiders swooped into the City Hall. A dozen of them stamped into Thompson's office, seizing letters and all records they could lay their hands on.

Before Sam Ettelson, with loud threats of legal action, and Chief Healey's police reserves, with upraised clubs, could halt the raiders, they had ransacked Healey's office and also Major Funkhouser's. This last raid was most important of all, since it produced records of payments by vice bosses to police officials, records gathered by Francis D. Hanna, a former Morals Division inspector. Hanna had been fired by Thompson early in his term because he dared offer a list of brothels running wide-open with police protection, and it was Hanna who had furnished Hoyne with the exact information about where to find the incriminating evidence. After the raids, Hoyne announced he was presenting his mass of records to the grand jury. "I expect some hot action," he said.

Although Hoyne's onslaught frightened Big Bill—"He is scared half to death," commented the *Journal*—he went through the motions of supporting Harry B. Miller, his city prosecutor, as Hoyne's opponent. Miller, who had once carried a drum in a Salvation Army band, was an inoffensive sort. Charles Merriam, quickly springing forward, called him "Bill Thompson's poodle dog" and "the Lundin-Thompson Mannikin." The *Tribune*, frowning on both Hoyne and Miller, declared its support for the Socialist candidate, William A. Cunnea.

There was glee in the Lundin-Thompson headquarters on election night, for Lowden defeated his Democratic rival, Edward F. Dunne, by 140,000 votes. And there was gloom, for Hoyne beat Miller by 40,000 votes, and immediately declared he was pressing for indictments against "certain high officials."

Thompson, who always spoke so highly of the will of the people when he won, now mildly berated them. "Hoyne's victory is a triumph of the forces of evil. The public is indifferent to law enforcement. If the public is indifferent, I don't want to stay in office." Responding quickly to this first of Big Bill's many threats to quit politics if he or his candidates lost, Hoyne retorted, "The mayor would do the city a service if he kept his word to quit."

6

In these hours of woe Thompson was without the support of his old friend, Jim Pugh.

After that glorious election night in 1915—"Bill Thompson," Pugh had cried, "we'll make you governor and senator and President, you old sonofabitch!"—Pugh's influence had been slowly sapped. He and Lundin quarreled frequently over statements and appointments, following the disagreement over the appointment of Ettelson. Another vital blow to Pugh grew out of Thompson's promise to fight for five-cent streetcar fares. Samuel Insull and the newspapers opposed such a move, but Pugh thought he could get James Keeley, who had left the *Tribune* to become editor of the *Herald*, to support the mayor. He let himself and Keeley into Big Bill's office one day by a side door and the three sat chatting affably about this proposal and about the possibility of compromising with the streetcar lines. But when Pugh told Big Bill that one condition on which Keeley's support hinged was that he rid himself of Fred Lundin, Thompson lumbered to his feet. "You're a couple of crooked Jims," he yelled. "Get the hell out of my office!"

Gradually Pugh was shoved out of Thompson's inner circle. Lundin's power grew as Pugh's diminished, then vanished. Heartbroken at what he considered his betrayal, Pugh spent most of his final years until his death in 1925 at Eastman Springs, near Benton Harbor, Michigan. There, to visiting reporters, he spoke sadly of his "purpling twilight of frustration," denounced Lundin as an atheist and Thompson as a drunk and, pointing to his small zoo of blooded airedales, goats, geese, monkeys and chickens, always muttered, "I keep only animals around me now because they are the only ones a fellow can trust."

7

With Hoyne promising indictments hourly, agitation developed among Thompson's leaders for Chief Healey's dismissal. But Thompson hesitated and Healey himself insisted, "I'm going to fight. I may go down, but I'll go down fighting. Hasn't Bill Thompson told me that I am the best chief this city ever had?"

The grand jurors thought otherwise. They smacked Healey with a mighty indictment charging him, among many offenses, with being entangled in a graft conspiracy with underworld characters like "Mike de Pike" Heitler, a vice boss, and Billy Skidmore. Healey then resigned and was replaced by honest Herman Schuettler, his first deputy, who sang a familiar tune about driving out the crooks, closing the saloons and completely suppressing all criminal activities.

Healey's trial early in 1917 produced sensation after sensation. One police captain admitted he had been Healey's collector. Another testified that Healey ordered him to keep away from certain South Side dives because "big people" in the City Hall preferred they be unmolested. A "little green book" turned up; it listed dozens of brothels and protection prices ranging from $40 to $150 a week, vice joints marked with "the Chief's places" and other illicit establishments, unprotected by graft payments or political friends, with the notation, "Can be raided." But Clarence Darrow and Charles Erbstein, most skillful of criminal lawyers, managed to win an acquittal for the chief. For extra measure, the jury also freed Skidmore and the other defendants.

In another trial growing out of Hoyne's raids, one of the defendants was the ubiquitous Oscar de Priest, the Second Ward's Negro alderman. A man revered by his people, who often followed him in admiring crowds down South State Street, De Priest was one of Thompson's most loyal supporters. He had tried to secure civil-rights legislation in the city council and had been influential in getting many jobs for Negroes in city departments. But at his trial he was accused of being a protector of crime and vice in his district. Several gamblers testified they were free from police raids only after paying cash to De Priest's agents. Henry Jones, owner of a popular gambling house called the Elite Café, told of giving $2,500 to De Priest from gambling operators and brothel owners. Under skillful questioning by Darrow, De Priest claimed he considered the money a campaign contribution in the Miller-Hoyne race and was unaware it had come from such disreputable elements. After an impassioned plea by Darrow, in which he warned against race prejudice, the jury acquitted De Priest.

Big Bill remained undisturbed by the revelations of the trials. He was absorbed in other matters. He soon managed to hurl himself into a new controversy that would make previous troubles seem as nothing, and would earn him a peculiar kind of world fame.

13 ||| Kaiser Bill

I

ON A STEAMING AUGUST DAY IN 1915
Bill Thompson had been introduced to a cheering throng of pic-
nickers at a Republican rally in Aurora. Other speakers on the flag-
decked platform had assailed Woodrow Wilson for his European
War policies, shuddering with anger at the President's statement,
after the *Lusitania* had been sunk the previous May, implying that
the United States was "too proud to fight."

Thompson disagreed with them. He even commended Wilson's
neutrality policy, but added, "We have not gone far enough into the
middle of the road. I believe we should not send any armaments or
munitions. Such a move would tend to encourage the dreadful
carnage which has drenched the soil of Europe with human blood,
brought misery and agony of mind and body to untold millions, and
put the blush of shame on the cheek of outraged civilization!"

Many in the crowd cheered. "It matters not to me," Thompson
continued, "who may for the time being be in the ascendancy in
Europe, and it matters not to me whether one brand or another of
the many revolutionary parties in Mexico be the underdog in that
fight. There are no exceptions to the divine commandment—'Thou
shalt not kill.' "

More cheers. Soon Big Bill finished with the booming advice that
the American government say to the fighting nations: "We will sell
you food, we will sell you clothing. We will sell you medicine and
hospital supplies. We will sell you anything out of our bursting

granaries, our enormous warehouses and depots that will relieve human suffering or distress. But we will not sell death-dealing implements of war with which to kill, maim or wound your fellow human beings!"

The public pronouncement evoked no outcry from his newspaper critics or his political foes, for the war fever in the Middle West was low. Although the general sentiment favored the Allies, the hope was still strong that America would keep out of the conflict.

Aware of this, Fred Lundin had persuaded Big Bill to speak out on the subject of America's involvement. The move was intended as another in the line of maneuvers to bring Big Bill national attention. It was Lundin's idea that Thompson, young and vigorous and outspoken, could become the leader of those opposing all warlike action, and in the coming Republican convention, if all went as he planned, Big Bill could be put forward as the best candidate to oppose any war-minded Democrat. To bolster the cause and spread Big Bill's antiwar views, Lundin started publication, in December, of a weekly newspaper, *The Republican*. Walter Rohm, one of Lundin's many relatives, was named editor, and Lundin often wrote editorials expressing the same views Big Bill had espoused on the Aurora picnic platform. To finance this journal all temporary workers given jobs by Lundin were obliged to become steady subscribers, and the $100,-000 war chest of the William Hale Thompson Republican Club also was tapped frequently.

2

In 1915 few cared what Big Bill Thompson thought about war or what abuse *The Republican* sprayed on President Wilson.

But as the hectic months passed, sentiment altered swiftly and an intense nationalism spread in waves over the country, inundating even the isolationist-minded Middle West. Clergymen indicted "the shameful doctrine of pacifism," Teddy Roosevelt stumped the nation exhorting young men to learn how to shoulder arms and General Leonard Wood cried for a bigger army and more training camps. The National Security League came into being, casting a sharp but often wild eye about for German agents. When Germany, early in 1917, unleashed its unrestricted warfare on the seas, the editorialists could write: "The cloud of war looms large on our nation's horizon." When notes and protests failed, Wilson declared for war: "We must fight for justice and right."

In Chicago, after war was declared on April 4, there were many hysterical spy roundups and, as Edgar Lee Masters later wrote: "A tensity of feeling was observed, a capacity for hate was manifested, a desire to demonstrate patriotism came forth from men who had never shown either courage, honor or integrity." The streets resounded with bands playing "Tipperary" and "Over There" and the "Marseillaise." Samuel Insull and other industrialists led the Chicago Council of National Defense. A *Tribune* reporter discovered to everyone's fiery indignation that a spelling book used in Chicago schools carried a eulogy of the Kaiser, and, with photographs and charts and instructions, the newspaper showed exactly how the offending paragraphs could be cut away without harming the rest of the book. Teachers who dared suggest that peace was better than war were denounced by Jacob Loeb, President of the Board of Education. The American Protective League snooped through German neighborhoods looking for enemy agents. The handsome monument to Goethe in Lincoln Park was disfigured and marked with red chalk. A movie showing the redcoats being driven back at Concord was denounced as "anti-British." Enlistment officers reported slack business, despite all the patriotic fervor, and hinted angrily that too many "slackers" and "yellow bellies" were going to the movies instead of to the recruiting stations.

Amid all this hullabaloo Big Bill did not change his views. The original motive had long since evaporated, since the Presidential push had died before it could work up the slightest steam. But Lundin still felt that if Thompson persisted in his antiwar stand he might yet win national acclaim, perhaps in 1918, perhaps later, but certainly, as Lundin put it, "when the people realize what's happened to them and they start to think about things."

For the moment Thompson made no antiwar comment. He even marched in several Preparedness Parades, strutting down Michigan Boulevard, a high silk hat perched jauntily atop his head, a small

American flag carried daintily over one shoulder. In one interview, he also proposed a "defense move" to thwart any German attacks by sea; this could be done, said he, by organizing thousands of power-boats on the Great Lakes and elsewhere in the United States into a scouting fleet equipped with rapid-fire guns and torpedo tubes and devices to detect, run down and destroy enemy submarines.

3

But soon he spoke out, with words that reverberated through the country and into the European capitals and battlefields.

In the first part of April, Thompson was too busy with political matters, he told reporters, to talk about the war. He was involved in a quarrel with L. A. Busby, head of the Chicago Surface Lines, who, he claimed, was thwarting his efforts to start building a sub-way. "If this crowd thinks it is going to make a monkey out of me," he said, "they have got another guess coming. I'm going to get going on this subway right away, believe me." In the aldermanic elections he found pleasure in the defeat of Charles Merriam, but this joy was quickly erased by the ouster of several of his own supporters.

Then, on April 15, the reporters asked if he intended to issue, as other mayors had been asked to, a proclamation for Paul Revere Day, three days away, designed to spur enlistments. "You'd come to the conclusion from the number of enlistments," commented Big Bill, "that the people of the United States do not favor sending an army to Europe. I do believe, though, that the people of the United States would go the limit in defending this country from invasion."

Did the mayor, asked a reporter, approve the proposal to pin yellow ribbons on those "cupid recruits," the men mobbing the marriage license bureau since plans for conscription had been announced in Washington?

"I do not!" he snapped. "I'm against such foolishness. I don't think that will encourage anyone to enlist."

So far, so good. Surely he had said nothing very extreme, nothing subversive, certainly nothing treasonable.

Then, several days later, there was another interview. Big Bill was asked if he had issued the formal invitation to Marshal Joffre, hero of the Marne, and René Viviani, French minister of justice, to visit Chicago on May 7 during their nationwide tour.

Thompson hedged. He ducked behind technicalities, claiming that it was the city council's duty to present such an invitation. Sam Ettelson had told him so, he declared. "Besides, some of our people might not be so wildly enthusiastic about it." Instead of extending the invitation, Thompson used the occasion to make a strong attack on the draft—"a drastic measure which should never be invoked until the life of the republic is threatened"—and to question the motives of the French mission. "It has never been explained yet what the purpose of these distinguished visitors is. We have pending in Congress a bill which means the drafting of 50,000 young men as Chicago's share of the quota, and maybe more. Are these distinguished visitors coming here to encourage the doing of things to make our people suffer or have they some other purpose?"

Banging his fist on the top of his desk, he called to Charles Fitzmorris, his secretary, to bring to him the school census of 1914. This showed, he told the reporters, that there were more foreign-born parents of school children in Chicago than American-born. "Chicago," he said, "is the sixth largest German city in the world, the second largest Bohemian, the second largest Norwegian and the second largest Polish. When, in time of war, an invitation is sent to some nation in the name of all the people I think a mayor is presuming considerably when he takes the position that all the people are in favor of such an invitation."

4

The outcry was loud and angry and violent.

"Bill the Big, mayor in these parts, seems unable to follow the American nation," jibed the *Tribune*. "The Big 'Un, after reflection, has decided to remain neutral. As a neutral, he perceives the indelicacy of inviting Marshal Joffre to Chicago. The Germans

might be offended. Couldn't Bill preserve his neutrality and make it
50-50 by inviting Joffre and Von Hindenburg?"

"We are too big to cry," commented the *Herald*, "and he hurts
us too much to laugh. Chicago is in no mood to drag the dregs from
the cup of gall and wormwood prest to her lips when Bill Thompson
became her mayor."

"Mayor Thompson," intoned the *News*, "does not fit in with
the needs of a city as an intelligent self-governing community
or as part of the United States." And in Philadelphia, the *North
American* asked, "Is Chicago for the United States or for Germany?
Why hasn't Thompson been arrested as mayor of a German city,
openly sympathizing with the nation with which we are at war?"

Teddy Roosevelt, arriving in Chicago on his country-wide tour
to spur enlistments, addressed himself to the matter from the Stock
Yards Pavilion where his audience sang, "We'll hang old Thompson
to a sour apple tree!" Said Teddy: "Now that we are at war with
Germany let us not, at the same time, try to curry favor with the
Germans by meeching meanness to General Joffre. Never hit soft!
Put the flag on the firing line and keep it there! Let us show that
we are eager to prove that those who are fit to live are not afraid
to die!"

A committee of three superpatriots hurried to the office of U. S.
District Attorney Charles F. Clyne and asked that he investigate
Thompson's loyalty. When Clyne said he would do so, Big Bill
retorted, "Why doesn't Clyne read the Constitution? That has
something in it about free speech." And Clyne: "I'll bet the mayor
has never read the Constitution in his life." And Joseph B. Fleming,
Clyne's first assistant: "If Thompson has read the Constitution then
he knows that the penalty for treason is hanging."

Bishop Samuel Fallows called Big Bill "a traitor of the worst kind,"
and at the Chicago Sunday Evening Club 3,000 worshipers heard
their leader, Clifford Barnes, declare, "We in Chicago hang our
heads in shame." William Wrigley, the chewing-gum magnate, decreed that Thompson had made "a grave mistake" and Jim Pugh,
scooting temporarily out of retirement, yelled, "This is our town
and we want the French officials to visit us. To hell with anybody
who doesn't think the way we do!"

5

An invitation finally was sent in the name of the city council. By the time Joffre, Viviani and their associates arrived on May 7 the hubbub had quieted. Thompson, in high hat and with toothy grin, greeted them at the station, drove them to their hotel and that night, at a meeting in the Auditorium Theater, offered the city's official welcome to the visitors.

But within hours after the Frenchmen, having made their plea for men and money, had left, the furor started anew. Each day Lundin's *Republican* made a fresh assault. The war, it shouted, was "a moneybags' war." America was fighting England's battle. The American people had been fooled by a subsidized press, a scheming Wilson and the war profiteers. "Is Democracy running amuck? Shall the Demos rule the world? Are we going to reform all the monarchies? Where will it all end? What is the limit in this Wilson game of benevolence?" Another front-page editorial read:

We may, of course, be mistaken, but we are strongly imbued with the idea that our entrance into the great war at this time was unnecessary, unwise, unwarranted, and contrary to the self-interest of this country and its people.

Shall we as a nation gain in wealth, honor, territory or influence, and if so, is the anticipated benefit worth the price in human blood that is likely to be demanded?

Thompson added to the running battle with frequent barbs: "This is the federal government's war, isn't it?" and "The closer you get to Wall Street the more flags you see" and "This war is a needless sacrifice of the best blood of the nation on foreign battlefields." He refused at first to permit solicitors for war bonds to canvass the City Hall offices and when he grudgingly gave in he refused to buy any bonds. Six months later he finally purchased $5,000 in Liberty bonds.

The barrage against him continued. The Rotary Club voted to expel him from membership. The Illinois Athletic Club removed his photograph from its walls and replaced it with an American flag.

He was called "Kaiser Bill" and "Wilhelm der Grosse" and "Burgo-master Bill" and a group of draftees marched off to training camp bearing a placard that read:

To the Hon. William H. Thompson, Mayor of Chicago: We, who are about to go, members of the National Army, District 78, Chicago, salute you. By the grace of God, we hope to get to Berlin and see Big Bill there. If we do we shall tender him the warm re-gards and tender solicitude of the burgomaster of the sixth German city of the world.

From the war front Colonel John V. Clinnin, a former Thompson ward leader, reported that the Germans were dropping toy balloons behind the French lines bearing extracts from *The Republican* and Thompson's statements. Floyd Gibbons, the *Tribune's* intrepid cor-respondent, wrote Big Bill that his stand against sending more troops to Europe was causing "ill comment." "I do not write to you as one of your constituents," read Gibbons' letter. "This is a matter you will have to settle with my mother. She voted for you. I can tell you, though, that United States troops here are coupling your name with language hot enough to explode the ammunition dumps at long range."

Even after Thompson greeted a Belgian war mission the criticism did not diminish. Clergymen continued to be the most virulent attackers. "Anyone who questions the justice of America's part in the war," declared Dr. Shailer Matthews, dean of the University of Chicago's divinity school, "must be idiotic, blind, pro-German—or the Mayor of Chicago." In Baltimore, Bishop George Herbert Kin-solving of the Texas diocese had the most violent proposal of all. "I think," said the churchman, "that Mayor Thompson is guilty of treason and ought to be shot. There is only one way of punishing treason: that is by death to the man that is guilty. I am in favor of the firing squad and a stone wall as the proper means of combating treachery to the United States. What this country needs is a few first-class hangings. Then we could go on with our work of mo-bilization without fear of being stabbed in the back."

The bitterness of the conflict over international issues spilled over into the city council, many of whose members were constantly embroiled with Big Bill over local issues.

On the night of June 22, Thompson was unable to quiet the rebels in an involved dispute over recent appointments he had made to the Board of Education. When they demanded a roll call on a vote affirming the selections, he refused to grant it. The crowded galleries hooted and jeered and aldermen leaped atop their desks to shout at Thompson. As the mayor fled, closely followed by Sam Ettelson, he was struck on the arm by one of a barrage of books hurled at him by such ordinarily dignified councilmen as Otto Kerner, A. A. McCormick and Thomas O. Wallace.

A week later the rebels sought to introduce a resolution of censure against the man they labeled "a low-down double-crosser," "a disgrace to the city" and "the laughingstock of America." But two friendly aldermen, "Foxy Ed" Cullerton and Stanley Kunz, a pair of old-time Gray Wolves, came to Thompson's rescue. They kept introducing other business in meeting after meeting, meanwhile seeing to it that middle-of-the-road aldermen were granted all the favors they had been seeking for months. By the time the vote of censure came up, the rebel forces were beaten. Kunz made a quick motion for summer adjournment and the council shut down for the regular eleven-week vacation.

6

The uproar over Thompson's war views was far from finished.

In July he went to Pittsburgh to attend the convention of the Loyal Order of Moose. Learning that Theodore Roosevelt was staying at the William Penn Hotel, Thompson sought to have breakfast with him. But Roosevelt rebuffed him. When Thompson heard a report that Roosevelt would not speak at an open-air meeting in front of the Allegheny Court House if he did, Thompson was furious.

"I'm as good an American as Roosevelt ever was, even if I am not in favor of crossing the Atlantic to hunt for trouble," he raged. "Tell him to put that in his pipe and smoke it. Any man who says I am pro-German doesn't tell the truth. I'm pro-American and I am ready to match my patriotism with that of any man in Chicago or any place, T.R. included."

The report about Roosevelt's refusal to speak turned out to be false, and he made his usual drum-beating oration. As for Thompson, his speech was scrutinized by a "committee of safety" for any "offensive or unpatriotic statements." The committee's work was wasted, for Thompson's address was harmless, stressing only the idea of brotherly love and the humanity of the Moose movement.

But when he returned to Chicago he continued to issue his strong statements. He threatened all the newspapers with libel suits and did file one against the *Tribune* and another against the *News*. Again and again he stated his opposition to sending more troops to Europe. His critics were really the unpatriotic ones, he charged, because they favored "looting America of food, men, money and resources." "I yield to no one in my loyalty," he said in one speech to his followers. "My enemies have been trying to put me in bad. My views are my own, and I never hesitate to express them. It was Europe's fight and not ours. I claim the right to differ with other people and I accord other people the same privilege of differing with me, and I do not propose to be influenced by threats of personal violence or of political annihilation."

He had one more opportunity to yield to his accusers in September. A pacifist group calling itself the People's Council of America for Democracy and Terms of Peace, barred from holding its meetings in other Midwestern cities and chased out of some with threats of tarring and feathering, asked Big Bill for permission to stage a rally in Chicago. He consulted Ettelson, and Ettelson advised that he had no legal right to forbid such a meeting. The delegates, led by Louis Lochner, who had been aboard Henry Ford's ineffectual Peace Ship, trooped into the city and registered at the Fort Dearborn Hotel. Immediately there were feverish reports that they were scribbling seditious phrases on the walls of their rooms. Peter Dratzberg, a Secret Service man, came to investigate, accompanied by a bellboy carrying a pail of water and a scrub rag. But no statements dangerous or otherwise were found.

When word of the meeting spread, the patriots set up a mighty clamor. In a move that opened a long and angry feud, Governor

Frank Lowden ordered troops into Chicago to halt the pacifists. Thompson bristled and threatened to stop the troops with his own police force. Before the battle between soldiers and policemen could occur, the pacifists held their rally, made speeches that sounded much like those of Thompson's, and quietly scurried out of Chicago.

Thompson's action inspired irate aldermen to irate words. Two days after the meeting John Toman offered a resolution rebuking Thompson and praising Lowden. In the hot debate the Socialist alderman, William O. Rodriguez, normally an anti-Thompson man, argued against the resolution. So did the Thompson loyalists, led by A. A. Michaelson. At one point the debate grew so furious that James J. Bowler, a hard-muscled athlete, advanced on Michaelson with fists up. "You're all a bunch of dogs! You're all a bunch of skunks!" Bowler cried. Before he could be pulled away from Michaelson, Bowler howled: "Who do you want to win the war, America or Germany?" After other aldermen had accused Rodriguez of sanctioning "Prussian destruction of innocent men and women and children" and he had been given the advice, "If you don't like it here why don't you go back to Russia?" the resolution was passed overwhelmingly.

The resolution, which also urged Thompson and other city officials not to permit any other such meetings, was promptly vetoed by Big Bill. "I regret," he wrote, "that the City Council of Chicago has thus seen fit to place itself on record before the world as criticizing the officials of this city for upholding the majesty of the law and requesting that they violate not only the law but their oath of office."

That night Big Bill was hanged in effigy on the lake front by the Society of the Veterans of Foreign Wars while thousands cheered and sang: "Hang Big Bill! Hang Kaiser Bill!"

7

All through the rest of 1917 Big Bill remained mute on the shipment of troops and on most of the other issues that stirred such violent responses. He started a relief fund for soldiers' wives and children. He finally showed up to bid farewell to draftees leaving for Camp Grant. He issued a proclamation calling on his fellow citizens "to show to our soldiers and sailors who are leaving for the front that our hearts, our hopes, our prayers go with them."

There was undoubtedly a touch of sincerity in his new attitudes. But, also, the role of the Popular Man pleased Big Bill more than the role of the Man Hung in Effigy, and then, too, there was political meaning and purpose.

For Fred Lundin had decided that the time was near to move Big Bill ahead. The prize now was a seat in the United States Senate, and Lundin was sure he could win Big Bill the Republican nomination and the election in 1918, "Kaiser Bill" notwithstanding. Actually, Lundin theorized, the antiwar stand had been no mistake at all, certainly not one like the Sunday saloon-closing order. Big Bill already had the support of the anti-British, Socialists, pacifists, antiwar Republicans, anti-Wilson Democrats, pro-Germans. Now was the time to turn off the unpopular speeches and sound as patriotic as the next candidate. As he had done so many times before, Big Bill listened to Lundin's advice, and hoped Poor Swede was right.

Big Bill the Builder—Thompson and Richard Wolfe, his public works commissioner, at the switches to start a construction project.

"What was good enough for George Washington is good enough for Big Bill Thompson!"

14 |||| A Remarkable Victory

I

THE DECISION MADE, BIG BILL PUFFED
out his big chest and roared. First he assailed the Democrats, a logical beginning for a Republican primary candidate. "I condemn the
Democratic party," he said, "because I sincerely believe that it was
through their inability, their inefficiency, their indecision, their wab-
bling diplomacy, their administrative blunders, their total inability
to cope with problems of great magnitude that we are now at war."

He spoke more cautiously about the progress of the fighting in
Europe, insisting only that he was for a just and honorable peace.
He made few references to his rival candidates, Congressman Medill
McCormick of the *Tribune* family, or Charles E. Foss, a downstate
politician. He cried often for conscription of all excess wealth and
excess war profits. And when the war was over, he told an audience
in the Loyal Order of Moose Hall in Rockford, he wanted America
to stay free of all foreign alliances. "I'm for America first!" was his
shout.

In Kankakee jeering mobs tore the banners from the cars in
Thompson's caravan. In Peoria a parade of his followers was joined
by another crowd carrying banners: "Big Pro-German Rally Tonight! Gas Attack Expected at the Majestic Theater!" In Edwards-
ville the manager of a theater where Big Bill was to speak canceled the
engagement, saying, "No man who is not 100 per cent loyal can speak
in my theater." In some downstate hamlets boys threw stones and

in all of them the epithet of "Kaiser Bill" rang. In Momence the caravan was greeted by signs reading: ALL AMERICANS HERE. THOMPSON NOT WANTED. THIS WAY OUT! In Springfield Theodore Roosevelt warned that Thompson's nomination would be a great calamity. "It will give satisfaction to Germany and pro-Germans and be hailed with joy and be misinterpreted to the detriment of America by disloyal people here and our enemies abroad."

Through the summer Thompson's cause grew more hopeless, but he plodded on. Replying to Roosevelt, he called the statement "the foolish tirade of a common scold." He tried every sort of special appeal, from a promise to vote against the importation of "Chinese paupers to compete with the labor of freemen and citizens" to a vow to seek legislation that would take wealth from "the privileged few who are a menace to every nation, a cancer gnawing at its heart." Lundin organized wives of loyal City Hall workers into "flying vote-getting squadrons" and everyone who did business with the city was compelled to sign pledges asserting firm support of Big Bill.

But it was all futile. In the primary election, McCormick, who had campaigned on his record as a progressive and patriotic legislator, overwhelmed Thompson, then went on in the fall to defeat Senator J. Hamilton Lewis, the dandified Democrat incumbent. Among those who refused to lend McCormick support against Lewis was Big Bill, who denounced his fellow Republican as a spokesman for war profiteers. It was a rash act that drove another wedge in the split between Thompson and the *Tribune* branch of the Illinois Republicans.

2

Again Fred Lundin had erred in his judgments of Illinois voters. "Kaiser Bill" was still too vivid a memory. Thompson's only successes had been in the city's strong German wards and in the Second Ward, whose Negroes hailed Big Bill as "a second Abe Lincoln." Even Thompson's own ward had failed to support his senatorial bid.

But Lundin remained calm and undaunted. Beyond this defeat there lay other elections, other opportunities. The important task now was to keep the local machine strong and powerful, consolidate the political gains, stay in power. "We're at the feedbox now!" was Lundin's cry. "And we're going to keep eating!"

So, on November 30, 1918, a deputation led by Lundin appeared at Thompson's office. Solemnly, Lundin read the official call to duty. "Because you have given Chicago a clean, constructive and economical administration, because honesty has been the rule and not the exception in municipal service, because you have appointed competent administrators and heads of departments, because you have followed the law yourself and enjoined its obedience on others; because you have stood against the encroachment on human rights of all powerful interests and thereby incurred enmity and vengeance as reflected in Chicago's daily newspapers, we join in urging you to become a candidate for re-election!"

Big Bill beamed and replied, "I am honored that you ask me. It is my duty to obey. I will run."

To oppose Big Bill the Republican faction led by Charles Deneen and Ed Brundage put forth his adversary of the 1915 primary, Judge Harry Olson, who promptly dubbed himself "the harmony candidate." The party's mavericks persuaded Charles E. Merriam to run. His supporters included Jane Addams, the founder of Hull House; Harold L. Ickes, the cantankerous Progressive; Donald L. Richberg, a lawyer who had often fought the Insull utility firms; and none other than Jim Pugh, ready with funds and advice.

Olson set out immediately to attack Thompson's war record, displaying letters from soldiers still in Europe offering their moral support. But now that the war was over, this tactic seemed suddenly to have lost much of its effectiveness. So the judge concentrated primarily on the profligacy of Thompson's administration. He directed most of his force at the fees paid to "experts" hired to guide the various street-widening and bridge-building projects initiated by Michael J. Faherty, chairman of the Board of Local Improvements.

One of the experts, Frank H. Mesce, had received $25,560 in 1915 and $10,046 in 1916 for his services as head of Faherty's fees bureau. Was there any significance in the naked fact, asked Olson, that Mesce came from Lundin's ward or that he had lived for a time in the home of Alderman A. A. Michaelson, one of Thompson's council floor leaders?

"These so-called experts have taken more than a million dollars out of the city treasury in the past four years!" shouted Olson. As an example of this disgraceful activity, he cited fees poured out in connection with the widening of Twelfth Street, which Thompson listed as one of his most important accomplishments. According to the indignant jurist, John M. Kantor, owner of the Moulin Rouge Café and a former Democrat who had become a loyal Thompsonite, got $5,000 as an expert real-estate appraiser. Morris Greenspan, a saloonkeeper who hustled votes for Thompson, received $2,470. Nate de Lue, secretary for a distillery, was on the rolls for $800. William A. Bither, a bulky lawyer destined for appointment as school-board attorney, was listed, though he got only $27 for his experting.

Judge Olson, replied Big Bill, was "a self-appointed savior unwanted by the people." His old enemy, the Municipal Voters' League, again critical of him, he labeled "the cat's-paw of rich tax dodgers" and "silk-hat Reds." Thompson fought back hard, speaking often and everywhere. He long since had forgotten his temperance vows to Lundin. He showed up flushed and exuberant for meetings, dressed usually in a dark sack suit, wearing his ten-gallon hat. Then he sat sleepily through his introduction, toying with his heavy gold watch chain. Once, roused suddenly from torpor, he got halfway through an oration on the Lakes-to-Gulf waterway before he remembered that he was in the midst of a campaign rally. Usually his crowds heard first a tirade against the newspapers: "The crooked, rotten, lying newspapers of Chicago are continually throwing a wet blanket on our beloved city. They would kill Chicago if Chicago could be killed!" Then followed a quick summary of his platform: "I'm for home rule, I'm for reduced gas rates, I'm for the five-cent streetcar fare. I'm for the people and against the selfish interests! Bill Thompson is for you!" At the meetings ushers distributed pamphlets titled "A Record of Progress," which glowed with the story of achievement, of money saved, of streets paved, alleys cleaned, bridges built, parks planned.

Merriam denounced these claims as "sheer fiction." Chicago's streets and alleys were the filthiest in America, he cried, and were clean now only because hundreds of temporary workers had been put on the pay rolls for election time. A new garbage plant had indeed been built, but only with padded pay rolls. "No more cynical attempt to delude an exploited people can be imagined," he declared.

At first Thompson refused even to reply to Merriam, except to call him "a scratcher and a wagger." Loyal old Dr. John Dill Robertson defended his idol: "The trouble with the professor is that he is katabolic while Bill Thompson is anabolic. Big Bill looks up. He has vision. He is a builder. He is clean and courageous. His heart is clean. His mind is clean."

Merriam challenged Thompson to engage in a series of debates with him, and Bill accepted. The first, held in the Masonic Temple, Michigan Avenue and Fifty-fifth Street, nearly ended in a riot.

Thompson spoke first, assailing, as usual, the newspapers ("corrupt, lying, commercialized, rotten") and corporations, "food pirates" and public utilities. His supporters, who had mobbed the hall, cheered every sentence. Thompson, having finished his tirade, waved his sombrero and marched off the stage and out of the hall.

When Merriam started to speak, the audience hissed, booed and catcalled. When it refused to stop, Merriam took a step forward, his lips pale, his fists doubled up. On the stage Sam Ettelson hid a smile behind his hand, and in the front row Bill Bither and Percy Coffin winked at him.

"I'll tell you what's the matter!" cried Merriam. "I'm going to say it to you—say it to your teeth—I'm going to say to you that Mayor Thompson has disgraced Chicago!"

"Boo! Boo! Go back to your school, Professor!"

"William Hale Thompson has been a shirker in times of peace and a slacker in times of war. He——"

"Shame! Shame!"

Above the clamor, Merriam finished. "William Hale Thompson is sound and fury accompanied by nothing. He is a disgrace to his city and his country!"

A week before the primary Merriam and a group of his followers, led by Captain L. M. Thorpe, who had been wounded in action, boarded an army transport truck, drove to the corner of Randolph and Clark streets, and parked beneath the windows of Thompson's campaign headquarters in the Union Hotel.

"We want a clean, red-blooded American in the vacant chair!" shouted Thorpe. "Is there anybody up there for Thompson?"

There was no reply from the window.

Turning to the crowd that had gathered about the truck, Thorpe asked, "Are any of you for Thompson?"

"I am," replied a man.

"Why? Why?"

"All I can say is that I admire him."

"Do you admire him because he was pro-German in the war?" shouted Thorpe. "We men who went across are tired of apologizing for Chicago. We want a new deal and a good clean man who stands for American principles for mayor."

Later that week Thorpe appeared at a Thompson afternoon rally, arising to challenge Big Bill's criticism of Merriam for staging this street-corner incident with uniformed men. "Can I speak?" Thorpe demanded.

With a wave of his hand, Big Bill invited him to the platform. "I served over there with the Fifth Division," Thorpe began. "I want to tell you how our soldiers felt when they received newspapers telling of the pro-Germanism of your mayor."

Caught by surprise, Thompson could think of nothing to say but "Soldier, have you received your discharge?"

"I have, and let me tell you now that——"

"Meeting is dismissed!" yelled Thompson.

That night Thorpe was in the front row of another Thompson meeting. When Big Bill saw him he howled, "You are here to make trouble!"

"No, I am here to defend the uniform you say is being disgraced by efforts to help elect an American mayor and defeat pro-Germans. Can I come up?"

Thoroughly upset, Thompson bellowed, "No, you cannot! Officer, remove that man from the hall!"

But there were few like Thorpe to offset Thompson's popularity and Lundin's patronage army. In the primary Big Bill ran 40,000 votes ahead of Olson, and Merriam's vote was slight. In his headquarters on election night, the mayor exulted: "We beat them today and we'll beat them on April 1." Among the celebrants at the victory meeting was a Thomas P. Westendorf, who humbly presented an acrostic to his idol. It read:

> To run a town and run it right
> He's on the job from morn till night.
> Old-fashioned graft won't get a bite,
> Make sure we re-elect him.
> Pure politics must stand the test,
> So let each voter do his best.
> On him the mighty task will rest,
> Nor can we now reject him.

3

That man with the ready handshake and the round-faced grin, Robert Sweitzer, was Big Bill's Democratic opponent, as in 1915. His selection had been pushed through by the new party boss, George E. Brennan, the strategist who had taken command on the death of Roger Sullivan. Brennan had chosen Sweitzer over the nagging protests of Maclay Hoyne, who had steadily built himself, with his indictments and raids and forays against Thompson favorites, into a more logical and dramatic candidate. But Brennan decreed Sweitzer was "safe"; he disliked Hoyne's independent spirit.

Rebuffed, Hoyne immediately declared he would run as an independent against both Sweitzer and Thompson. Accusing Thompson of bipartisan deals with the machine Democrats, Hoyne called on the voters to elect him, "an unfettered man." "I entertain the belief," he said, in the voice of all men who have ever set out to defeat political machines, "that the city of Chicago is big enough and alert enough to select a candidate for mayor who is not controlled by the politicians and whose sole aim, if elected, will be to serve the people of Chicago to the best of his ability."

Fred Lundin, determined to err no more, planned Big Bill's campaign with canny care. For weeks he studied the vote returns in every local election since Thompson's triumph in 1915, noting where enthusiasm had remained persistent, where it had lagged, where it had grown. Finally he decided that Thompson should concentrate on winning big margins in the "minority wards," those where thousands of Negroes dwelt after their migration from the South before and during the war years, those populated by the anti-British Irish and the German-born, who still remembered and approved Big Bill's blasts at the Allies and Woodrow Wilson.

For reasons both sincere and coldly political, Thompson had always cultivated the Negro vote. They loved him for his flamboyant ways and for the manner in which he upbraided those foes of his who had shown the slightest sign of race bigotry. In his first term as mayor, he appointed one of his most rabid backers, the Reverend Archibald J. Carey, a flaming orator, to a post as investigator in the city law department, and he had named two Negroes as assistant corporation counsels, the brilliant Edward H. Wright and Louis B. Anderson. In words clear and sure and remarkably progressive, Thompson had replied to those who protested such selections: "The persons appointed were qualified for the positions. In the name of humanity it is my duty to do what I can to elevate rather than degrade any class of American citizens. I am under obligations to this people for their continued friendship and confidence while I have been in this community."

To make sure of the continued support of the Negroes, George F. Harding, once the "millionaire alderman" of the Second Ward, again went to work for Thompson. Unlike most millionaires or politicians, Harding was free of race prejudice. As a young man out of Harvard, where he had been a football star, he had made many friends among Negro workers on his father's real-estate projects, and he also had helped finance the early career of the great Negro prize fighter, Jack Johnson. As an alderman, Harding often rose in the middle of the night to furnish bail for an arrested constituent, and he was always available for anyone who needed help in an emergency, whether it was a lawyer, a doctor, a Christmas basket or a few dollars on election days. Other South Side property owners had fled during the heavy Negro migration, disposing of their properties or letting their buildings deteriorate while they exploited the new tenants through high rents and unsanitary living conditions. But Harding remained, buying all the dwellings he could, so that he now owned some four hundred buildings, all occupied by Negro families who paid reasonable rents. The least these citizens and their friends could do, Harding made clear, was to cast their votes for his good friend and fellow athlete, Big Bill Thompson. The result could be an important one. The Second Ward was now seventy per cent Negro, an increase from twenty-seven per cent nine years before.

There was little more Thompson could do or say for the German voters, Lundin theorized. "If they're not convinced Bill's for them, they never will be," he said. But among the Irish communities there was much that could be done and needed to be done, since Sweitzer, a prominent Catholic layman and an official of the Knights of Columbus, would sway many votes.

In this endeavor there was available to Thompson that dynamic Irish patriot, Michael J. Faherty. The Galway-born chairman of Big Bill's Board of Local Improvements had been active for years in Irish societies. In 1908 he had succeeded in bringing to Chicago President William Howard Taft to deliver the address at the St. Patrick's Day dinner of the Irish Fellowship Club. Faherty had imported earth from Ireland on that occasion, so that Taft delivered his address standing on the genuine ould sod. For this deed, Faherty had received from the Irish leader, T. P. O'Connor, a cable reading, "Michael, the Irish people will never forget you!"

Lundin did not deem it wise for Faherty to campaign as actively for Big Bill among the Irish as Harding was doing among the South Side Negroes. Both of Thompson's foes were aiming some of their fire at Faherty's department, as Olson and Merriam had done in the primary. They called sharp and irritating attention to those fees paid to the real-estate experts. Sweitzer pointed out that while such payments in the last three years of Carter Harrison's regime had amounted to $456,000, the fees in the first three years of Thompson's term for a similar amount of experting by Lundin-picked men came to $1,700,000.

But Faherty did offer advice to Thompson on how he could make sure of the hearts and votes of the city's Irish. And Big Bill took the advice, crying out loud and often on an issue that had not the slightest relationship to a Chicago mayor's duties. He took a stand, firmly and unequivocably, for home rule for Ireland and the "dissolution of the British yoke of oppression."

4

This time Fred Lundin planned well and guessed right.

In the election—held, amusingly enough, on April Fool's day—Big Bill Thompson eked out a victory over his nearest rival, Sweitzer, by a margin of 21,000 votes. Of these, 11,000 came from the Second Ward alone, a feat for which George Harding would soon be rewarded by succeeding Eugene Pike as city comptroller. The rest of the slim plurality issued from precisely the places where Lundin had predicted they would, with the aid of his thousands of temporary city appointees, who worked the precincts and manned the polls.

Lundin serenely accepted Big Bill's flushed gratitude. As newspapers around the country howled their astonishment at the outcome of the election, Chicagoans sought to defend themselves. Enemies of Thompson repeated the complaint, "You can't beat the machine," especially when it so successfully exploited the special interests of the minorities. Besides, it was pointed out, the Democratic vote had been split by the Hoyne candidacy, and Sweitzer's backer, Boss Brennan, had no lilylike reputation himself.

But critics outside Chicago, unaware of the cold statistics and special circumstances of the campaign, or perhaps seeing beyond them, found the re-election of Thompson incredible. William Chenery, in the New York *Times*, thought he detected in Big Bill's triumph "a state of mind very close to that out of which Bolshevism arises overseas." The people who had voted for Thompson, according to Chenery's analysis, thought they were selecting the lesser of two evils, since Sweitzer had been linked to the public-utility interests. "These sad people," wrote the disgusted Chenery, "have the desperation of disillusion. . . . Not until the sources of what the people of that populous city believe to be injustices have been removed will the discontent which eventuates in Thompson-ism be eradicated."

"Poor Old Chicago!" lamented the Kansas City *Star*. "Chicago is joined to her pro-German idols, and instead of letting her alone, she is to be watched in the future," rumbled the Philadelphia *Inquirer*. "CHICAGO's SHAME!" was the editorial heading in the New Haven *Journal-Courier*. Said the Lincoln, Nebraska, *State Journal:* "Everybody to his own taste, as the old woman said when she kissed the cow."

But *The Republican* in Chicago had its own blaring explanation. Thompson's triumph was not his alone; it belonged to all of Chicago. He had conquered his enemies because he was a man who "could be neither BOUGHT, BOSSED NOR BLUFFED."

"The people of Chicago," declared Lundin's paper, "have won a great victory. It spells the defeat of vicious newspaper control. It means that the defenses of the insincere public utility organiza-tion—the Municipal Voters' League—have been shattered. It means that Chicago will come into its own and that, with the defeat of time-honored corrupt influence and institutions, the great period of reconstruction about to ensue will reflect its glory and achievements in dear old Chicago."

Thompson himself spoke of the future after a curt reference to the past. "I have been maligned. I have been misunderstood. I hope during the ensuing four years to be understood. I want to make Chicago a great city, the summer resort of the United States. I want to build her a lake front, to finish widening streets and building bridges. I love this city! My love for her was inherited! I love Chicago with all my heart!"

15 ║ Cream Cheese vs. Limburger

I

ALL THAT JOYOUS SPRING OF 1919 BIG
Bill worked with diligence to speed these ambitions into reality.

Bubbling with the spirit of the booster, he urged Faherty to hasten those improvements which had been started in his first term. More streets were widened, more viaducts were built, more sewers were constructed. Thompson was especially eager to see the rapid completion of the big steel-and-limestone bridge across the Chicago River at Michigan Boulevard, the main artery of the lake-front area. True enough, the original estimates of the bridge's cost had more than doubled, what with experts' fees and high bids and many expenses. But Thompson, waving aside the newspaper complaints against the outrageous cost, was calm and confident. "This bridge'll bring property values up around here by the millions," he predicted, and accurately so. "They'll be building big skyscrapers here when that bridge is finished, and some of them that'll build them will be the very ones that are howling at me now."

Another project he helped push toward completion was the electrification of the Illinois Central Railroad tracks running along the impressive lake front. This idea had been the foundation of Daniel H. Burnham's original Chicago Plan,* but legal delays, squabbles over property rights and obstinacy of both railroad officials and

---

* This was an immense program to beautify and improve the city with boulevards, parks, bridges and other construction projects. It had been devised by many of the men involved in the World's Fair of 1893 and was officially organized in 1909.

various aldermen had delayed the ordinance granting the railroad electrification rights. After Alderman Ulysses S. Schwartz introduced an enabling ordinance in July, Thompson made speeches, argued with recalcitrant councilmen, won the support of doubting merchants. The ordinance was passed, ultimately allowing the citizens a sight of their handsome lake front without peering through dusky billows of locomotive smoke.

Delighted with the progress, Big Bill shaped a new slogan. He would use it then and later and again and again, long after it had become a mockery of the activities that inspired it. "Be a Chicago booster!" he clamored. "Throw away your hammer! Get a horn and blow loud for Chicago!"

2

The summer was less gleeful.

On the torrid afternoon of July 27 the growing tension between Negroes and whites on the South Side suddenly snapped. At the Twenty-ninth Street beach a Negro boy swam across a so-called segregation line. Several white bathers threw rocks at him, and one struck him, knocking him from a raft onto which he had clambered for safety. A policeman near by refused to arrest any of the rock hurlers, nor would he budge even after other missiles were thrown at Negroes and whites who were removing the drowned boy's body from the water onto the beach.

Rumors and reports, evil and vicious, coursed through the Black Belt and adjoining white territory. From the Stock Yards district came such hoodlums as Ragen's Colts, armed with torch and gun, looting and shooting at random all over the Black Belt. Negro war veterans took their service revolvers from the bottom drawers of bedroom dressers and went looking for white marauders. Negro houses were set afire or dynamited, as they had been intermittently in the preceding months. Vandals, black and white, roamed the streets, overturning automobiles, invading streetcars, smashing store windows, fighting, robbing, shooting and killing.

For three full days the fury raged. To persistent demands by newspapers and city leaders that he ask Governor Lowden for a detachment of state militia, Thompson paid no heed. "Our police can handle this," he snapped. "They're in full command." But the police were actually powerless to do much but stop sporadic fights. Worse yet, some of the uniformed men were in sympathy with the white rioters and a few, according to later testimony at investigations into the riot, shot wildly into crowds of peaceable Negroes. State's Attorney Hoyne injected his opinions, careful to give them a political slant. "The police department has been demoralized to such an extent by the politicians, both black and white, on the South Side," went his analysis, "that they are afraid to arrest and prosecute men with political backing or who claim to have political influence."

When the rioting was in its fourth dark day, having diminished slightly, Bishop Archibald J. Carey, the Thompson booster of boosters among Negroes, led a committee into the mayor's office. They pleaded that he get in touch with Lowden and secure the state militia. This Thompson finally did, but before the 6,000 men summoned by Lowden could march into the riot area, the terror had subsided.

When the frenzy was spent, twenty Negroes and fourteen whites were dead, over 500 injured, and scores of houses in the Black Belt destroyed by fire. For years to come Big Bill's opponents, whenever they sought to sell their political wares to the city's Negro voters, never failed to remind their audiences how laggard Thompson had been in summoning state troopers.

3

Before the summer was over, another trouble beset Big Bill, and he sought to solve it in his typical blunderbuss fashion. Now it was his long-continued interference with the affairs of the city's schools that came to be the first of many climaxes.

When Thompson was elected in 1915, he promptly forgot his pledge to put a mother on the school board and to give the schools a business administration. Instead, he attempted to push political hacks into important school jobs. When his demands were resisted by the board, Thompson appointed new members, named Jacob Loeb, an insurance executive, as president. Loeb, however, developed his own brand of independence. When a new superintendent of schools was needed, he did not consult Thompson or Lundin, but appointed a commission of nine civic leaders to find the best man available. After canvassing the country, the commission proposed Charles E. Chadsey, an able educator then directing the Detroit schools.

While Thompson was in the midst of his strenuous campaign in 1919, the Board of Education appointed Chadsey. The mayor made no protest then, but he promised Lundin he would fire Chadsey as soon as the campaign ended. This he did, naming Peter A. Mortenson, a big, genial high-school principal, to the job. Chadsey, goaded by the anti-Thompson forces, filed suit to oust Mortenson, and Judge Kickham Scanlan, an independent Republican, ordered Chadsey reinstated.

Defiantly Thompson's man refused to yield his office to Chadsey. City detectives were assigned to school headquarters to turn back Chadsey if he sought to enter. Samuel Ettelson took Judge Scanlan's decision to the Appellate Court and was rebuffed. Chadsey marched into office again and Mortenson was named his assistant.

The series of skirmishes continued through the summer. By fall Thompson was ready to counterattack. He persuaded, and easily enough, his six key supporters on the board—the newspapers called them the "Solid Six"—to swing through a series of directives against Chadsey which would strip him of his powers. At a meeting early in November Chadsey appeared before the board to read a list of proposals he had drawn up for improving the schools, the most important of which he deemed the raising of teachers' salaries. He had barely finished his first sentence when Hart Hanson, one of the Thompsonites, leaped to his feet.

"I propose we refer these proposals to the school administration committee!" he shouted. "I have another matter to bring up." Then he introduced an order giving Mortenson power to select textbooks, promote or transfer teachers, pick sites for schools.

Loeb, aware of what such an action presaged, yelled against "this daylight burglary." But he was definitely a minority on this scheming day. The board members hurriedly approved Hanson's order and trooped out.

Chadsey had had enough. On the next morning he resigned, attacking the City Hall's "political wrecking machine." His last official act before he hurried off to accept a post as dean of education at the comparatively placid University of Illinois was to scrub his name off the superintendent's door with wood alcohol. "The life and the works of the school board," growled the *Tribune,* "proceed with the restraint of a Hottentot war dance."

Thompson's triumph over Chadsey and Loeb had a sour aftertaste. Inveighing "A crime has been committed," State's Attorney Hoyne thrust sharply at his foes. He brought contempt charges against the "Solid Six" and the board's bulbous attorney, William A. Bither, that loyal soldier in the Thompson forces. After a long trial Bither was ordered to serve five days in jail and pay a fine of $500 as the legal agent in the plot against Chadsey. The others received slighter sentences or fines ranging from $300 to $750.

The judge who presided at the trial was the same Kickham Scanlan that had ruled earlier for Chadsey over Mortenson. Big Bill, scowling in the rear of the courtroom, marked down that name in his memory, certain that a time would come when he could pay back this righteous fellow tenfold.

4

With his customary resiliency, Thompson quickly bounced back from his troubles.

Now he was the Big Booster again, for it was time to make the city's bid for the Republican National Convention. His florid eloquence remained undimmed as he stood before his fellow committeemen. He paid tribute to George Washington, Abraham Lincoln and William McKinley, damned Woodrow Wilson, lauded the Constitution. His peroration mesmerized the committeemen:

"Come to Chicago, where the people support real Republicans who loyally stand for the principles of the Republican party, and where frauds and counterfeits are repudiated!

"Come to Chicago, and let us revive our Republicanism at its fountainhead, and there, in the words of my father's old commander, Admiral Farragut, with full steam ahead we will sail into the fray.

"Come to Chicago, where the people stand resolutely for the Americanism of our forefathers and believe in getting out of Europe and staying out. Nothing can shake their American faith!

"Come to Chicago, where the Constitution in fair weather and in storm is the supreme law of the land!

"Come to Chicago, the city that stands for America First, for our country and our flag, Old Glory, and where our great Republic is not rated as one-sixth the importance of another country!

"Come to Chicago, where our people are one hundred per cent in their proud Americanism and never will agree that any nation the sun shines upon is six times as important as their own country!"

The Republican committeemen, evidently as impressed by this chauvinistic paean as by the incontrovertible fact that the city's central location was ideal for such an important convention, chose Chicago.

There was nothing, however, that Big Bill could do or say when the rambunctious bravos of the new American Legion met in St. Louis to select their 1920 convention city. When Chicago's name came up for discussion, T. F. Herbert of the Massachusetts delegation cried, "To hell with Bill Thompson! My state will not agree to having a convention of soldiers in the great war go to a city that has as its first citizen by vote one who cannot measure up in any small part to the test of 100 per cent Americanism."

There were plenty of Herbert's comrades who agreed, and the meeting broke up with crowds of Legionnaires sweeping down the aisles ripping from the walls bright signs reading: CHICAGO WANTS YOU!

5

If Big Bill the Booster chortled happily over snaring the party's Presidential convention for Chicago, Big Bill the Avenger throbbed with conspiratorial glee. For one of the certain aspirants to the nomination was Frank O. Lowden, and Thompson was bitterly determined to thwart that ambition in any way he knew and by any means.

The friendship that began back in 1904 had grown frayed.

Thompson and Lundin had built a long list of grievances against
the man they had helped elect governor in 1916, a list underscored
with their frequent plaint—"He's not a good party man, he's not
grateful to us."

It was true, indeed, that Lowden had rebuffed the pair again and
again since his election. They came asking for patronage over
which Lowden held command—jobs in local divisions of state offices and in the various Chicago park districts—and Lowden usually
sent them away empty-handed. Sometimes he refused to see them.
He had upset all traditions by appointing to the post of Cook County
administrator, a plum that previously fell to the City Hall machine
in power, a political unknown named A. Gordon Ramsay, who
had not a shred of affiliation with anyone in the Thompson-Lundin
camp. Besides such a politically sacrilegious act, Lowden had sent
those troops into Chicago in 1917 to stand by for the meeting of
the mild-mannered pacifists to whom Thompson had granted permission to assemble. And he had irritated Thompson and Lundin
in that wild year by saying privately that Big Bill was "pro-
German."

Lowden was busily lining up delegates in his behalf. He was
spending heavily, and so was another hopeful, General Leonard
Wood; both would later be embarrassed when Senate investigators
queried them about their extensive expenditures in quest of delegates. Lowden already had the support of Victor Lawson's *News*,
Lawson having written to his editor, Charles H. Dennis, "Personally I want to do anything I can to further Lowden's candidacy.
. . . I think the country would be very much better served by a
practical businessman at its head. Governor Lowden has shown
his business sense and his good executive ability in the way he has
reorganized conditions in Illinois, and I believe he would be a 'safe
and sane' man as President."

Big Bill Thompson thought otherwise.

Before returning from Washington after securing the convention
for Chicago, he and his party of seventy-five Republicans took over
the whole seventh floor of the Pennsylvania Hotel in New York.
Amid the jubilation and revelry of the celebration, Thompson
granted interviews to the New York reporters.

"The fact that the convention is to be in Chicago should give Lowden a decided advantage, shouldn't it?" they asked.

"Maybe so."

"You'll back his boom, won't you?"

"We have not seen his platform yet. We know what he has stood for as governor, but the time has come when he should declare himself on national issues, and some of his friends are saying he has no intentions of doing that before nominations are made. This is hardly satisfactory."

Then Big Bill sang his familiar political lyric. "We all want to know, and we have a right to know, whether he is for America first, or whether, like so many other statesmen, he is willing to subordinate the interests of his own country to the interests of three or four countries across the water. We want to know—" and his voice throbbed huskily—"whether he will abide by the policy laid down by George Washington and pursued by every other President since Washington's time, which provides for friendly relations with all foreign powers and entangling alliances with none."

Even this bold challenge failed to arouse Lowden to a reply. But one of his followers had his own sarcastic answer. Said Reed Landis, the war ace and son of the stern-visaged Federal Judge Kenesaw Mountain Landis, "In this matter of Americanism, Lowden versus Thompson is like the odor of cream cheese versus the smell of limburger."

6

The division between Lowden and Thompson soon grew deeper and wider.

In April 1920, two months before the convention, Lowden received a clear majority in the state's advisory Presidential primary. But Big Bill and Lundin were the really triumphant ones. For in thirty-four of Chicago's thirty-five wards, their candidates for ward committeemen had won, a clear and significant sign to the Lowdenites of how the winds blew in Chicago, the garden city where their champion was preparing to fight for the party's nomination.

The platform on which Thompson and Lundin had built their

victory was a shrewd mixture of strong isolationist beliefs and special appeals. It stood against any affiliation by the United States with the League of Nations. It was for exempting all incomes of $5,000 or less from tax payments. It demanded conscription of all excess war profits and all inheritances of more than $1,000,000, bonuses for war veterans, jail terms for war profiteers. It called for the United States to "get out of Europe and stay out." Remembering Lowden's dispatching of troops to Chicago during the war, it made a special thrust at him, calling for "no abridgment of the constitutional right of free speech."

In May, Thompson and Lundin, armed with these tenets and the impressive voting figures, marched to Springfield for the Republican State Convention. "The people of Chicago and Cook County have declared for these principles," said Thompson. "I certainly am going to give the people of the state a chance to do the same."

But the Lowden forces, in control of the downstate majority, managed to reject this platform. They adjourned quickly until September after selecting delegates-at-large—Thompson among them—to the convention. Officially the delegates were instructed to vote for Lowden, but at least one of them had other plans.

16 ||| The Big Triumph

I

IT LOOKED LIKE A GOOD YEAR FOR
Republicans, this 1920. Postwar disillusionment spread steadily, and
with it the dissolution of the spurious unity of the war years. The
origins of a depression were at hand. War-goods factories had
closed, Europe was again tilling its fields and the American farmer
could no longer sell his surplus abroad. The enormous national debt
kept taxes high and the exorbitant prices of wartime failed to follow
a downward trend in wages. The Democrats in power took much
of the blame. There were strikes, frazzled national nerves, and a
search, diffuse and vagrant, for political scapegoats.

It looked, despite his temporary setback in Springfield, like a good
year for Big Bill Thompson. Only three weeks before the G.O.P.
clan assembled for its big convention, he received what he called,
with burbling pleasure, "the most wonderful birthday present of my
whole life." On May 14, decked in high silk hat and lavish smile, he
drove with Charles H. Wacker, head of the Chicago Plan, in a big
parade along Michigan Boulevard toward the splendid new bridge
that had been under construction all the past year. There he snipped
a silk ribbon. Bands blared, people shouted: "Hooray for Bill
Thompson!" and the first automobile crossed the bridge to the north
link of the boulevard. The crowd sang "The Star-Spangled Banner,"
trying to make itself heard above the wild tooting of boat whistles in
the river below and the eerie cry of a fire-boat siren. In a reviewing
stand on the site where William Wrigley would soon build a porce-

lain-white skyscraper, opposite the spot where Thompson's bitter foe, the *Tribune*, would later erect its Gothic tower, the mayor sat and beamed and waved and smiled. And he nodded briskly when floats swept by, their signs and banners hailing him: ALL HATS OFF TO OUR MAYOR! WHAT DO WE LIVE FOR?

2

A greater personal triumph, filled with a kind of vengeful satisfaction, was still to be realized.

As the Republicans streamed into the city the two favorites, each with one third of the delegates pledged to him, were Governor Lowden and General Wood. Into town, too, strode William Randolph Hearst, marshaling forces and followers at the Blackstone Hotel, intent on pushing forward Hiram Johnson, that most irreconcilable of "Senate Irreconcilables," a small but volatile band of men passionately opposed to the League of Nations. Somewhere, almost everywhere, was that wily politician named Harry M. Daugherty, buttonholing delegates, talking swiftly and smoothly about his dark-horse candidate, Warren G. Harding, the handsome, poker-playing senator from Ohio.

Thompson quickly made clear how he felt about the candidacy of his state's chief executive. Through the lobbies of the hotels where delegates were quartered he went, visiting one delegation after another presumably as the city's official host. But wherever he appeared he informed the delegates how low was his esteem of Lowden—"His word's no good. You can't count on him, believe me." At the Illinois preconvention caucus on the evening before the delegates trooped into the big Coliseum, he introduced a resolution withholding support of any candidate whom the Senate investigators had criticized for excessive spending in preferential Presidential primaries. Since this was a direct slap at Lowden, the thirty-eight pro-Lowden delegates rejected it, while Thompson's seventeen followers approved it. By a similar vote the delegation also turned down a resolution denouncing the League of Nations. That night Thompson was busy warning delegates who visited his headquarters in the

Congress Hotel: "You nominate Lowden, and the Republicans'll lose Illinois in the election!"

The convention balloting began shortly after the Republicans approved a platform with an ambiguous plank on the League of Nations. General Wood took and held a slim lead over Governor Lowden. Following the third ballot, which produced no shift in votes, Bill Thompson was urged to exploit his excellent opportunity to start a landslide to Lowden by swinging his seventeen delegates to the Illinois governor, perhaps with an eloquent eulogy, or at least a strong plea for party unity.

Instead, Thompson struck hard at his enemy. With a sudden statement that he could not remain in the Illinois delegation because of the "moral issue" that had arisen over Lowden's expenditures in the preconvention campaign, Thompson resigned as delegate-at-large. So did Samuel Ettelson. The two of them stomped from the convention hall, to spend the rest of the steaming afternoon in the annex of the Coliseum where Dr. John Dill Robertson had set up an emergency hospital to care for victims of the heat.

Big Bill's action was thoroughly approved by William Randolph Hearst, who strongly shared Thompson's view on American foreign policy. Hearst's *American* blared the Thompson resignation from its front page, and newsboys were sped to the Coliseum to distribute free copies as the delegates were being polled for the fourth time. Again the count favored Wood, with Lowden still second and Johnson third. Senator Henry Cabot Lodge, chairman of the session, called for a recess until the next morning, and perspiring delegates gratefully voted to end the day's deliberations.

Wood's managers had little doubt that in the morning their man would get the nomination. Lowden's strategists were equally confident. But that night there was the inevitable meeting in a "smoke-filled room," one in the Blackstone Hotel occupied by Colonel George Harvey, an ex-Democrat and veteran political manipulator. There Harry Daugherty huddled with faction leaders. Shortly after 2:00 A.M., Senator Harding was sent for, and informed he would be the Republican nominee. "Well," remarked Harding to Daugherty as they departed, "looks like we drew to a pair of deuces and filled."

In the morning there were a few perfunctory ballots to permit

Wood and Lowden to save political face. Then orders came from party bosses. The Harding band wagon started to roll and roll. Late that afternoon he was nominated.

Thompson was exultant. He would have preferred Hiram Johnson, the candidate backed by Hearst, but this was a secondary consideration. What pleased him was that Lowden's ambitions for the Presidency had been squelched and he had had a part in squelching them.

To prepare for new contests in his own political territory, Thompson visited Harding at his home in Marion, Ohio, where he discussed the handsome candidate's ideas about international affairs. When he departed he carried with him Harding's silken assurance that he was opposed to the League of Nations as Thompson was, the memory of watching Mrs. Harding sweep the front porch of her home ("Where but in America could that happen?") and the less-than-valid feeling that Harding would be "one of our great Presidents."

3

In July, Thompson and Lundin made known their candidates for the important primary in September. A new governor was to be selected, and a state's attorney for Cook County, and a county judge who controlled election machinery, and a state's attorney general, and a Sanitary District Board with a passel of jobs for worthy payrollers, and a host of minor officials, all woven into the broad pattern of power and control.

For governor, Len Small was their man. This veteran among downstate politicos had gone over completely to the Lundin-Thompson forces. He was always obedient, always subservient, always ready to perform willingly and capably for Poor Swede and Big Bill.

For state's attorney, Lundin urged Thompson to select a pugnacious fellow named Robert Emmett Crowe, a man with great oratorical strength, a desire for power, and a good record as a judge, having been the youngest chief justice in the history of the Criminal Court. Thompson agreed that Crowe was just the man to replace that obstreperous Maclay Hoyne.

For county judge their choice was a lean, sly machine politician,

Frank S. Righeimer, whose uncle, John, owned the popular saloon across from the City Hall, a politicians' hangout patronized by Lundin. Into other niches went the faithful, the deserving, those whose loyalties to Thompson and Lundin were sure and steadfast.

Not since his failure at the convention had Governor Lowden publicly uttered a word against Thompson. But now he announced his intention to wage war and smash this "Thompson Tammany."

"An extraordinary situation confronts this state," he declared. "The situation, if not met firmly and courageously, is a real menace to the state of Illinois." Thompson was building a Chicago Tammany, said Lowden, that surpassed New York's original. "Drunk with power, he seeks to extend its rule over the affairs of the entire state." He had to be stopped.

Lowden entered no county ticket, but to oppose Len Small as his successor he picked his able lieutenant governor, John G. Oglesby, the son of "Honest Dick" Oglesby, one of the state's revered governors. Against State Senator Richard J. Barr for attorney general, he named an old Thompson foe, Edward J. Brundage. "If they are successful at the primaries and the polls," said Lowden, "Illinois will be insured a sane, honest and economical administration of its affairs, and Thompson's Tammany will be stopped at the Cook County line."

4

As if he himself were opposing Lowden for the state's highest office, Big Bill hurled himself vigorously into this primary campaign.

At meeting after meeting in Chicago, whenever Len Small and Big Bill shared a platform, the candidate, a sad-faced man in a rumpled suit, always made a short, dull speech, ending, "I'm sorry to be taking up your time, for I know you want to hear the greatest mayor Chicago ever had—the greatest man in the United States."

Thompson responded with a wave of his sombrero, then lashed into Lowden. He scored the state utilities commission for granting the streetcar lines a seven-cent fare after he himself had succeeded in blocking the traction ordinance of 1918, in which the company had sought such an increase. One of Small's promises was to sign legislation, if it was introduced, to make "Mayor Thompson's rapid-transit, five-cent fare plan a living reality." Thompson also called Lowden "a fake patriot" and "a crook whose word is no good."

When such newspapers as the *News* and the *Tribune*, stronger than ever in their opposition to Thompson's candidates, charged that the city was bankrupt and cited figures to show that it had $1,000,000 in unpaid bills, Thompson presented his comptroller, George F. Harding, to refute the accusation. Chicago, grumbled Harding, was in good financial condition, its indebtedness per capita at least $150 below New York's, smaller even than in staid, old Boston. "These newspapers are professional knockers," said Harding. "The time has come when some citizen should nail the lies which have been circulated in them against the name and reputation of our city. These calumnies have been published for cheap political purposes."

When Lowdenites charged Thompson with reckless spending, Big Bill gleefully replied, citing the Senate investigators' chastisement of Lowden. When Oglesby called Thompson "seditious" and "unpatriotic" Thompson roared into court to file another libel suit—actions were already pending against the *Tribune, News, Herald* and assorted critics—and to tell campaign crowds precisely how good an American he was. "I'll tell you the kind of patriot Bill Thompson is!" he rumbled. "Bill Thompson is the kind of patriot that beseeched Congress to place an embargo on foodstuffs, to save the surplus so that men, women and babies of America would not starve and so that the war hogs might not fill their pockets with the millions taken from the pockets of the helpless in America! Bill Thompson's patriotism is the kind that demands that we bring our boys home from Europe and keep them home! That we pay them the bonus which we owe them, and that we forever pledge ourselves against the making of any foreign entangling alliances! Sure, it's not the patriotism of the *Tribune* or the *Daily News*! But if Bill Thompson has got to jump to his feet and sing 'God Save the King' to please the *Tribune* and the *News*, then they can both go straight to hell!"

On primary day, the bitter citizens had their say and by their votes drove scores of men out of office. Three hours after the polls closed in Chicago, Thompson was on a telephone, phoning first to

THE RAMIFICATIONS OF CITY HALL POLITICS

[Copyright: 1922: By The Chicago Tribune.]

Small, awaiting results on his Kankakee farm, and congratulating him on his victory, then to Lundin, informing him of other winners. Only one result displeased Thompson, for Brundage had defeated Barr. But Big Bill wasted little time in worrying over this lone Lowden man among the winners. He was sure that Brundage, if elected, would be amenable to reason.

5

In the November elections Len Small's Democratic rival was the dapper orator, bewhiskered Senator J. Hamilton Lewis. While Small continued to promise support of Thompson's legislation for five-cent fares and to inveigh against the League of Nations, Lewis warned that if Small won, Thompson would control a "super-army of pay-rollers." He called his own campaign "a people's crusade, a fight against the bosses."

In Cook County, Crowe and Michael L. Igoe, who had bested Maclay Hoyne in an embittered primary, waged a loud battle, but rarely against each other. Crowe cited his record as a hard-fighting assistant state's attorney and as Criminal Court justice, noting proudly that an old Thompson opponent, Judge Harry Olson, and twenty-two other jurists were backing him. He attacked the news-papers, in the style of Thompson, singling out Victor F. Lawson, the *Daily News* publisher, for special censure. Lawson, according to Crowe, owed the county taxes on his Lake Shore Drive house—a charge made previously by Thompson and fully refuted by the pub-lisher. "I am going to try to make him pay his taxes," spoke Crowe. "I am going to try to make him run a decent newspaper. Of course, that is going to be a hard job and if I don't succeed in doing it I am going to put an additional burden on the taxpayers of this state. For if Victor Lawson doesn't do these things, I am going to make the taxpayers buy him a railroad ticket to the penitentiary at Joliet and I am going to give Victor a free ride and then we are going to keep him at public expense until he learns how to behave himself."

In its answer the *News* scoffed at Bob Crowe's oft-repeated charges that the newspaper had assigned detectives to shadow him and plague him. "Judge Crowe," read one editorial, "is rash thus to reveal to intelligent voters that his conception of his office is that of an agency for the persecution of those who have the temerity to oppose his political methods, or the political methods of his master, rather than the great instrument of the law by which the public should be protected against vice and the evil deeds of the vicious, against crime and the merciless acts of criminals."

Igoe pointed a shaking finger at Thompson as "Crowe's boss."

Recalling Thompson's parentage and background, he deplored the mayor's "revolutionary metamorphosis" since his first election. "His present position is a tragic commentary upon the evils of bad associations," lamented Igoe. Thompson disregarded these and other statements. But when those sterling statesmen of the First Ward, Bathhouse John Coughlin and Hinky Dink Kenna, came out in support of Igoe, Chief John J. Garrity's police suddenly discovered evil in their rip-roaring district. A week before the election, squads raided Big Jim Colosimo's restaurant and Ike Bloom's Midnight Frolics because of complaints that liquor was sold in these establishments owned by two of the stalwarts in the Coughlin-Kenna organization.

This was the year—alas for Lewis, Igoe and Democrats everywhere—of the Harding landslide. Every county and every office in the state went to the Republicans. Small, winner by half a million votes, orated: "We face a new dawn, which will bring peace, prosperity and happiness." Crowe, defeating Igoe by over a quarter of a million votes, made no new promises to prosecute Lawson. Righeimer triumphed over Francis X. Busch, a prominent lawyer, by 175,000 votes.

On this victorious night Big Bill held court on the fifth floor of the City Hall, outside his office. "The roof is off!" he yelled as the first returns came in.

Hundreds of persons packed the corridors. Notables arrived to offer congratulations, some of them winning candidates, some of them influential businessmen, like Samuel Insull, the utilities monarch. To keep the crowd from mobbing their hero, an extra cordon of police guarded Big Bill as he stood behind a big oak table and waved his arms excitedly. "We ate 'em alive!" Thompson shrieked. "We ate 'em alive with their clothes on!" He beckoned to a group of musicians unloading their instruments. "Put on a big party! Let the jazz band play! Let's show 'em we're all live ones!"

While the horns shrilled and the bandsmen blew and Big Bill blared his greetings and his gratitude to the party workers, Fred Lundin sat quietly in his Hotel Sherman room, dining alone. When the reporters came to ask him the secret of this great success, he grinned coyly and shrugged in mock bewilderment. "Oh, I don't mix in politics, y' know. I'm only a private citizen, y' know." And then he and the reporters laughed and laughed, and someone passed around a bottle of bourbon so that this citizen's victory might be properly toasted

On the next morning, behind a desk piled high with flowers, Thompson offered a familiar analysis and a familiar promise. "The issue was Thompsonism pure and simple, and I got most of the lambasting from the opposition," he said, with a hearty, all-forgiving laugh. "But that ship is gone. That was yesterday. Today is here and the thing to do now is to carry out our pledges to the people with as little delay as possible."

And in New York, that worshipful follower, Michael J. Faherty, broke into a prepared address he was making as president of the American Road Builders' Association. "William Hale Thompson is the greatest statesman Illinois has ever had since Abraham Lincoln! As a politician he is without a peer and we believe he will be President in four years!"

17 ||| Wrong Guesses

I

NEVER IN THEIR CAREERS, SEPARATELY
or jointly, had Big Bill and Poor Swede held so much potential power.
Soon Len Small would be Governor Small, ready and willing to let
Lundin select most of the men and women to fill hundreds of jobs in
Cook County. Through County Judge Righeimer, slated to serve
at least another year and a half until a new election for a full term,
they held watch over the election machinery. Bob Crowe seemed to
be just the perfect man for state's attorney, a sensible fellow who
would not give them the kind of trouble Maclay Hoyne had always
been stirring up; a bit aloof, this Crowe, not a man to jump and holler
for the sheer joy of the noise, but a fellow with class, learning and the
right connections. Ed Brundage, sole Lowdenite to win a state office?
"All by himself up there in that attorney general's job," scoffed Lundin. "We'll box him in when the right time comes."

Lundin had been content to let Thompson take credit for their political triumphs as long as Poor Swede held the power. Now, puffed
up with adulation, Big Bill chose to make a major move without consulting Lundin. It was the first wide crack in their partnership.

Prohibition had arrived in the city on January 16, 1920. In a local-
option vote the previous spring the town had already indicated its
feelings about the Volstead Act by casting a three-to-one ballot
against the closing of saloons. Even the citizens of the Hyde Park
district, which included the University of Chicago, had voted wet.
The city's hoodlums were wise enough to see, by these portents, that
fat profits could be made by slaking such a thirst. With passage of the

191

Volstead Act, rival gangs were busy organizing a beer and liquor supply not only for Chicago, but for much of the Middle West.

By election time Chicago was dripping wet. Many policemen hired out to guard the cars and trucks of the beer and whisky runners. Federal agents slapped their "booze lids" on cabarets. A federal grand jury was listening to evidence that some city policemen were in a league with "Mike de Pike" Heitler, a notorious pander turned booze baron, to run $250,000 worth of liquor into the city every month. A local banker, John A. Carroll, complained on the front pages of every newspaper that to arrest one of the three men who had robbed his Hyde Park State Bank of $272,000 in securities he was forced to hire his own detectives. Thompson's police, he growled, were "indolent, incompetent, stupid."

While he was basking in the post-election sunlight at West Baden, Indiana, Thompson received additional reports that Chief Garrity's police force was more hopeless and helpless than ever. Angrily he decided to name his own man to the chief's job. He wired orders to Garrity, brusquely dismissing him "for the good of the service." As his successor, Thompson named his secretary, the popular Charles C. Fitzmorris, who, through his experience as a reporter and city editor for Hearst's *American* and his service under Harrison and Thompson, surely had a good understanding of the city's crime problems. As before, Thompson's message to his new chief was "Clear out the crooks!"

Fitzmorris set out like a whirlwind, as if he really could dig into the complex conditions that produced periodic crime waves and the anarchic state of the police department. "Get results or get out" was his first order to the force. Then he declared he would break up cliques and combines where favored policemen received lucrative districts. In a noble effort to show the men under his command exactly what he meant by swift action, he and his new chief of detectives, Michael (Go Get 'Em) Hughes, led a picked group of 110 detectives on important raids. They invaded well-known gambling joints: the North Clark Street establishment of "Prince Artie" Quinn, son of the loquacious "Hot Stove Jimmy" Quinn; the Roosevelt Road cardrooms of "Lovin' Putty" Annixter; a big gambling house on Halsted Street run by "Nails" Morton and Herschie Miller,

Big Bill (right) and Len Small, the man he helped make governor.

Big Bill and his cohorts set out to inspect the Mississippi River.

Big Bill and his cronies join in a favorite campaign song—"America First, Last and Always!"

the precious pair recently acquitted of shooting a policeman in a brawl in the Beaux Arts night club; and Clarence (Izzy) Lazarus' Monte Carlo, a lavish place on Grand Boulevard. In twenty-four hours of raiding they seized 800 men and women and, although all but a few who were fined $25 were freed the next morning because of lack of sufficient evidence or warrants, Big Bill, hearing of Fitzmorris' activity, expressed his great satisfaction. "Wonderful!" he said as he prepared to return to the city. "Charlie is making a good start! He's sure some chief, isn't he? In the language of the cowboy, he's a bird."

At last the newspapers found something to praise, although each noted that surface cleanups and superficial raids, even if carried on daily, would hardly eradicate the mess that had been allowed to thrive and grow in the five years since Big Bill had been elected mayor.

But Thompson was still happy over the election and over Fitzmorris' action. He cared little that Fred Lundin had not been asked if he approved Fitzmorris' appointment, nor that Bob Crowe, drawing up and organizing his own force of raiders and investigators, was making still-subdued complaints about the dapper chief's excessive eagerness to carry out the bidding of the man who had given him this difficult assignment.

Big Bill was busy now with his plans for the big pageant of which he had talked ever since he first had thought of the slogan, "Throw Away Your Hammer! Get a Horn! Be a Booster for Chicago!" It would be a Pageant of Progress, depicting the city's past, present and, most notably, its future as viewed by Big Bill. To prepare it he had organized the Chicago Boosters' Club on the eve of his big year by persuading a score of highly reputable businessmen to raise at least $1,000,000 which would be spent to yodel the praises of Chicago in the next four years, through such a show as he now planned for Municipal Pier, the outdoor exposition palace jutting into Lake Michigan; through a network of roadside billboards along New York-to-Chicago railroad tracks; through pamphlets, articles, movies, photographs and the establishment of an information booth in the City Hall. It would be, he glowingly told these businessmen, a national, even an international, campaign to build up Chicago as a place to live in, to establish industry, to lure business. His campaign, said

Thompson, would compel people to forget the slurs and slanders about crime and criminals, although at that very hour the police were fighting rampaging auto bandits, burglars, robbers and liquor hijackers.

More than 1,200 businessmen fell in with the plan. D. F. Kelly, then manager of Mandel Brothers department store, was a codirector of the club, along with Everett C. Brown, president of the National Live Stock Association, Frederick H. Bartlett, a real-estate man, and R. J. McLaughlin, hardware merchant and Thompson's friend from the Illinois Athletic Club.

The pageant would be held at Municipal Pier in the summer, when the children could come to see the exhibits. "We'll sell Chicago to Chicagoans," bawled Big Bill, "and sell Chicago to the outside world. We're the greatest town there is and we're going to let people know about it."

2

Again, in the midst of good things, while the exhibit booths for the Pageant of Progress were being installed and while Fred Lundin was quietly placing his grateful underlings in new jobs, there came misfortune. Some of it was of Thompson's and Lundin's own making, some brought on by sworn enemies, some created by those within the political family, whose loyalty and obedience the two men had thought more steady.

In April the *Tribune*, acting as a Chicago taxpayer, began the long litigation that became known as the "experts' fees case." It filed a suit charging that George F. Harding, Michael J. Faherty and Thompson were involved in a conspiracy with two city building specialists, Frank H. Mesce and Austin J. Lynch, to defraud the city of $2,876,-063, a sum that represented, according to the suit, overpayment in fees to these and others for work in connection with the building of the Michigan Avenue Bridge and other projects under Faherty's direction. There were charges of kickbacks and illegal payments and contributions to the city machine for favors offered and accepted.

So confident and cocky was Thompson that this suit, a long way from trial at the moment, bothered him very little. What he and

Lundin were more concerned with was the forthcoming election of twenty Circuit Court judges and a judge of the Superior Court.

One of the jurists scheduled to be placed on the regular Republican ticket was Kickham Scanlan, the stern man who had dared to give back to Charles E. Chadsey his school superintendent's job after Thompson had thrown the dignified professor out of the school system. Thompson had never forgiven Scanlan for this breach of political manners, and he was determined to keep the judge from reelection.

Lundin had more sanguine reasons for deciding to draw up a new slate of candidates who would hearken to his command and direction. Under the law, the Circuit Court had domain over the South Park Commission, then preparing to embark on a $3,000,000 beautification program on the lake shore. The prospect of all this money and all the jobs and contracts whetted Lundin's eagerness to control the commission, and to do so he needed judges who would listen to his suave reason. Moreover, judges made many patronage appointments in selecting referees and masters in chancery to hear special cases, and these too Lundin yearned to control.

So he and Thompson, in full control since the last election of the G.O.P. county central committee, chose to pick only "safe men." The Democrats, smelling victory, conferred with the Chicago Bar Association, and a coalition slate was drawn, composed of sitting Democratic judges and those Republicans rejected by Lundin. Their cry was "Stop the City Hall from Seizing the Judiciary!"

The campaign was unlike any other for the election of judges. Scores of women, inspired by the coalition idea, stumped for the combined-ticket judges. At first Lundin was sneeringly contemptuous of the furor. "It'll die down," he scoffed. "No one stays excited about a judicial election." Always ready to predict, he estimated that the total vote would amount to a bare 200,000.

But as election day neared there were indications that the vote would be much greater. Lundin attempted some maneuvers. "Go out to the Democrats," he told the Republican poll watchers, "and tell them they are suckers if they have any dealings with Republicans." To make it more difficult for the independent voters to cast their ballots he ordered a last-minute switch of polling places. On election day many voters showed up at their regular places, only to be told that they must walk another mile to new ones; many did so, grim and determined to beat the steal by Lundin.

The day's results proved Lundin miserably wrong in his estimates. More than 600,000 citizens trooped to the polls, a record vote for such an election. His ticket was soundly defeated. Even Thompson's own ward went against the Republican regulars, and all through the county there were reports of heavy balloting for the coalition judges and scant ones for Lundin's, with the coalition winning finally by 100,000 votes.

"Thompsonism has been dealt a smashing blow between the eyes!" sang the *News*. Others spoke of the city's moral awakening, praising the role played by the women, who were voting for the first time in a judicial election. Hearst's *American*, now friendly to Thompson, commented sadly that Big Bill had erred in "abdicating too much power to his ward committeemen" and those who had put patronage above principle.

3

A wrong guess, a careless grab for more power—and disaster followed on disaster.

Reeling from the blow in the election, Thompson and Lundin journeyed to Springfield to plot passage of their "five-cent fare" transportation bill. Prior to the judicial contest, they had been assured by Samuel Ettelson, the corporation counsel who also served as state senator, that the bill, setting up a local commission to establish fares and regulations for the streetcar lines, would pass easily.

But such political assurances depend on success in the field, and Lundin and Thompson had failed. When the measure came up for a vote, it was two short of a required majority. Alarmed, Thompson suggested that another try be made later in the day, and he and Lundin scurried to Len Small to press him into action in rounding up more votes.

That afternoon, while Thompson and Lundin, as was customary, sat behind Fred E. Sterling, the new lieutenant governor, on the rostrum, a new state senator from downstate Murphysboro, Otis F.

WHEN RIGHEIMER FELL

[Copyright: 1923: By The Chicago Tribune.]

Glenn, arose to denounce the pair. He upbraided them for daring to come to Springfield to influence legislation. He called on them to leave the rostrum and the chamber. When he was finished and another vote was taken, the bill was doomed.

Soon Ed Brundage, the only anti-Thompson man to win in the 1920 election, was heard from. Early in his new term Governor Small had received the order from Lundin to cut the appropriation for Brundage's office. Not only was the attorney general a faithful follower of the *Tribune's* Medill McCormick and a sworn enemy of Lundin and Thompson, but he was friendly to Senator Glenn and he had aspirations to be the next governor. "We've got to stop him" was Lundin's edict. Small, of course, had complied by slashing the appropriation, through his veto powers, by $700,000, and Brundage swore vengeance.

Now Ed Brundage brought up his heaviest weapons. He had probed deeply into Small's background and had discovered what he considered to be irregularities in Small's handling of funds when he served as state treasurer. The amounts involved came to over $2,000,000 which, according to Brundage, represented interest earned on state funds kept in private banks owned by a good friend of Small's. No interest had been paid the state on this money, said Brundage, and this was a direct violation of state laws. He brought the case before the Sangamon County grand jury and indictments were soon returned charging Small and several others in the case with conspiracy to embezzle the money.

From Small came the plaint, "I am the victim of a political plot engineered by big business and public utilities." His good friend, Big Bill, spoke up heatedly. "Len Small and I will see you all in hell first! Whether this is a government of the people, for the people and by the people, or whether this is a government of money, of newspapers and of crooked political bosses against the people, is to be proved. We will go on!"

4

Even New York, traditionally aloof from the provincial political squabblings beyond the west banks of the Hudson River, took note of what the *Times* called "sagging Thompsonism." It was quite clear, commented its august editorialist, that the City Hall machine, "of which Fred Lundin is the brains and William Hale Thompson the figurehead," was heading for disaster. "The wicked prosper for a season, but the 'close' season seems to be coming on in Cook County and Illinois. Mayor Thompson's motley following and curious record are only too well known. After all, he is not much more than a puppet of abler men. Spoils, demagoguery, inefficiency, waste—that is the sort of administration he has given Chicago. It must put up with him for about two years and a half more. But the power of his machine is waning and his capacity for mischief is diminishing. This is encouraging to civilized governments in all cities."

As if in direct reply, Lundin staged a banquet at the Congress Hotel in the week of Small's indictment. It was to be a "unity dinner," with invitations sent to 350 City Hall machine stalwarts. But so swiftly had the forces been dispersed by these few, sudden calamities that only 100 persons came. Lundin blandly asked for $3,000 from each guest "to fight future battles." All he received was $200 in personal notes. Yet he orated as if the party war chest was stuffed with dollar bills. "Where do they get that noise about our City Hall ship sinking?" he wanted to know. "Why, instead of that, we are going to keep right on sailing into the port of success every election!"

5

Brave words—and futile ones. Even as they echoed through the half-filled hotel dining room, even while Brundage prepared to take Small to court and Small's friends raced to his defense—some even urged him to refuse to accept the indictment papers—a slow-smoldering feud burst open, sending new tremors through the ranks of the Thompson-Lundin fold.

In the early weeks of his term State's Attorney Crowe had watched with anguished eye the free-swinging activities of Police Chief Fitzmorris. Never one to get close to Big Bill or his appointees, Crowe had his own ideas about how to subdue the vice rings and the bootleggers. He knew also that Fitzmorris had been chosen by Thompson without Lundin's approval, and he heard that Lundin was much distressed over the appointment.

Fitzmorris' drive slackened after the first fine burst of endeavor. Truck hijackings soon were as plentiful as always, and vice joints flourished under the averted eyes of police captains. In the aldermanic elections of February 1921 several bombings occurred, principally in the old Nineteenth Ward, where the veteran boodler, John

(Johnny de Pow) Powers, was opposed by Anthony d'Andrea, president of the Hod Carriers' Union and of the Unione Sicilione. D'Andrea, an unfrocked priest who had been active on the Levee in its palmier days, was threatened with Black Hand letters after Powers beat him, but the police told him to disregard them. On May 11 D'Andrea was slain by assassins carrying sawed-off shotguns.

This slaying, so typical of many others in the decade to follow, prompted fresh criticism of Fitzmorris' police. He promised new arrests, but no one was ever charged with D'Andrea's murder. Nor was any suspect found to be connected with the many bombings in the weeks before the election.

That violence gave Crowe his opportunity to take up the cry, openly and critically, against Fitzmorris. He demanded that forty policemen from Fitzmorris' department be assigned to a special investigative staff under his command. With it, he asserted, he would wipe out the crime and vice that was being tolerated by Fitzmorris. The police chief refused to grant his request until Thompson, eager to keep peace, ordered him to assign the men to Crowe. How Crowe expected to carry out his announced intentions remained a mystery, for his chief investigator to head this force was an unsavory character named Ben Newmark. Crowe himself later referred to Newmark and his men as "Ali Baba and his forty thieves." Newmark did carry out raids, but he was just as quick at accepting bribes from brothel owners and gamblers. Despite such reports, Crowe insisted he was powerless to fire Newmark. "Certain political leaders," he said, had compelled him to take Newmark on, and there was no way of getting rid of the rascal without incurring the wrath of these important politicians.

As Crowe continued his quarrel with Fitzmorris, Big Bill finally came to the defense of his chief. He dared Crowe to indict Fitzmorris if the charges of laxity were true. He also sent Crowe a letter reminding him that he had helped elect him state's attorney, and asking for party unity and co-operation. "I have no quarrel with the mayor" was Crowe's response, "but I must say that his letter is filled with glittering generalities."

The fight between Crowe and Fitzmorris soon veered from its

single track as Crowe, moving farther apart from the two men who had indeed aided him in reaching his power-wielding eminence, looked about for new means to demolish his rivals' tottering stronghold. He made no pretense of allegiance to the Lundin-Thompson group now. He turned his sharp and eager attention to persistent reports that much was amiss in the activities of the Board of Education.

To Crowe's office early in 1922 there came three members of that board, J. Lewis (Iron-Handed Jack) Coath, Francis E. Croarkin and Hart Hanson. They had interesting details to relate. On April 26, Charles E. Springer, a real-estate operator, had written to Hanson charging school officials deliberately ignored a chance to buy the site for a new Wendell Phillips High School on the city's South Side for $60,000. But, after the ownership of the site had changed hands, the board did buy it for $90,000. "Who got the $30,000?" Springer asked. Hanson had read this letter at the next board meeting and demanded an investigation. President Edwin S. Davis had called a special meeting, at which William A. Bither, the old-time Thompson hack who served as the board's attorney, offered a long and devious explanation.

"We're not satisfied," Hanson told Crowe. "Will you investigate?"

Crowe would, and did. Soon he was before the grand jury, armed with evidence that went beyond the claims in Springer's letter. He informed the jurors that Bither, in 1920, when he was in charge of acquiring land adjacent to the old Wendell Phillips High School, managed to turn title over to a Henry W. Kaup, a good friend of Albert W. Severinghaus, one of Thompson's original Solid Six on the school board. This was done, according to Crowe, by the neat device of buying the land from tenants who lived on it, then inserting Kaup's name in each sale contract. Until the board bought the land at a higher price, Kaup collected rents and split his profits with Bither. From such peculations grew the first of several "school-board scandal" trials. Tried for conspiring to obtain school funds fraudulently, Bither was sentenced to a one-to-five-year term and fined $2,000, while Kaup received a similar fine and a nine-month term.

Both men appealed and two years later their sentences and fines were reversed. Then, however, Crowe no longer was interested in pressing the case, for the damage to his foes had been done.

6

Thompson and Lundin were disturbed by the convictions. Ominous whispers issued from Crowe's office that even more interesting information had turned up in the course of the school-board investigation. Crowe said nothing, but the cry of "Scandal!" started to haunt Thompson. In a rash move he tried to fire the entire school board, but the city council forced him to renege.

This setback came just as the second of his Pageants of Progress was drawing to an end. The first one in 1921 had been a notable success, with 55,000 persons thronging Municipal Pier every day for two weeks. Bill had reveled in the crowds and its cheers. He munched hot dogs with them, paraded up and down the end of the pier waving his sombrero, made happy speeches, and the profits had totaled $300,000. But this year's pageant was a failure. Harassed by a streetcar strike, it registered a much lower attendance, and its profits were less than $50,000. Worse yet, a pesky citizen named Samuel Grossman filed suit to discover if any of the two years' earnings had gone into the pockets of Thompson, Dr. John Dill Robertson or their associates. In the next few months Grossman's litigation brought out the fact that Dr. Robertson had a financial interest in the clinic that was to have been established—and never was—for the free treatment of children's teeth, and that certain men friendly to Thompson had made handsome side money on contracts for construction work and in leasing pageant concessions.

Another fiasco that sad summer bothered Thompson. To the annoyance of Chief Fitzmorris, he appointed the Reverend John H. Williamson, known in church circles as the "Fighting Parson," to a $10,000-a-year job as law-enforcement commissioner "to care for the city's moral welfare." Under broad powers bestowed by Big Bill, the young minister carried on energetically but with minor effect for several months. He visited cafés where bootleg liquor was reported to be sold, clashed with Chief Fitzmorris over which of them had the legal right to seek out and destroy such establishments, and received the sneering jibes of the anti-Thompson newspapers. Once he made the tactless error of citing the great number of gambling houses flourishing in the bailiwick of Alderman Louis B. Anderson, one of Thompson's strongest Negro backers. An obviously sincere crusader, the Reverend Mr. Williamson found himself balked at every turn, and before the end of the year he resigned.

Then, too, there was another legal victory for the *Tribune*. An earlier libel suit by Thompson for no less than $10,000,000 because the newspaper had declared the city to be "bankrupt, insolvent, broke, in a bad financial condition and improperly and corruptly administered by its officers" had been dismissed by Circuit Judge Harry M. Fisher in a mighty opinion guaranteeing every citizen the right to criticize the city government as long as there was no advocacy of overthrowing that government by force.

This year's action was for $500,000. Thompson charged the *Tribune* had called him "disloyal" during the war and had carried on "a persistent campaign of misrepresentation and abuse." All the turmoil of 1917 was revived, with Thompson's lawyer, David H. Jackson, denying that Big Bill had ever made the statements attributed to him, and with Weymouth Kirkland, the *Tribune's* lawyer, producing witness after witness to testify that he had. Thompson himself testified that he was no traitor—"I never had but one intention and purpose in mind, and that was to protect the United States of America and the people of this great country of ours!" The trial ended abruptly when two of the jurors fell ill and Judge Francis Wilson was forced to dismiss the case. It never was resumed.

7

In this time of travail there was only one bright note, the outcome of Len Small's trial.

Arguing that it would be impossible to get a fair hearing in his heavily Democratic home county, Small had been successful in shifting the trial to Waukegan. The defense made careful preparations. Before the jury was selected, salesmen hired by Small's friends visited the homes of every potential juror in the area, offering

an amazing photographic bargain. Each salesman carried an album
of samples, one of which was a portrait of Small. The reaction of
each prospective customer to a glimpse of this photograph was
noted by the salesmen and carefully reported to the defense attor-
neys, who thereby gained a useful guide in selecting the jury.

After weeks of complex testimony Small was found not guilty.
But there were several aftermaths. On the night of his narrow victory, Small's wife, Ida, dropped dead in the excitement from a
heart attack. Later Brundage filed a civil suit and Small eventually
was forced to return $600,000 to the state treasury. In addition, a
grand jury opened an inquiry into charges that the jury was fixed.
When "Umbrella Mike" Boyle, the labor racketeer who derived
his nickname from his custom of collecting graft in an umbrella,
and Ben Newmark, the erstwhile Crowe investigator, refused to
testify before this group, they were sentenced to six months in jail
for contempt. Small pardoned them both after thirty days.

8

In November there was more sadness for Thompson. Judge Righeimer, running for his first full term, was beaten by a popular
Democrat, Edmund K. Jarecki. Other Democrats—Robert Sweitzer for county clerk, Paddy Carr for county treasurer, Henry
Horner for probate judge—overwhelmed the Lundin-Thompson
candidates.

Even Big Bill's comrades in the Ancient and Mystic Order of
the Nobles of the Shrine turned against him. On one woeful evening they gathered in the Medinah Temple to protest the city's
refusal to allow a paddle-wheel lottery at the annual Shrine circus.
The chief spokesman against Thompson for this heinous offense
was Imperial Potentate Will H. Wade, a close friend of Brundage
and Medill McCormick.

When Wade completed his harangue, William H. Wesbey, a
Thompson adherent, arose. "Mayor Thompson is present. Give
him a hearing."

Thompson bounded heavily onto the stage and faced his hostile
audience. "Mr. Wade is mistaken. I never——"

Hissing and shouting stopped him. As he stood, mouth agape, the noise continued for ten minutes. He gave his tormentors a long, sullen stare, then walked out of the hall. Later he hit back at Wade by ordering Governor Small to fire Wade's business partner, Thomas J. Houston, as State Insurance Commissioner. But the hostile reception still vexed him. "That Shrine affair," he told all who would listen, "really cut me to the heart."

18 | Scandal—and More Scandal

A DEMOCRATIC VICTORY IN COOK County was bad enough, but perfidy in the Republican ranks was worse. And perfidy is what Bob Crowe, in the angry eyes of Thompson and Lundin, was preparing to commit as he and Ed Brundage went before the grand jury with bales of records and evidence linking Lundin to scandalous happenings in the administration of the schools.

Fred Lundin promptly left town. Thompson was bewildered and dismayed. A new mayoral primary was swiftly approaching. In the previous summer he had informally announced his candidacy. But now this ugly talk of new school scandals plagued him. Worse yet, George Harding and Sam Ettelson, asked for their estimates of his chances, told him, "You won't come within 50,000 of beating a Democrat." Crowe and Charles V. Barrett, another anti-Lundin party boss, came out for Arthur C. Lueder, the city's federal postmaster, as their candidate for the mayoral nomination.

Then, late in January, Bill learned more definitely about the case Crowe was so energetically presenting to the grand jury. Aimed at Lundin, it would air the whole evil business of school scandals and wreck any campaign Bill Thompson might undertake. So on January 25 Thompson withdrew his name. Publicly he declared, "I wish to make plain my continued interest in public affairs and my willingness to lead or follow in any contests the people may make manifest their desires." Privately he damned Lundin, Crowe, Brundage. Then he announced that he and Mrs. Thompson would take a long vacation on a Pacific island after a new mayor was elected and his term was over.

2

On the day after Big Bill's withdrawal, the grand jurors smashed through their indictments.

There were enough charges and hints of scandal to satisfy every

THE SILENT PARTNER

[Copyright: 1922: By The Chicago Tribune.]

one of the foes of Fred Lundin and Big Bill Thompson. Lundin was named as the master of a ring of twenty-three conspirators who had robbed the school treasury of over a million dollars. They had operated, said the indictments, through fake contracts, false bids and excessive purchase prices for school supplies. They had secured graft payments through direct shakedowns and bribery. They had demanded campaign funds from all those who did business with the schools. They had sought to establish a dictatorial reign over all school affairs, from the classrooms to the business offices.

Indicted with Lundin were Virtus Rohm, his nephew and patronage assistant; Edwin S. Davis, ex-president of the Board of Education; Albert Severinghaus, ex-vice-president; Charles Forsberg, former business manager; William A. Bither, the hapless school attorney already under sentence for his fake land deals; Patrick J. Moynihan, a Thompson committeeman and member of the State Commerce Commission; Charles Ward, an old-time Lundin leader and speech writer for Thompson; and a host of minor officials, all members of the Thompson-Lundin organization.

These culprits, said the stern indictment, had conspired to defraud the taxpayers, and Crowe and Brundage vowed swift and strong prosecution. The case languished for weeks, giving rise to rumors that there was insufficient evidence to back up the charges and that deals were being made between Crowe and Lundin to minimize the accusations. Lundin stayed away. He was now in upper Minnesota, now in Havana, now at French Lick. Thompson had no comment, although later he would grumble, "My friends have crucified me. I believed in them and I did everything I could to help them make good to the people. And they betrayed me. I am happy in one thing, and that is that I have given Chicago the best administration it ever had."

Finally Lundin suddenly appeared, flanked by Clarence Darrow and Charles Erbstein, the city's finest criminal lawyers. He strode into the Criminal Courts Building with a silver-handled walking stick and quickly laid down $10,000 as his bond money. Then he vanished again after a swift smile for the photographers.

3

The trial was set for April Fool's Day, a week after Lueder won the Republican primary and honest, stolid Judge William E. Dever was chosen the Democratic mayoral candidate. But following motions to dismiss the indictments and denial of the motions there was a postponement. Lundin broke his silence at the brief hearing to assert his innocence. "If the state will produce one honest man who will testify that I have ever taken one dirty dollar," he said, "I will call on the judge to halt the trial and sentence me immediately. One man and one dollar—but it must be an honest man and a dirty dollar!"

Finally the selection of a jury began before Judge Charles A. McDonald. This caused new delays, for many of the potential jurors expressed strong feelings about Lundin and Thompson, and some about Crowe, and some about Darrow, and some about all politicians. A jury finally was chosen and Assistant Attorney General Marvin E. Barnhart arose to call Lundin and his associates "pirates." He would prove, cried he, that they stole more than a million dollars through graft in the purchase of coal, boilers, insurance, doors, varnish, beds, blankets, electric driers, drawing instruments, plumbing, printing supplies, light bulbs, furniture, books and phonographs.

One of the first witnesses against Lundin, who slouched in a chair near the counsel table fingering his black Windsor tie, was Jacob Loeb, once president of the school board. A meticulous man with a torrent of facts and figures, he appeared eager to repay Lundin and, indirectly, Thompson for the many days of misery they had caused him.

Loeb remembered the first days of his presidency, when Lundin, discussing the selection of new members, had told him, "We don't want highbrows on the school board. We want fellows who will vote the way we want them to." He told of meetings at which Lundin gave orders to discard those who had proved themselves unfaithful to the organization. For his pains Loeb heard himself described by Erbstein, under cross-examination, as a "Uriah Heep" and "a chronic malcontent" and he was perspiring profusely when he left the witness chair.

Hart Hanson was a talkative witness against Lundin. He compared Poor Swede to a marionette master. When he had been appointed in 1917, said Hanson, he was told to take orders from Edwin S. Davis, the president. "He's a good little fellow," Lundin had told Hanson, "and he does what he is told when he gets his orders from headquarters." It was Hanson who disclosed that Lundin, when receiving his protests that the public might not be happy over a certain overpayment for school textbooks, yelled, "To hell with the public! We're at the trough now, and we are going to feed. You do what Davis tells you."

From John Howatt, the school engineer, the jury heard that boilers worth $4,000 had been purchased for $7,500 or more. A favorite of Lundin's in the boiler business, said Howatt, had been paid $165,000 for boilers that could have been purchased elsewhere for $60,000. Dr. Frank G. Bruner, director of special schools, testified he had a chance to rent busses for crippled pupils at $12.50 a day but that the contract was awarded to a Lundin-sponsored firm for $28.50 a day.

There were, of course, many other witnesses and many other accusations.

Davis' board had approved the purchase of potato peelers at $133 each, kitchen tables for $106, electric hand driers for $133. Phonographs worth $70 had been bought for $187 each from a company owned by Moynihan. Contracts for doors in new school buildings were awarded only to the Central Metallic Door Company, owned by none other than Fred Lundin. Davis, by demanding fifty cents on every ton of coal bought by the city, had received $7,500, testified Timothy J. Charles, president of a coal company. O. W. Huncke, an insurance broker, testified that he handled all insurance for the school system through Lundin and Rohm, and that they got thirty per cent of the premiums and he ten per cent.

Whenever Lundin's name was mentioned, he chuckled and smoothed his black tie. He sat placidly near his lawyers, augmented by the oracular Patrick O'Donnell and the crafty Benedict J. Short, as they hammered away at each state's witness and then began the defense. In Darrow's words, the case was "a conspiracy engineered by the enemies of William Hale Thompson and Fred Lundin." While it was true that Lundin had engaged in business enterprises, he did no business with the board. "His sense of honor prevented him from doing that! This is political prosecution!"

Of the witnesses ready to damn the accusers, two were most vital to Lundin's case. One, of course, was the accused himself. The other, rushing from his Hawaii vacation, was Big Bill Thompson.

THE BAD EXAMPLE

[Copyright: 192?: By The Chicago Tribune.]

With the bland stare of a child, Big Bill denied that Lundin had ever interfered with any of the city's business. He certainly had not injected his opinions into the affairs of the school board. "He took the position that the Republican party should guard against politics in the police and on the school board. It was a religion with him." He delineated for Darrow and his associates, for the audience and for the goggle-eyed jurors his theories about selecting men for city office who were "serviceably sound," quoting advice an old Texas cowhand had given him in his cowboy days. Thompson the young cowboy had sought to buy a perfect horse, but the rancher told him: "My boy, if you want to make a success in your life, you want to change your point of view. You do not want to look for perfect countries, perfect climate, perfect men or perfect women, for if you do all you will do all your life is hunt, and you will never find them. Now, if you will change your standard and look for things that are serviceably sound, then you will always find them, and you will accomplish things and get somewhere."

In his session on the stand Lundin was masterfully guided by Darrow. Here was Poor Swede, Insignificant Me, the fortunate medicine man, the Loyal Patriot, the Misjudged Citizen, all in one bucktoothed man, with persuasion in his soft voice and self-pity in every word.

He related the familiar story of his youth as a bootblack, of selling newspapers, of years as a pill peddler and purveyor of his Juniper Ade, of his early ventures into politics.

Bill Thompson? "A man of strong character, integrity and courage, and so few have that in public life."

Patronage? "Oh, yes, I was on a patronage committee that really had no name. I called it a committee of kicks, you know, to take the abuse of disappointed office seekers."

Influence? "I never asked the mayor or any other official in connection with the city government for any favor, nor recommended any man for any position. I never have accepted any appointment because, if I did, I would have to do as I was told and I can't do that."

Politics? "It has been my chief hobby and my duty. I love it, I dream it, I live it. So few people are willing to explore the pretenses of uplifters. Someone that does not love money, or golf, or to shine at dinner in full dress has to take the job. That's the pleasure I get out of it."

Enemies? "Ed Brundage has started all these myths about me. The newspapers have haunted me for thirty years. I was the cuspidor for all the abuse of Mayor Thompson's political opponents."

And the defense rested. Lundin was the only one of the twenty-three defendants permitted by the smart legal battery to testify.

4

As the jurors filed into their chambers, the cries of the Lundin lawyers still resounded in their ears. Erbstein: "All they've shown here was that Fred Lundin was Bill Thompson's campaign manager and that all the defendants were members of their organization." Short: "This is the most monstrous legal hippodrome ever aired in any courtroom! Hanson is an ingrate! He is a schemer and a perjurer! Loeb is a liar! Charles is a thief, an embezzler, a con man and a boozer!" O'Donnell, his deep voice echoing through the building as he denounced Brundage for his "attempt to rule Chicago by political oligarchy," rumbled, "Sing your songs, O ye Patricians, sing your proud paeans of glory, but for me the Te Deum and the Miserere of God's unfortunate people!" Finally Darrow: "If Fred Lundin or any other man in this case could be convicted on this evidence, made up of suspicions and cobwebs, then I want to retire to a cannibal island and be safe! This is an infamous conspiracy against the liberties of man!"

The jurors agreed. In less than four hours they were ready with a verdict that found all the defendants not guilty. Crowe fulminated and promised new indictments. But Lundin, grinning, intoned, "Truth crushed to earth will rise again," and when his wife, who had sat in the front row throughout the trial, started to weep, he said, "C'mon, kid, let's go home."

5

The trial was over, but so was the Lundin-Thompson power and the glory. Never again would Fred Lundin refer to Big Bill Thompson as a "man of strong character." Never again would Big Bill say sparkling words about the selflessness of Fred Lundin.

Despite his defense of Lundin in the courtroom, Thompson held Poor Swede responsible for the ruin of his re-election plans. Had Lundin been more circumspect, Crowe could not have brought the indictment which had forced Thompson to withdraw from the campaign for the mayoral nomination in January. Besides that, Lundin had dissipated their campaign funds, collected for the mayoral race, in a futile attempt to elect Righeimer to a full term as county judge. Lundin betrayed him, Thompson told friends, when he brought down the wrath of the public by his greedy patronage methods and his demands for more and more city contracts and accounts. Ever since he appointed Fitzmorris police chief without consulting Lundin, Big Bill had sought to expand his balky independence without much success. The newspapers constantly irked him with their cry that he was merely a Trilby to Lundin's Svengali. Since his own regime was on trial he had no choice but to come to the aid of Poor Swede in court. Bitterly he told his cronies that he had saved Lundin from the penitentiary. But he was through. Henceforth, Big Bill intended to be his own man.

A Democrat now sat in the City Hall: Dever had defeated Lueder. Out in the street were many who had been with Thompson and Lundin since the beginning. Dever's new corporation counsel, Francis X. Busch, vowed to sue the firms that had evaded payments for use of city streets, to catch up with all wrongdoers. Len Small was being hounded by Brundage to explain $10,000 paid to the governor's relatives for their labors as "inheritance tax investigators." The Dever ax fell everywhere, on school trustees and on those lowliest beneficiaries of political largess, the "chop suey wagon" men who gathered the city's ashes and garbage.

Lundin allowed himself the harsh statement, "I'm through with Chicago forever," and went off to sulk for a while. His protégé offered one final gift for the citizenry, his record of accomplishments. These were lavishly described in a pamphlet titled "Eight Years of Progress," thousands of copies of which were distributed in Thompson's final week as mayor. Each carried a handsome photograph of Big Bill, sporting his Shriner's pin, that resembled only faintly the heavy-jowled, fleshy man he had actually become. It cited the many projects carried on at what so many of Thompson's critics considered excessive costs—89 streets widened, 832 miles of streets paved, 402 miles of sewers constructed, the Michigan Avenue Bridge completed, 55 new playgrounds, a fish hatchery in Lincoln Park. Even the two Pageants of Progress were adjudged huge successes and the Police Department was decreed to be forever divorced from politics. "I bear no ill will toward any person or persons," said Big Bill in his farewell message to the city council. "I shall forget any apparent injuries and shall ever remember all friendships and kindnesses."

6

In a few short months Thompson was back in the political maelstrom. Len Small was ready to announce his candidacy for reelection and Lundin was still in temporary retirement. Big Bill thought the time had come to seize leadership in the Small camp and assert his new independence.

Flanked by scores of his faithful, Bill swept into Springfield late in 1923 and took over the meeting at which Small formally declared himself a candidate. In an aggressive speech, Thompson railed against the *Tribune*, against those who would divide the Republican party, against all who had ever spoken an unkind word against him or Small. He led his listeners by the hundreds to the cemetery where Mrs. Small lay buried. Tears streaming from his eyes, he stood over her grave and throbbed, "I swear to avenge Mrs. Small's death by seeing to it that Ed Brundage is defeated! He'll live to regret the day he caused the death of this fine woman!"

In the primary Thompson heaped great abuse on Brundage, whose opponent was Oscar E. Carlstrom, a member of the State Tax Commission. Carlstrom, hailing Thompson as "one of our greatest patriots and greatest Americans," promised that he would knock out

Brundage's suit to recover money from Small in connection with the bank case. Thompson also blasted away at Crowe, who was seeking re-election as state's attorney, and at Medill McCormick, whom Thompson detested even more than he hated McCormick's opponent, Charles S. Deneen. "Anytime you'll find that I'm in the same political bed with Bobby Crowe, the Barrett brothers, Ed Brundage who was the cause of killing Governor Small's wife, the Chicago *Tribune*, profiteering from Canadian free lands for their pulp paper, and their Medill McCormick who voted for war, then you'll know that Bill Thompson has turned out to be a crook!"

Although Thompson's efforts were mighty, the results were not all to his satisfaction. Small's enemies had sung "Oh, Pardon Me!" to the tune of the traditional "Oh, Promise Me!" because of the thousands of pardons and paroles he had granted, but he won by 60,000 votes. So did Carlstrom, and so did Deneen, who eked out a 6,000-vote victory over McCormick. But in Cook County, where Thompson needed a victory to give him equality with Small, Bob Crowe was elected.

7

Yet Big Bill still hoped to recapture Chicago as the bastion from which to attack Crowe or force a truce. Most of all, he needed to stay in the public eye through a publicity build-up like that of his early days when he was a champion athlete and winner of boat races. He soon found just the thing, conceived by a press agent for the cypress-wood industry. He informed Chicago that he would lead an expedition to the South Seas to hunt tree-climbing fish.

He had read of such fish, he insisted, in a scientific treatise. "I have strong reason to believe," he declared with great solemnity, "that there are fish that come out of the water, can live on land, will jump three feet to catch a grasshopper and will actually climb trees. I figure to take moving pictures of them. Pictures of fish ought to be profitable. There are millions of people interested in fish. One million passed through the Lincoln Park aquarium in 129 days, and 51 million through the Battery aquarium in New York in 26 years. Recent jungle pictures have made a profit of half a million dollars."

A cypress yawl, the *Big Bill*, was especially constructed for the expedition. Its figurehead was a full face of Thompson carved in oak. It was launched from Riverview Amusement Park on Memorial Day and set out for shakedown cruises in the Great Lakes. Thompson, replying to scoffers, offered to bet $25,000 on the success of his expedition, but found no takers. He also staged a mass meeting in the Fish Fans Club, an organization he had founded at Belmont Harbor in 1922 which, among other things, was committed "to urge and encourage the propagation of fish in American waters." Here he presented Billy Lorimer, no longer the mighty boss but a seedy has-been, grateful for coming out of murky retirement. At the meeting it was clear there was another motive in the fantastic expedition, for Lorimer again sounded his cry for the Lakes-to-Gulf waterway and hailed Thompson as the "leader in this great cause."

Before the expedition sailed, Thompson caused a mild flurry at the Republican National Convention, held in Cleveland in June. He threatened to bolt the Republicans and support Senator Robert M. LaFollette, the Progressives' "Fighting Bob," instead of Calvin Coolidge, the regulars' choice. "I like Bob's ideas about breaking the big monopoly that's strangling the American people," he explained.

He was still in this frame of mind when, early in July, the *Big Bill* set out to hunt tree-climbing fish. Thousands of Chicagoans stood on the Michigan Avenue Bridge as the craft sailed down the Chicago River into Lake Michigan. Out of sight of land, Thompson relaxed with determined vigor. He donned dungarees, which he held up with a rope belt, wore a cut-down fire marshal's hat and drank and sang commands day and night. George Harding, sedate and prim in a black business suit and stiff white collar, derived some private joy from the excitement and confusion. Strangest of the passengers was Urbine J. (Sport) Herrmann, owner of the Cort Theater and an irrepressible playboy. He wore a yachting cap, tennis shoes and an athletic supporter. When Captain A. J. Aiken Duken, Big Bill's skipper, touched port, Herrmann was stowed out of sight and Thompson put on more presentable clothes to speak on the need for a waterway that would compete with railroads along the route. Long before the craft reached New Orleans, Thompson and his companions were on their way home. Captain Duken, without promised funds to carry on, sold part of the ship's gear and sailed to Panama, where he settled down in Cristobal to charter the *Big Bill* for fishing parties.

8

Despite its notable lack of success, the tree-climbing-fish expedition had done what Big Bill wanted it to. He had received columns of newspaper space, he was talked about again and remembered, unlike other politicians who had dropped out of the warfare of campaigning. He gave up his mild flirtation with the Progressives, and threw himself into the fight to elect Small and Carlstrom. He even put out peace feelers to Crowe, who received them quite willingly, now that he was convinced Fred Lundin was out of Big Bill's political life. Thompson toured the state, shouting for Small and the entire ticket.

There were no answering cries from Small. When he entered the spring primaries, Thompson had asked for and received Small's pledge to support his transportation plan for Chicago: legislation to permit the city to establish a transportation authority which would consolidate the surface and elevated lines and fix a uniform five-cent fare. The scheme was favored by Samuel Insull, who had worked it out with Thompson, Sam Ettelson and Frank L. Smith, chairman of the Illinois Commerce Commission, which regulated public utilities. Such a program, successfully put through the legislature, with Thompson given the credit, would enable Big Bill to spring back into the City Hall with ease, or, at any rate, with the help of Insull money.

But Len Small uttered no word about the traction-authority plan in his speeches. In the Coolidge landslide, he went on to win without any public commitment to Thompson, smothering Judge Norman L. Jones, his Democratic rival, by 345,000 votes. In Cook County, and up and down the state, other Republicans went into office with him.

When Thompson sought a pledge for the streetcar legislation in the governor's inaugural address, Small was evasive. He did not expand the patronage Big Bill and his friends already held. There were reports from Springfield that Fred Lundin had been seen there on his way to the governor's mansion. A deal was in the making.

Thompson was hurt, for he genuinely liked Small. And he was angry over the developing double cross. He loaded a roaring band of followers into a special train and set out for Springfield for Governor Small's inaugural. That night he staged a banquet in the Leland Hotel—a victory feast not attended by the governor. At the height of a noisy celebration, Richard W. Wolfe, a former La Follette leader in the state and a man given to orotund prose, arose to toast a trio he referred to as "The Three Horsemen."

Head high, Wolfe rolled out his phrases. "Gentlemen, I give you for senator, United States senator, in 1926, the honorable Frank L. Smith, of Dwight!" Smith, the lanky chairman of the Commerce Commission, beamed and bowed while the crowd cheered.

"And I also give you, for governor in 1928, Oscar E. Carlstrom, our new attorney general!" Carlstrom, broad-faced, smiling, waved his hand to acknowledge the yells. A few at the table sat appalled. This, unquestionably, was Thompson's declaration of war on Small.

"And for mayor of the great city of Chicago in 1927," Wolfe went on, "I give you, my good friends, William Hale Thompson, a great American!"

Now the cheering split the smoke-filled air as Thompson arose and held both arms aloft. Even the doubtful and fearful ones joined in the yelling. An accordion sounded, playing "Hail! Hail! the Gang's All Here!" George Harding leaped to his feet to lead more cheers. When the cries died down, Thompson briefly thanked the assemblage and vowed to serve his constituents well.

There were no joyous acclamations from the statehouse. Big Bill had chosen inauguration day in Len Small's own state capital to declare the re-elected governor out of future campaigns. Small struck fast and hard. He withdrew the patronage he had doled out to Thompson. Gene Pike, Big Bill's old friend, was fired as boss of the Lincoln Park Board and replaced by Attorney David H. Jackson, Lundin's friend. Thompson's sister, Mrs. William Pelouze, was dismissed from the same board. Dr. John Dill Robertson, who had made his peace with Lundin, got the job of president of the West

Parks. Percy Coffin, who also had hastened to welcome Lundin back from exile, replaced a Harding associate as public administrator, a job good for $100,000 annually in fees.

Thompson was left with nothing but his chairmanship of the Illinois Waterways Commission, a position that paid no money and carried no patronage. The premature challenge to Small had proved foolhardy and disastrous. Without patronage, his followers, even the most loyal, would melt away. Without precinct workers, he was lost. In grabbing for downstate power with his bid to Carlstrom and Smith, he had thrown away nearly all of what little he possessed in Cook County, the precise place where he needed votes and strength. He had driven Small into Lundin's willing arms, and he had left only his personal popularity, Harding's Negro wards and money and the dimming possibility of financial help from Insull.

9

The full effect of his ridiculous mistake was too much for Thompson. Pleading illness, he left Chicago with Mrs. Thompson for Palm Beach. Even there he was dogged by bad luck. A few hours after they registered, their hotel burned to the ground, destroying all their clothes and possessions. At another hotel, freshly supplied with clothes, Thompson brooded and gloomed about, refusing to go sailing or fishing. Occasionally he was cheered by a telephone call from faithful Harding or Pike. And some solace was derived from an amazing document dispatched by Richard Wolfe, the orator who had touched off all the trouble. With other members of the William Hale Thompson Real Estate Men's League of Chicago, Wolfe was on a world cruise. In Jerusalem he had been moved to indite this tribute:

Whereas, the historic places we have visited—Carthage, Rome, Athens, Jerusalem, Thebes—are graveyards not of cities or towns but of dead empires and civilizations; and

Whereas, these ruins and graveyards and empires were in no instance due to the faults of the working and producing peoples of their times, but instead were in every instance due to the sins of the exploiters, profiteers, profligates and tyrants at the top; and

Whereas, the hungry faces and ragged clothes of children, the worried faces of mothers, and the hopeless looks of the thousands of unemployed men and women we have seen everywhere on our travels are due in large measure to the World War brought on by the blind greed of the exploiters and profiteers of our times; and

Whereas, our American republic, American institutions and the peace, security and prosperity of the American people are now threatened by the alien-hearted, native-born American Tory in alliance with the autocracy of Europe; and

Whereas, these Tories, in alliance with the European capitalists, have seized control of our public utilities, insurance companies, banks and natural resources and many newspapers, with an army of hirelings and propagandists ever intriguing to supplant in America the rule of the grand dukes for the democracy of Jefferson and Lincoln; and

Whereas, through control of our money and business they therefore control our government, legislature and courts; and

Whereas, Honorable William Hale Thompson is a genuine native American who has inherited the love of liberty possessed by the fathers who founded the republic; therefore be it

Resolved, that we, here in the shadows of the temples and scenes of the great ones who labored and died for love of mankind, urge Honorable William Hale Thompson to offer himself as candidate for re-election to the office of mayor of Chicago, not only for the service he may render the people of Chicago as their mayor, but also for the opportunity it will give him to help preserve the American Republic and its institutions and safeguard the people against their enemy.

19 ||| No Longer a Trilby

I

WHEN HIS VACATION WAS OVER, Thompson had worked out the broad details of a plan for his comeback. He would need help, though, and that help, to begin with, would come from his loyal friend, George Harding.

As city comptroller, Harding had been a strong defender of Thompson, dazzling the public with statistics and rows of figures when anyone raised the charge that Big Bill was hurrying Chicago toward bankruptcy. Now Harding was eager to be Cook County treasurer, and ready to dip into his millions to attain that office.

Harding's ambition was Thompson's opportunity. Big Bill sent word to Charles Deneen in Washington that he and Harding would support and contribute to Deneen's county ticket in the 1926 primary if Harding had a place on that ticket and Deneen would support Thompson for mayor in 1927. Stunned by this proposition from his persistent enemy, Deneen declined, principally because one of his own men, the vigorous Edward R. Litsinger, had already made known his intention of running for mayor.

Rebuffed, Thompson made new overtures. This time the object of his sudden affection was even more shocking, for he proposed to join the Crowe-Barrett faction, despite the recent affiliation of Ed Brundage, who had run to Crowe after the sudden death of Medill McCormick with, as the *News* put it, "the agility of a startled fawn."

Crowe had little fondness for Thompson, but he did want a highly reputable fellow with a highly reputable bank account on his ticket. That need had grown suddenly acute when his candidate for county treasurer, Sheriff Peter B. Hoffman, had been publicly revealed as an ultrafine host to two notorious bootleggers in his custody, Frankie Lake and Terry Druggan. Both were discovered to be getting fancy privileges, a scandal that forced Crowe to drop Hoffman. George Harding, Crowe and his co-leaders of the faction agreed, would be a capital candidate for county treasurer to replace Hoffman. Harding, loyal as always to Big Bill, agreed to run if Thompson received a pledge of aid and support for his mayoral race in 1927. Crowe consented, and so did his lieutenants, and early in 1926 the men who had called one another "skunk" and "rat" and "thief" and "crook" and "liar" and "bluffer" and worse were allies in a grand union to win new power and help Big Bill return to the City Hall.

2

Before a month passed, it was clear that Big Bill, snorting with the pleasure of political conflict, intended to take charge of the county campaign.

He provided the main issue, a strange one, indeed, for a flock of county candidates, although a more logical one for Frank L. Smith, who was in the primary against Senator William McKinley. The issue: "No World Court!" President Coolidge and Congress had been moving closer to membership in the organization, and in the isolationist Middle West, suspicious of foreign alliances, the slogan seemed psychologically sound. It took little urging on Thompson's part to convince Crowe and Barrett to adopt his idea, for both had often expressed their anti-British and anti-internationalist viewpoints.

Over the protests of Brundage, Big Bill took charge of the county convention. In the manner he had learned from Lundin, Thompson staged a pageant with former servicemen parading through the aisles bearing papier-mâché statues of George Washington and Abraham Lincoln, followed by a trio dressed as the figures in the "Spirit of '76." The platform adopted at the meeting bore all the characteristics of a standard Thompson oration.

"We stand for Home Rule in CITY, COUNTY, STATE AND NATION!

AMERICA FIRST! NO WORLD COURT!" read its major plank. It continued:

We believe that the interests of our country can best be promoted by adhering strictly to the wise policy laid down by George Washington, of maintaining friendly alliances with all foreign nations, but entering into entangling alliances with none, and that it should be maintained as a permanent policy of the United States. We believe that the participation of our government as a member of the Permanent Court of International Justice, commonly called the World Court, is fraught with grave danger to our peace and prosperity, because in our judgment such course would ultimately result in making this country a part of the League of Nations. We protest against any situation which would require the American boy and American wealth to be drafted for the purpose of settling quarrels between foreign governments, in which quarrels we have no interest.

Thompson was platform builder, speaker, showman, impresario, organizer, appearing everywhere, bustling and hustling and happy. Late in January the new alliance of Crowe, Barrett, Brundage and Thompson—now called the C-B-B-T—invited the Senate's chief spokesman against the World Court, William E. Borah, to a big anti-World Court rally in Chicago. When Borah accepted, Thompson sent letters to thousands all over Illinois and adjoining states, asking them to help "in keeping Old Glory at the masthead." They could do this, he advised, by taking part in an automobile parade when Borah arrived.

The senator came on Washington's Birthday, fittingly enough. At the railroad station Thompson and Crowe were in the welcoming committee. Ten bands, paid for by the various C-B-B-T candidates, blared and tootled. More than 2,000 decorated cars streamed along in a procession that ended at the Field Museum, where seventeen guns boomed a Congressional salute. Then, after another parade down Chicago's new Outer Drive, the senator was installed in the Presidential suite atop Hotel Sherman.

That night in Fred Mann's Rainbo Gardens, Borah set the tone for all local campaigners using the World Court as an issue. The court, said he, was a device to entrap the United States into "the scheme of international domination and control" of "the Old World." That world was filled with hate and intrigue, said Borah. "We cannot trust European nations. Imperialism flourishes and wars still rage." He berated England, condemned the League of Nations, and yelled that opponents of European alliances had been gagged in the Senate. He was cheered mightily. "Thank God for Chicago!" Borah exclaimed when he returned to Washington next morning.

Flushed with the success of the Borah rally—even the *Evening Post*, habitually against Thompson and for the World Court, admitted, "It was a big and highly successful show"—Thompson invited another foe of European alliances to Chicago. But this orator, Senator Henrik Shipstead, the Minnesota radical, had less personal appeal than Borah. In his speech on St. Patrick's Day he bored his listeners with a complicated constitutional analysis of the situation, evoking applause only when he cried, "The League of Nations is an imperialistic superdictatorship of the world based on force. It will bring war, not peace!"

Big Bill's introduction of Shipstead was so long and so repetitiously filled with sentiments expressed by Borah that the senator was left only ten minutes of an allotted half-hour broadcast on a local radio station.

This tendency by Thompson to push himself forward at every public meeting on the World Court issue developed rumors that he and Crowe had quarreled, with Big Bill threatening to punch the state's attorney, a much smaller man. Both denied this canard volubly. Crowe took special pains at a meeting of precinct workers to joke, "Anyone who knows what a little fellow Thompson is and how big I am knows that it would have been reversed."

The incident soon blew over. But Crowe found a new irritant in Thompson's tactics. With no great enthusiasm Crowe's group was nominally supporting Senator McKinley, who had cast a tentative vote for limited membership in the World Court. But Thompson, openly and enthusiastically, was out in behalf of Frank L. Smith, who shared his opinions on the World Court. Crowe had no enmity toward Smith, but Thompson's support of his own candidate's rival was embarrassing. Yet he reasoned that it would be more embarrassing, and perhaps disastrous, if he argued openly with Thompson, who, with three and four speeches every day in the week, was rousing the loudest cheers and the biggest applause. Besides, Crowe had far less interest in the senatorial primary than in the race for county jobs.

3

So Big Bill was given his full way, free to fulminate against McKinley, against Deneen, against enemies local and enemies international—and against Fred Lundin.

The Poor Swede had remained quiet in the early part of the heated primary. Content with his control of all state patronage in Cook County, he wished no share of the factional strife and bitterness. He scoffed when Thompson, threshing desperately for new allies, sought union with Crowe and Barrett; he continued to scoff when Thompson made his first statements on the World Court.

But now the time for scorn was over. Thompson was running away with the campaign, attracting the most attention, waving the banner for Smith so furiously that Crowe and Barrett did not dare drop him or even censure him unless they wanted to go down to defeat.

Lundin was forced to fight. His first open attack on Thompson came early in April. In the Lundin-Small newspaper, the *Illinois Republican Council Bulletin*, Thompson was excoriated for going into the stronghold of his enemies, Crowe and Barrett and Brundage. He was reminded that Crowe, in 1922, had declared of Thompson: "Any man that is interested in protecting gambling and vice and protected prostitution I refuse to travel along with, politically or otherwise." He was asked to remember that he had once called Brundage "this hypocritical lickspittle of the traction interests." He was reminded of how Barrett had fought him and Lundin when the pair worked for a bill shrinking the powers of Barrett's County Board of Review.

Big Bill quickly replied with a piece of showmanship that won him national notoriety. Scheduled to speak with Smith on the stage of the Cort Theater in Chicago's Loop, he proposed to bring two caged rats with him, one to represent Lundin and the other Dr. Robertson. But Smith's friends dissuaded him because they felt it would be an affront to the senatorial candidate's dignity. So Thompson delayed his act until the next night, April 6.

He placed the caged rats on a table in the center of the stage. Standing behind the table, Thompson spoke mildly on general issues. Then, with a quivering finger, he pointed to the rats. "I want you all to meet a couple of fellows you've all heard about. This one here on the left is Doc. I can tell him because he hadn't had a bath for twenty years until we washed him yesterday. But we did wash him and he doesn't smell like a billy goat any longer."

The audience gasped, then howled. "Some of my friends," continued Thompson, "have advised me against doing this. They tell me it is a political blunder. But I don't think so. Do you?"

"No! No! Go on! Go on, Bill!"

Waggling his finger at the other rat, Big Bill bellowed, "Fred, let me ask you something. Wasn't I the best friend you ever had? Isn't it true that I came home from Honolulu to save you from the penitentiary? Isn't it a fact, Fred Lundin, that it took Clarence Darrow, Patrick O'Donnell, Ben Short, Charlie Erbstein and Bill Thompson to keep you out of the penitentiary? I have learned, Fred, that you are going to flood Chicago with 500,000 copies of a newspaper called the *Bulletin* full of lies about me. I know that for many years you have been referred to as 'The Fox' in politics. But now I think this justifies my saying that your monicker ought not to be 'The Fox' but 'The Rat.'"

"More! More!" yelled the listeners.

"Doc," continued Thompson, glowering at the first rat, "do you remember how thousands came to me to protest the appointment of yourself as health commissioner? Do you remember, Doc, how a newspaper said I was sacrificing the lives of Chicago children to fulfill a political debt by appointing an incompetent health commissioner? Do you remember how I stood up against them and honored you with that great office? If you do remember you know now why I now call you a rat for turning against me with Lundin!"

No reply to this astonishing outburst issued from either Lundin or Robertson, but the Swedish Club of Chicago, of which Lundin was an official, passed a resolution in which its membership did "resent and hereby censure William Hale Thompson" for his ungentlemanly conduct.

The "rat show" was the talk of Chicago the next day. It had done more than smash dramatically at Lundin and his lackey. It had disclosed a part of the truth behind all the charges made against Lundin and Thompson in Big Bill's first and second terms. Thompson had admitted his great indebtedness to Lundin, that Robertson had been an inept choice for health commissioner—as his much-hated reform foes charged when the appointment was made—and that Lundin, despite his acquittal, had been involved in the school graft that brought about his indictment and trial.

4

Even more of a revelation, psychologically, emotionally and politically, was a speech two days later in the Olympic Theater. Here, in a long harangue, was embodied all of Thompson's techniques of obfuscation, confusion of ideas, shrewd slanting toward class appeals and prejudices of his listeners, gutter language and irrelevancies. And his listeners cheered and cheered as he cried out his hoarse imprecations:

"All this argument for the World Court is a lot of propaganda for the King of England. They tell us that we oughta trust England, that she is our friend. Well, the King got control of all the rubber and raised the price enough to pay all their debt to us. That shows they're pretty friendly, doesn't it? The King got control of coffee and is doing the same thing. I shouldn't be surprised if the King had something to do with slipping over the Volstead Act on us so that all their distillers can make fortunes selling us bootleg liquor. You are paying them a billion dollars on those three items alone!

"How do they do it? By using our pro-British senators to vote down Old Glory! I admit I never expected much of McKinley, with his running over to see the King every summer. He likes it so well that with your help we'll fix it on April thirteenth so that he can spend his winters there too!

"I helped elect Charley Deneen senator. I thought he was an American. But he hadn't been in Washington a year before the King got him. I apologize for what I did."

Like Borah, he roared against the "gag rule" in the Senate. He sneered at McKinley as "that bell-hop" and "that poor, miserable reprobate."

"I hear McKinley is on his second million now. They say he's a good business man. What kind of business do you call it to spend a million to get a $7,500 job—unless there's some business going on we don't know about. You might expect anything of a man who voted to haul down the flag and destroy American institutions. . . .

"Charlie and Willie think it takes seven Yankees to lick a Britisher. Well, I'm pretty old and fat, but I'll guarantee to lick any Britisher my weight. If they are so good, why don't they send someone over to lick Jack Dempsey? Why couldn't they lick Jim Jeffries? It seems to me I remember . . . John L. Sullivan used to go over to England and lick a couple of Britishers every night. . . .

"I'm not in this campaign for anything for myself. I think there is great danger ahead. We stand at the crossroads. You always stood by Bill when he needed you. When they called me Kaiser Bill and the newspapers bribed with British money called me a traitor you re-elected me as mayor to prove I was right. When you need me I owe it to you, and I'll be there! . . .

"After the war I saved Chicago from the bread line and the soup kitchen with my Pageant of Progress, and I don't ever want to see anything like that in America! All this may happen if you're not alert. McKinley and Deneen will vote you into the League. The flag of internationalism will be raised above Old Glory, the constitution nullified, all American institutions as laid down by the Founding Fathers struck down. They'll call the roll on the repudiation of all war debts, and what they don't pay, you've got to pay. Thirty billions! No wonder McKinley is willing to pay a million to save that much for the King!

"They've had twenty-eight wars since the Armistice, one for every ninety days. After they get Uncle Sam in they'll have one every sixty days. The King wants it so. McKinley and Deneen are voting so. Let's get rid of them at the first possible time.

"I'm here to prevent you from suffering. I need not be in this campaign at all. But I love our flag, and want nothing over it. I want us to be left alone!"

5

Five days after this speech the primary election was held. Thompson had served his new comrades well. Smith defeated McKinley by nearly 200,000 votes, and prepared to meet in the fall election none other than George E. Brennan, the Democratic boss who hungered for national prestige. And George Harding also was among the victors.

But Smith's triumph was brief. Late in July a Senate investigating committee headed by Senator James Reed came into Chicago in quest of information about contributions to Smith's campaign. An election scandal in Pennsylvania had led to the formation of this committee, and in the course of preliminary work reports had reached it of irregularities in the Smith-McKinley contest.

All through the summer the hearings went on. Thompson appeared to testify about his alliance with Crowe, and kept his eyes averted from Fred Lundin lounging in the rear of the hearing room awaiting his turn to testify. Crowe, his stubborn jaw set, declined to discuss his campaign expenditures, vowing only that he had supported Smith because of his feelings about the World Court. "I would have been for anyone who was against the World Court even if he had not contributed a dime," snapped Crowe. Charles Barrett, solemn and austere, told how the $175,000 under his watchful eye had been spent for county candidates; the sum, he revealed, included $25,000 Big Bill Thompson had obtained from the Smith organization. Homer K. Galpin, the slippery politician who was G.O.P. county chairman, admitted accepting $1,000 from the McKinley forces, although he was active in Smith's campaign. Ward leaders boasted of their "swell little organizations." Minor officials described the complex system of alliances and cross-alliances and double crossing in Illinois politics.

Samuel Insull, the droopy-eyed, all-powerful utilities magnate, was soon summoned by the investigators, for it had been reported that he was a heavy contributor to the campaign of Smith, the man who held life-or-death powers over all utilities matters as head of the state commerce commission. Insull was stubborn and recalcitrant in his first appearances. All he would say was that he was strongly opposed to the World Court and firm alliances with the British or other foreign governments. Ultimately, however, the truth came out that Insull had given $125,000 to Smith's campaign, and that from two other utilities executives who did business with the state—Ira Copley, president of the Western United Gas and Electric Company, and Clement Studebaker, Jr., president of the Illinois Power and Light Corporation—Smith had received $45,000.

The final outcome of this inquiry was that Smith, even after defeating Brennan, was denied his Senate seat because the use of Insull's huge fund was "contrary to sound public policy, harmful to the dignity and honor of the Senate" and "dangerous to the perpetuity of free government." Long after the controversy died, Smith charged that Julius Rosenwald, the merchant-philanthropist, had offered him $550,000 in Sears, Roebuck and Company stock if he would withdraw in the fall election and throw his support to the independent candidate, Hugh S. Magill. By this time Rosenwald was on his deathbed, unable to issue either a denial or confirmation of Smith's belated accusation.

6

Before the exciting summer of 1926 ended, any notion Bob Crowe may have had of bossing Cook County, with Bill Thompson as one of his stooges, was gone.

A few days after the fruitful primary, Crowe's dapper assistant, William McSwiggin, known as the "hanging prosecutor," was slain by gangsters outside a saloon in Cicero. Killed with him were two drinking companions, Tom Duffy, a bootlegger, and James Doherty, a South Side gangster. Myles O'Donnell, of the West Side O'Donnell clan, escaped death.

The uproar was tremendous. The newspapers and the public demanded answers: Why was McSwiggin in an illegal saloon? What was he doing in the company of two gangsters whom he had, without success, prosecuted a year before? Why did gangsters want to kill him?

"Who killed McSwiggin—and why?" was the question shouted at Crowe. Reform groups, citizens' associations, newspapers, ministers wanted action. Harry E. Kelly, president of the Union League Club, began a campaign to force the appointment of a special state's attorney to investigate the slaying.

Rarely had the city been so aroused. Crowe's political future, so bright only a few months back, seemed doomed. He refused to step aside for a special investigator, but he could not stop the outraged cries of press and public that his own inquiry would result in a whitewash.

Finally Crowe hit on a happy idea. He yielded to Attorney General Carlstrom as the man to carry on the investigation. Carlstrom was no friend of Crowe's, but he was an ally of Big Bill Thompson. With Thompson's approval, Carlstrom stepped into the case, and in time Crowe's notion bore its fruit. The special grand jury not only concluded that McSwiggin was guiltless of any wrongdoing or traffic with gangsters, but it took special pains to praise Crowe for his vigor and fairness in the inquiry. Then, for good measure, the jurors fired a few shots at Governor Len Small, blaming gang warfare partly on Small's lax policy of granting paroles and pardons.

So the summer ended happily for Big Bill. Crowe was in his debt. Len Small bore some of the onus of the McSwiggin murder. It was sad about Frank Smith's predicament, of course, but Thompson had his own future to think of now. Jauntily he looked ahead, and coyly he parried questions about the mayoralty in 1927. He merely admitted that pledge cards were being circulated. "If they show the people want me," he said modestly, "I will consider being a candidate."

20 Al Capone Moves In

I

SOON THE TIME FOR SUCH GENTLE
replies was over.

Early in October, when no sure statement of his candidacy had
yet come from Big Bill, Charles R. Francis, a Lundinite who had
been his public works commissioner, sent him a letter asking that he
support Dr. John Dill Robertson in the coming primary.

Francis received no formal reply, but on the night of October 13
he was made starkly aware of what Thompson and his cohorts
thought of such a preposterous bid. Five thousand of them gathered
in the Medinah Temple to make a mass plea that Big Bill be their candidate. Sophie Tucker, the night-club singer, entertained the crowd
and speaker after speaker extolled Thompson.

When he walked onto the stage, an organ blared, steamboat whistles shrilled and ship bells clanged. Behind him a curtain dropped;
on it, in huge letters, the message: BIG BILL, CHICAGO NEEDS YOU!
Then the frenzied audience, stamping and howling, sang a new song
written by Richard Wolfe and Milton Weil, a former boy minstrel
in vaudeville who fancied himself the "Mayor of Randolph Street."
It was called "America First, Last and Always" and it was sung
again and again by the happy throng. At its end Thompson spoke
briefly, promising to run if enough people wanted him to. Each
person received twenty-five pledge cards. "If you get them all
signed, I know I'll run!" cried Big Bill, and the listeners waved the
pledge cards and vowed, "We will, Bill! We will!"

2

The man whom Thompson hoped to supplant in the mayor's seat was weary of the arduous job.

William E. Dever had started his term with the good wishes of every respectable Chicago citizen. In his first days, encountering the morass of confusion and incompetency of the Thompson reign, he made noble promises about straightening out the "intolerable mess." He strove hard to accomplish this by appointing able men to important jobs, such citizens as Francis X. Busch as his corporation counsel, Colonel A. A. Sprague as his commissioner of public works, young Dr. Herman N. Bundesen, a Republican who switched easily to Dever's side, as his health commissioner. As good and as genuine a booster for his city as Big Bill, he had as his motto, "Chicago always is entitled to first place."

In his four years there had been no scandal, no public officials indicted, and only the bitter Thompsonites and Lundin men gathered in their meeting halls to gossip about graft and corruption in this paving project or that bridge job. With less ballyhoo, Dever had helped push through almost as many civic improvements. In his term the impressive double-decked Wacker Drive, extending westward from the Michigan Avenue Bridge, was finished, and important thoroughfares were widened and paved. The engineering feat of straightening the course of the Chicago River was accomplished. Hundreds of new traffic lights were installed in the Loop, 190 miles of streets and 50 miles of alleys paved. New school buildings, 68 in all, went up, adding over 25,000 seats. Despite Thompson's loud claims, construction, public and private, in both his first two terms, totaled $1,077,500,000, while in Dever's single term new building amounted to $1,377,211,040.

To bring order and quality into the chaotic school system Dever hired a new superintendent, a spade-bearded educator, tart and progressive, and his name was William McAndrew. Years before he had been principal of Chicago's Hyde Park High School, but at the time he was engaged he was associate superintendent of New York's schools.

Immediately after his appointment McAndrew made his progressive ideas known and his sharp temperament felt. He had no patience with incompetents or dawdlers or loafers. His slogan was "Every man on the job!" He reduced the number of holidays for teachers and students and instituted time checks for all employees of the Board of Education. He started a program of 100-per-cent mastery of reading, writing, spelling, punctuation and arithmetic after surveys he carried out showed him that elementary students in these basic subjects made appalling records. He was adamant against political interference, and any ward heeler who came with a supplication for special favors for a teaching applicant was quickly ushered out of his office.

The schools soon were being operated more efficiently, but his swift revolution won McAndrew the enmity of many teachers, especially Margaret Haley of the powerful Chicago Teachers' Federation. The union was annoyed and angered at McAndrew's dissolution, in September 1924, of the teachers' councils, which had been established to permit teachers to meet on classroom time to determine policies and procedures instead of taking their orders from principals and other superiors. This step prompted Miss Haley, who had first approved McAndrew's appointment, to call him an autocrat and demand his censure by Dever. But the mayor stood by his superintendent, who continued on his stubborn way, establishing junior high schools, demanding periodic ratings of teachers and principals, setting up the platoon system of school attendance—promptly assailed by Miss Haley as "a factory plan of education"—and generally provoking teachers and politicians.

One of those especially antagonistic to McAndrew was "Iron-Handed Jack" Coath, still on the school board. He derided McAndrew as an "outsider," despite his years of service to Chicago schools. He challenged him on every step. When McAndrew wrote an article in a teachers' magazine objecting to displays of war pictures and other "symbols of carnage" in public schools, Coath called him a "goddamned pacifist." At one session of the board, Coath arose to charge that McAndrew, as a slave to the "selfish interests" of the city, had taken away the school children's penny lunches and had transferred excellent gymnasium and classroom equipment to schools in the wealthy districts.

"I want to say to you," yelled Coath, "that you, Mr. McAndrew, are incompetent. The condition in the schools is due to your mismanagement."

The stubborn Scot glared at his accuser. "That's what you say every week, Mr. Coath."

Although Julius Smietanka, acting board president, denied Coath's charges, the voluble member went on. "I think the school board should erect a monkey house to put the superintendent in. He not only looks like a monkey, but he has been acting like one."

In an effort to end the trouble, Dever brought together McAndrew and Charles Merriam, an unofficial adviser now that he was back teaching political science at his University of Chicago. As gently as he could, Merriam tried to explain to the dour McAndrew the need for using more tact and diplomacy in dealing with teachers and board members. "You don't have to give in to them, but you can let them off more easily" was Merriam's advice. But McAndrew snorted at such simple counsel. He was the superintendent and it was his duty to carry out his ideas as he saw fit, whether the public or the teachers or the board liked it or not. He would persist in his ideas, he informed Merriam, to the very finish.

3

In another field Dever's well-meant programs had also gone awry, bringing disastrous results.

Determined to wipe out crime, Dever, early in his term, gave orders to his new chief, Morgan A. Collins, to intensify the drive against all violators of the prohibition laws. Soon many overzealous police were invading private homes to arrest citizens possessing an illicit bottle or two of bootleg gin. Such tactics gradually turned many Chicagoans into "cop haters." When a wispy hoodlum named Martin Durkin killed a policeman, then fled and was recaptured by federal agents, anti-police sentiment in the city was so strong that crowds gathered at the railroad station when his train arrived and yelled, "We're with you, Marty!" and hissed and shouted curses at the grim-faced policemen surrounding the killer.

This created such tumult that Dever banned the showing of the newsreel films of Durkin's recapture and return to Chicago.

Even more important and far-reaching in results for both Dever and Big Bill Thompson was Collins' constant campaign against the underworld. A man of iron integrity, Collins could not be bought by the gangsters, although he was often offered $1,000 a day and once $100,000 a month if he would not molest the beer-running operation of the supreme leader of the hoodlums, pasty-faced Johnny Torrio. Instead of playing along with the criminals, Collins carried on a persistent attack on such a powerful man as Mont Tennes, the handbook king whose establishments had been untouched during Thompson's terms. Within a year Collins closed 200 handbooks that had yielded Tennes a yearly profit of $370,000, and by the first week of January, Tennes was ready for retirement from active control of the betting parlors and poolrooms.

Ironically, Collins' intensive activities touched off a new series of conflicts in the underworld that made Chicago a fresh reputation as a bloody battlefield of crime. Worse yet, the warfare and carnage brought the emergence of the swarthy gangster, Scarface Al Capone, into a vastly important role as successor to Torrio and new overlord of the multimillion-dollar crime empire.

Despite sporadic outbreaks of purity, Thompson rarely interfered with either Torrio or Big Jim Colosimo, Torrio's first employer. Torrio had been brought to Chicago in 1908 by Colosimo to supervise and manage his various brothels. When the Levee was smashed by Carter Harrison, Torrio was dispatched to surrounding villages to set up entire communities of whore houses and gambling joints. By lavish corruption and buying of village officials, he built an empire of such establishments and fell heir to it and to all of the other illicit possessions of Big Jim after Colosimo was mysteriously slain in his Wabash Avenue café in 1920.

A master organizer, Torrio made certain that he would encounter as little interference in his endeavors as Colosimo had. He made the right contacts with City Hall politicians, distributed money in proper places, and soon he carried a membership card in the William Hale Thompson Republican Club. Late in 1920, while Chief Fitzmorris and State's Attorney Crowe had wrangled over who was the more enthusiastic fighter against crime and vice, Torrio had set up his shrewd plan for controlling the beer and liquor traffic of Chicago and Cook County.

After forcing himself into partnership with the owners of several pre-prohibition breweries, Torrio allotted to the various gangsters, robbers, bank thieves, burglars, kidnapers and murderers collected under his muddy banner, districts in which they would handle beer shipments, deliveries and collections. Those outsiders who dared to invade the respective bailiwicks would, of course, be dealt with in the manner commonly used by the Mafia assassins with whom Torrio had been associated back in the Five Points Gang area in Brooklyn before his arrival in Chicago. For the last three years of Thompson's regime, Torrio ruled in businesslike fashion over some 800 gangsters. In his technique of organization, he was not unlike a master politician, using the powers of patronage and favor when it suited his purpose, punishing when his purpose was thwarted, breaking and upsetting alliances when an underling sought to defy him.

In this first Torrio syndicate, Al Capone, imported by Torrio from Brooklyn in 1920 to be his bodyguard and enforcer of his stern edicts, was merely another district captain, handling a section of the West Side with such notables as Harry (Greasy Thumb) Guzik, an oldtime pimp, and Frankie Pope, the "Millionaire Newsboy." The North Side was commanded by a former choir boy named Dion O'Banion, ambitious and suave, a shrewd character who paid out thousands of dollars a week to policemen who guarded the Torrio beer trucks and acted as doormen at illicit gambling houses. On the South Side the Torrio assistants included "Polack Joe" Saltis, once an honest Joliet saloon owner; Ralph Sheldon, a leader in the 1919 race riots as a member of the notorious Ragen's Colts; and Frank McErlane, who relished his particular notoriety as the most brutal killer in the city's criminal history.

As long as Thompson was in office, despite all his fuss about driving out the criminals, this alliance progressed smoothly, in the businesslike way Torrio hoped it would. In a single year Torrio grossed $4,000,000 from his Chicago beer peddling, $3,000,000 from gambling, $2,000,000 from prostitution, and another $4,000,000 from similar enterprises in the suburbs. Chicago alone had more than 12,000 speak-easies, beer flats and brothels that sold illegal liquor. Payoffs to police officials and protecting politicians were high and frequent, but Torrio had no objections as long as he could carry on without too much harassment. So solid was he with the Thompson machine that he was able to secure a pardon from Len Small for Harry Guzik and his wife Alma before they had served a single day of a sentence for operating a ring that recruited inmates for the Torrio brothels.

4

But Torrio's syndicate shivered, shook and started to fall apart in 1923, when Thompson quit and Dever was elected. The new mayor ordered all-night cabarets to shut down. Every week he revoked liquor licenses in wholesale batches. Soon he had shut down 7,000 soft-drink parlors and restaurants operating as speak-easies.

Such activity had immediate and ironic results. Threatened by incessant police raids and by daily defections from his well-built syndicate, Torrio reached out for new territory. This area was Cicero, one of the largest suburbs yet unexploited, although Harry Guzik lived there, and so did Ike Bloom, once one of the Levee's powerful denizens. Early in 1924, Torrio assigned Al Capone and his hardiest hoodlums to capture Cicero. Then he and his wife and his mother went on a trip to his native Italy.

While Sheriff Peter Hoffman looked in all other directions for the criminals State's Attorney Crowe vowed hourly to bring to justice, Capone surged into the suburb. This was his first major opportunity to prove himself, and he made the best of it. He forced Eddie Vogel, the town's slot-machine boss and political leader, into an unwilling alliance. He offered his bold support to the pliant mayor, Joe Klenha, a Democrat. In the April election Capone sluggers and killers roamed the streets all day, driving Republican voters away from the polls and shooting up saloons owned by Klenha's enemies. At the end of that day, with Klenha elected again, Al Capone was the boss of Cicero. He soon set up brothels, imported hordes of prostitutes, established gambling houses, and ruled the terrorized town from his armored headquarters in the Hawthorne Inn.

When Torrio returned from Europe, where he had deposited bundles of securities against an uncertain future, he approved what Capone had done. But he soon discovered that his organization in Chicago was in revolt. Police pressure had cut down illicit profits and Torrio's district leaders were making their own deals with police captains and ward politicians in an effort to get protection. While Capone was preoccupied with Cicero, the subchiefs grew more independent and greedy. Soon they no longer hesitated to invade the territories of one another to hijack trucks, kill rivals, rob warehouses and force their beer on terrified customers. Mayor Dever's cleanup backfired. The machine guns came out again and the rifles and the shotguns, and warfare raged anew, and the infamy of Chicago increased.

There were casualties, many of them. One of the first to go was Dion O'Banion, the tough North Sider. Contemptuous of Torrio and especially of the six Genna brothers, rulers of a kingdom of alcohol cookers on the near West Side, he had expressed his feelings for them even when they were superficially at peace. Now he not only invaded Genna territory but defied them to enter his. Although friends warned him to be more circumspect, he cursed, "Ah, to hell with them Sicilians!"

In the political campaign of November 1924, O'Banion had been a central figure in an incident that brought embarrassment to Dever. When rumors developed that O'Banion intended to throw his considerable strength in two North Side wards to the Republicans, a dinner was held for him by Democrats in the Webster Hotel. Seated not far from such administration representatives as Dever's commissioner of public works, Colonel Sprague, and his chief of detectives, Michael Hughes, were such notorious hoodlums as "Big Tim" Murphy, George (Bugs) Moran, Vincent (Schemer) Drucci, Hymie Weiss and Louis Alterie. Hughes explained to the mayor that he had been under the impression the dinner was for a union official and not for O'Banion. When Dever rebuked him, Hughes resigned. The banquet proved to be a futile gesture, for O'Banion came through in his usual efficient fashion for the Republicans, carrying his wards by big margins for Senator Deneen and Crowe.

A week after that election O'Banion was in his flower shop across the street from Holy Name Cathedral on the near North Side. Two men strode in and he advanced toward them smiling, hand out-stretched. In a few seconds he was dead among his flowers, his chest, neck and jaw punctured by bullets. O'Banion's was the first of the big gangster funerals. Mounted police had to clear the streets for a cortege that included twenty-six truckloads of flowers, among them a basket of roses with a pink ribbon and a card: "From Al."

O'Banion's murder renewed the carnage that bloodied Mayor Dever's Chicago in 1925 and 1926. Hymie Weiss, an ill-tempered bandit with homicidal impulses, succeeded O'Banion. He vowed vengeance on Al Capone, whom all gangland knew to be the man who planned O'Banion's assassination. But first Weiss struck at Torrio. His gunmen surprised the gang boss in front of his home, wounding him severely in his arms, chest and stomach. In the hospital, shuddering with terror, Torrio summoned Al Capone to his bedside. He informed him that when he left the hospital he was turning over his realm to him, the brothels, the distilleries, the gambling houses, the night clubs. "It's all yours, Al," mumbled Torrio. "Me, I'm quittin' and it's me for Europe."

Capone accepted the slimy scepter. The warfare crackled on. Alliances shifted, and old friends and old associates shot at each other with the hatreds and rivalries of new enemies. In May 1925, Angelo Genna was killed by North Siders; a month later it was his brother, Mike, and then the handsome brother they called Tony the Gentleman. The McSwiggin slaying after the 1926 primary was one of the many in this series of murders. Gangland gossip said that Capone himself had handled the machine gun.

When it became evident after Torrio left for Europe that Capone was indeed his successor, Hymie Weiss, in reckless bravado, made an insane attempt to assassinate him. Eleven automobiles jammed with Weiss's gun-wielding gangsters drove to the Hawthorne Inn in Cicero and sprayed the building with more than 1,000 slugs and bullets. But Capone, eating in an adjoining restaurant, escaped death by falling flat on the floor. Twenty days later, Hymie Weiss was killed as he alighted with friends from an automobile near Holy

Name Cathedral. His slayers had aimed their machine guns at him from the window of a flat across the street where they had kept their grisly vigil since the week of Weiss's invasion of Cicero.

Now Capone was stronger in his rule of the fantastically rich domain. There were still other foes to be quelled by bullets and brutality. And there were new alliances to be built, with rival gang chiefs and with the politicians. Capone had learned well from Torrio the importance of organization and protection. He knew the vital need for cultivating the right friends in the right places, Republican or Democrat. It was clear that Mayor Dever could not be bought. His police captains may have been willing and grasping, but there could be no strong tieup with the City Hall for Capone if Dever ran again and won. Others, untried and unknown, might be dangerous to deal with, or too greedy. So Capone waited to see what Big Bill Thompson would do. Here, if anywhere, was a man to cultivate more closely than before; not directly, perhaps, but certainly through effective go-betweens. Capone waited to hear what Thompson would say, and to determine if he liked what he heard.

21 ||| Down with King George!

BY DECEMBER, AL CAPONE HEARD, and knew his man.

First came the inevitable pledge card meeting in the grand ballroom of the Hotel Sherman. "Bill Thompson," bawled Major Hamlet C. Ridgeway, a former prohibition agent, "look at that ring of cards!" The excited major pointed to a huge pile of cards arranged in a circle. "There aren't 125,000 pledge cards there. There aren't 250,000. There are 430,000!" Ridgeway strode to Thompson, removed his sombrero and tossed it onto the cards. "In behalf of the voters of Chicago," he yelled, "I throw your hat into the ring!"

Sniffling from a severe cold, Thompson began, "I accept, and with grateful thanks." Too ill to continue, he handed his prepared statement to Michael Feinberg, a ward worker and later a circuit judge, who called out loudly and clearly the first two planks in Big Bill's platform. "I'm going to run Superintendent McAndrew out of town. And if I catch a policeman crossing the threshold of a man's home or place of business, I will fire that policeman right off the force!"

Capone cared little about what happened to the superintendent of schools, but he was vitally concerned with Thompson's attitude toward the police. This assertion, as the gang chief read it in the next day's newspapers, indicated broadly that Thompson was for the wide-open town. A report of Thompson's statement at a ward meeting a few days later bolstered this feeling. Outlining the campaign, Big Bill said, "The Dever administration has made one of the greatest records in Chicago's history for closing up business. When I'm elected we will not only reopen places these people have closed, but we'll open 10,000 new ones." To Al Capone the meaning was unmistakable. More "places of business" meant more speakeasies and more customers and more revenue. Big Bill's friends might shout that the businesses were legal and legitimate ones, but Capone knew better, for the beer flats and illegal saloons were the only kinds of business Mayor Dever had shut. He needed no more speeches to assure himself that Bill Thompson was the man to support.

2

First to challenge Thompson in this 1927 primary was Fred Lundin. Espousing the candidacy of Dr. John Dill Robertson at the Swedish club, he called Thompson "an insincere demagogue."

"Thompson is shouting generalities and dodging the issues!" cried Lundin. "Ask him to state his position with regard to the alliance between crime and politics and you may expect him to reply, 'America First!' Ask him about the abandonment of people's ownership of the traction lines and the five-cent fare and he will answer, if at all, by crying, 'Down with the League of Nations!' I have never said anything derogatory about this man, whom I entertained and lived with much of the time in my home for eight years, who sat at my table and broke bread with myself and my family. I was taught by my mother and father, although humble peasants, that to qualify as a gentleman, I must act, speak and behave as a gentleman. The fact that William Hale Thompson called me a rat and made disparaging remarks about me has nothing at all to do with the part he or I may take in the performance of our duties as citizens."

He recalled Thompson's broken pledge to the United Societies when he closed the saloons on Sunday. "Will the people fooled by Thompson in 1915 permit themselves to be fooled again?" As for Thompson's promise of no interference with those who cared to defy the liquor laws, Lundin raged, "As a citizen I don't intend to let William Hale Thompson or any other man substitute his will for the law of the land, without my protest!"

Lundin wound up with a powerful plea to the club members to support the best man available for the nomination, crying, "And I believe that man is John Dill Robertson!"

To this Big Bill responded with a sneer. "Poor Fred Lundin! Imagine anyone thinking of electing a man mayor with a name like John Dill Pickle Robertson!"

3

Thompson's other rival in the primary was Senator Deneen's man, Edward R. Litsinger. His career in politics went back to the days when Deneen was state's attorney of Cook County and Litsinger was one of his assistants. He had been an alderman, an unsuccessful candidate for county treasurer, a member of the powerful board of review since 1916. A physical culturist and amateur athlete— in his aldermanic race in 1902 he had boxed four rounds with the president of a West Side political club to win its endorsement—he was handsome and robust and bursting with strong opinions about Big Bill Thompson. To spur him on, he now had in his entourage Ed Brundage, who had left Crowe after denouncing the state's attorney as "the Poo Bah of Cook County Republicanism."

Whirling through the city, Litsinger, introduced everywhere as "The Bridgeport Boy" because he had been born in that district, set up a persistent clamor against Thompson. He spoke on such subjects as "Why the Name 'Big Bill' Fits Bill Thompson" and "Chicago, the Crime Capital." He accused Thompsonites of trying to pocket $500,000 in proceeds from the two Pageants of Progress. He brought up the fees paid to real-estate experts. He derided Thompson's "America First!" slogan. "Bill Thompson's delusion is that he is a Christopher Columbus who discovered America first. Trying to come back to power, he feels he must cover up the stench of his record by raising a cry of 'America First!' The issue is clearly 'Chicago First!' Save this town from Thompsonism!"

Citing $2,700,000 paid out in experts' fees in 1920, as disclosed in the *Tribune's* suit then being heard before Judge Hugo Friend in Circuit Court, Litsinger produced a chart on which were listed the men who had received the money, and he cried, "Look it over! The name 'Big Bill' is right, isn't it? The Thompson administration's expert-fee scandal alone is sufficient explanation of why the name 'Big Bill' fits so well. But it is only one of a number of things that made eight years of boodle and blunders at the City Hall such a big bill of expense to every citizen and taxpayer. These figures are on the record. If Big Bill will appear on this platform with me and say these figures are off, I'll choke the figures down his Big Bill throat! Or he can sue me for libel tomorrow! If Big Bill wants to come with clean hands, should he not first return this $2,700,000 he owes the people of Chicago?"

"Litsinger is the biggest liar in Chicago politics," retorted Thompson before a throng in Lincoln-Turner Hall. "Litsinger has sunk into the slough of false criticism! The truth about the falsehoods on the experts is that when I became mayor I set the rate of real-estate advisers at fifty dollars a day. But at the instance of Charles E. Merriam, a noisy, destructive member of the council, a committee began flying over the country investigating construction programs of large cities. The committee came to the council and reported fifty dollars was not enough. It was Merriam and his crowd that boosted expenses, and not William Hale Thompson!"

An astonished Professor Merriam took time off from his university classes to respond. "I was never connected with such a committee. As a matter of fact I spent two years trying to keep the experts' fees down. Apparently Mr. Thompson has got things all balled up. As I remember, there was not even such a committee as he seems to think, but if there was I certainly had nothing to do with it."

4

The oratorical din grew louder.

Fred Lundin made another speech, claiming that it was he who had persuaded Thompson to use the "America First!" slogan in the Senatorial campaign of 1918. According to Lundin's account,

Thompson had asked, "What do you mean, Fred, by 'America First'?"

"Bill Thompson," Lundin said, "don't you know the people of this country are being fooled into sending money to support the rotten government of King Peter?"

"Who's King Peter?" Thompson had asked.

"He's the rotten monarch of Serbia."

At this, claimed Lundin, Big Bill had scratched his head and asked, "Fred, what is Serbia, or where is it?"

The slogan also drew an attack from Peter S. Lambros, editor of an influential Greek-language newspaper, when he addressed a meeting of a thousand members of the Greek-American Litsinger Club in the Hotel La Salle. "Thompson has no right to use the words 'America First.' These are sacred words and should not be taken in vain. No demagogue should be allowed to employ them for his own selfish reasons." At the same meeting Brundage introduced an appropriately Grecian note. "Socrates was forced to drink hemlock because he dared to expose the weak and corrupt governments of his city. He was fighting the Big Bills of his time!"

Nor was State's Attorney Crowe left out of the excoriations issuing from Litsinger and his advisers.

Chicago was the nation's crime capital, shouted "The Bridgeport Boy," because of Crowe's policies. "Bob Crowe has delusions of grandeur and believes himself destined to be boss of all Chicago and Cook County. Today he is Big Bill's boss. In the first two years Crowe controlled the Cook County law-enforcement machinery, and Thompson the police force, murders rose from 190 in 1921 to 228 in 1922, while there were but 55 convictions the first year and 73 the second full year of his term as prosecutor.

"The first business of government is to protect life and property, yet there was a murder a day and one over for each of every 24 hours of 1926—with convictions averaging barely twenty-six per cent. Why? Because Bob Crowe is too busy playing politics, trying to seize control of the county!"

Toward the end of the primary, Senator Deneen himself hurried to Chicago to orate about the alliance between crime and politics. "The facts are only too well known," he declared. "The criminal classes will use the most desperate means to nominate and elect their candidates. Vice and crime are in alliance with corrupt and powerful leaders. They employ gunmen and other violent means to nominate and elect candidates favorable to them. Litsinger would break up this unholy alliance!"

Dr. Robertson mumbled agreement with Doneen, but differed on the choice of the man for the job. He was the proper candidate, he insisted. "Murderers, morons, gunmen, gangsters and their political partners must be put out of business," said the political physician.

Big Bill brushed off both his rivals. "Litsinger is dry. And Doc Robertson is so dry he never even takes a bath. The Doc used to boast he didn't take a bath in years. But read Bill Thompson's platform—you can't find anything wetter than that in the middle of the Atlantic. It's the only wet platform in the campaign!"

His speeches were filled not only with snide remarks about Robertson and Litsinger, but he had taken on an additional enemy, the King of England, and the crowds pushed in for the show. When they finished singing "America First, Last and Always," and Bill had been introduced as one of the greatest living Americans, he lumbered forward, grinning his crooked-tooth grin, his brown eyes gleaming with pleasure. He drew his big hands from his pockets, cracked them together over his ample paunch, and warmed up the crowd with a few choice comments on the latest utterance of a rival, or Dr. Robertson's untidy eating habits. "You should see him with egg spattered over his tie and vest, it's enough to turn your stomach!" Then, after dealing with Dill Pickle Robertson, Litsinger the Liar, and assorted local issues, Big Bill tore into King George.

"I wanta make the King of England keep his snoot out of America!" he cried huskily. "That's what I want. I don't want the League of Nations! I don't want the World Court! America first, and last, and always! That's the issue of this campaign. That's what Big Bill Thompson wants!"

He advanced toward an American flag hanging from a staff on the platform, embraced it and shrieked, "This is the issue of this campaign! What was good enough for George Washington is good enough for Bill Thompson!

"I'm not a mud slinger. But the papers have been saying things about me that I can't let pass. And Ed Litsinger's been making statements about me. I've told you and I tell you again that he's the biggest liar that ever was a candidate for mayor. And you know what else? He plays handball in the semi-nude! That's right, with only a little pair of pants on. I know one thing. You won't find Bill Thompson having his picture taken in the semi-nude!"

Soon he returned to his "main issue." "If you want to keep that old American flag from bowing down before King George of England, I'm your man. If you want to invite King George and help his friends, I'm not. This fellow McAndrew in the schools! Teaching un-Americanism! If we don't look out our history books are going to have all kinds of things belittling George Washington, the great founder of our country. By God, if you elect me mayor, I'll tell you what I'll do! I'll fire McAndrew back to Wall Street. That's what I'll do!"

5

While Thompson played to the crowds, Harding, Barrett, Homer Galpin and Bob Crowe organized the wards and assigned pay-rollers to their election work in the precincts. Here they ran into trouble. Deneen held federal patronage. Lundin possessed state jobs provided by Governor Small. Even in the Negro wards, the stronghold of Thompson-Harding power, there was rebellion. The veteran Republican committeeman, Edward H. Wright, long an ally of Small, defied the Thompson crowd. "I'm no political slave," he told them, "and I don't propose to sell out my people to satisfy the whims of the downtown bosses." Wright was promptly deprived of all his county patronage. Into his place as ward leader went Daniel M. Jackson, head of a Negro underworld syndicate that included dozens of brothels, bootlegging gangs, cabarets, policy wheels and gambling dens. Jackson at once set out to collect campaign funds and to organize the thousands of Negro voters. He carried with him Thompson's promise to reopen the hundreds of policy stations closed by Dever's chief of police.

In Al Capone's Cicero and other suburbs hard-faced gentry appeared in scores of saloons, demanding tribute for the Crowe-

Thompson organization. Sometimes the callers said they were working for Thompson, sometimes Crowe. Either way saloon keepers without slot machines were obliged to kick in at least forty dollars. Those with machines who wanted to keep running had to pay no less than $250. Downtown in Chicago, where he had opened his sumptuous, heavily guarded headquarters in the Hotel Metropole on South Michigan Boulevard, Scarface Al Capone received a daily accounting of the growing collections. Pleased with the results, he indulged himself in an added bit of interior decoration for his private office. Three big portraits were hung on the bullet-proof walls: one was of George Washington, one of Abraham Lincoln, and the third a flattering photograph of William Hale Thompson.

6

Toward the end of the campaign it became clear to Lundin that he could not hope to match the Thompson-Crowe job holders or money at the polls on primary day. Doc Robertson withdrew, with denunciation of Thompson tactics and a threat to run as an independent. Such a promise pleased George Brennan, boss of the Democrats, since he expected no trouble in securing Dever's nomination. A division in Republican votes after the primaries would work to his advantage.

Dever's opposition in the primary was only perfunctory, and he won easily. He had been reluctant to run again but Thompson's accusations and wild charges had stung him into angry acceptance of Brennan's bid to try for another term. Big Bill's victory was an overwhelming one, too. His 180,000-vote margin over Litsinger set a new record in any Republican primary ever held in Chicago.

On his day of victory Thompson instantly reaffirmed his vow to get rid of McAndrew. Crowe gloated over his triumph, saying, "I hope it will teach character assassins like Brundage and Litsinger that it doesn't pay to lie about decent citizens who oppose them politically." Litsinger promptly closed ranks with the Thompsonites to help defeat Dever. Senator Deneen, answering a question in thousands of minds, sent a telegram to the newspapers: "I am a Republican and accept the verdict of the Republicans at the primaries." As for the *Tribune*, girding for a new battle with its enemy, its editorial after Thompson's great victory concluded:

> Thompson is a buffoon in a tommyrot foundry, but when his crowd gets loose in the City Hall, Chicago has more need of Marines than any Nicaraguan town.
>
> No one is obliged to guess as to Thompson or as to Dever. The city has had experience with both and knows exactly what to expect. It is not exploring unknown territory. Both regions are mapped and sign-posted.
>
> The issue is between common sense and plain bunk. It is between decency and disreputability, between sensible people and political defectives, between honesty in administration and the percentage system.

22 ||| America First and America's Thirst

I

NOW BRENNAN AND DEVER WERE the enemies. The mayor of Chicago, asserted Big Bill, was a puny puppet in the hands of the Democratic boss. Before departing on a brief vacation trip to Georgia, he fired a barrage.

Boss Brennan, Thompson charged, was a "left-handed Irishman" who had, through his insurance company, milked the city and county of much money in bonding certain officials at double the usual rates. "Left-handed George, doesn't it make you laugh when the mayor says there is no gambling in Chicago? Left-handed George, you know and the people of Chicago know that with Charles C. Fitzmorris as superintendent of police I drove the crooks out of Chicago in ninety days, and it is you and Mayor Dever who are responsible for their return, and nothing else!" Replying to Brennan's assertion that every hoodlum in Chicago supported Thompson, Big Bill urged women voters to study photographs of himself and Brennan side by side. "You do that and you'll see that left-handed George carries all the earmarks of the hoodlum."

While Thompson lolled in Georgia, with the election a month off, the Deverites, both professionals and amateurs, got busy. Reformers and other respectable citizens, who characteristically had not made a serious attempt to beat Thompson in the primary, now thought they could do it in the election. This George Brennan had anticipated. A reform front had carried Brennan's organization to power four years previously, and he expected to repeat. Hundreds of Republicans refused to back Thompson and many of them organized the Nonpartisan People's Dever for Mayor Committee. Its members included Max Mason, president of the University of Chicago; Walter Dill Scott, president of Northwestern University; Dr. Frank Billings; the Reverend John Timothy Stone of the First Methodist Church; Harold L. Ickes, the former Progressive; Raymond Robins, the reform leader; and Donald Richberg, the anti-utilities lawyer. Its orator and chief spokesman was that implacable opponent of Thompson's, Charles E. Merriam.

This group's first contribution was the party's campaign slogan, "Dever and Decency." Brennan considered it limp and uninspiring, but he was too busy to devise a better one. He tightened his organization of the wards, assigned election jobs to the City Hall pay-rollers, provided help and encouragement to Lundin to insure that Dr. Robertson would run as an independent. Noting that Thompson got 45,000 of his primary votes in the Negro wards, Brennan prepared strong measures for those areas.

Just before Big Bill returned from Georgia, the Nonpartisan Peoples' Committee issued a mock communique titled "Big Bill, the Shrinking Violet." It read:

Citizens are advised that William Hale Thompson will arrive in Chicago shortly. With his usual modesty, he will attempt to slip into town unnoticed. Only one or two bands will be at the station to meet him. An appreciative citizenry ought to disregard William's shrinking habits and aversion to publicity. They ought to turn out in countless thousands to greet this heroic return from Georgia (named for King George). As they march down the street the citizenry will be able to tell William and the band apart if they look closely. William will be wearing a cowboy hat.

Less frivolous was the action directed by Brennan. Raiders were dispatched into the Second and Third Wards, where lived thousands of Thompson's Negro partisans. The policemen broke into gambling houses, brothels, saloons, and pool rooms, and invaded private homes. More than 1,000 men and women were arrested and held in jail over the week end. All were discharged on Monday morning. In Thompson's absence, Homer K. Galpin, chairman of his campaign, and Bernard W. Snow, Municipal Court bailiff active in his support, drafted a statement calling the raids "a plot . . . to terrorize and intimidate the colored voters so they will be deprived of their vote at the mayoralty election."

Chief of Police Collins issued a tight-lipped denial, insisting that since Thompson's triumph in the primary the entire Black Belt had come alive with new vice and gambling dens. "Unless I had acted and sent my best squads into the district to clean up things," he explained, "it would have been necessary to call out the militia."

Brennan was satisfied. The outlaws who had plumped for Thompson in whatever ward they infested would now think twice before trying it again. No hoodlum could mistake the punishment meted out in the South Side wards. Brennan had become the active boss. If they guessed wrong, and Thompson lost, he would continue to be boss for four more years.

2

"I'm in fighting trim to hit up a hot pace twenty hours a day," announced Thompson when he returned. And then he was off, determined to prove it.

He paid his compliments to the nonpartisan group as "traducers and liars and lily-white gentlemen." Informed that Merriam was in the wards speaking for Dever, he snorted, "That crook! Why, he runs our schools. That's why no picture of George Washington hangs in the classrooms any more!"

He made his opening speech in the Eighth Regiment Armory, drill hall for the city's Negro troops. For a full seven minutes his audience of 6,000 stomped and yelled when he appeared on the rostrum. Then, removing a fat cigar from his mouth, he touched off his campaign, hitting on every theme in his political litany.

"We stand for America First! We stand for Old Glory!" he boomed, his voice growing hoarser the longer he spoke. "And we stand for kicking out of office the Cossack mayor who doesn't keep his oath to God! We'll kick him out! We'll kick him out so far, he'll go so high——"

New cheers drowned out the rest of the statement. After a pause,

PREPARING FOR ONE OF THOSE APRIL SHOWERS

Big Bill continued: "Dever threw 1,000 innocent citizens in jail who white judges said were innocent. You have been patient as I asked you to be. You have accepted your persecution. When the time comes we'll show this Cossack mayor that he's up against a buzz saw, and a buzz saw isn't any joke!"

Jestingly Thompson continued. "I don't say that those arrests wouldn't have taken place if I had been here. But I sent out word when I got back to get those star numbers and I notice that nobody has been arrested since. You keep taking down those numbers. I want them. I'll have use for them on the day after election."

After charging that some members of Dever's cabinet received money for protecting gamblers, he upbraided the police. "Elect me and I'll turn the police from sneaking under the mattresses of your homes, looking for a little evidence of a minor infraction of the Volstead Act, to driving the crooks out. And they won't have to guess whether they'll get in bad by arresting or not arresting a crook the way they do now, with the orders from the City Hall changing so fast that it makes a policeman's head dizzy!"

Roscoe Conklin Simmons, a fervid Negro orator and attorney, denounced Brennan for the raids. "He's an Irishman. It's the first time a son of Erin ever placed the heel of the oppressor on the neck of a fellow man. This demonstration is to show how a friendly people can greet their friend. America only is the platform of the American Negro!"

And an old relic of the political past had his say too. "Get that man Dever out of the mayor's chair in the City Hall," wheezed William Lorimer, "and put in Thompson and you won't have to wonder whether you'll be recognized."

Before the meeting was over Thompson leaned over to embrace a handsome Negro child, the nephew of Oscar de Priest, one of his firmest backers. This gesture was duly reported to Brennan, who instantly had cartoons drawn of Thompson kissing Negro children. The drawings were distributed in neighborhoods where restrictive covenants prevailed and where there was strong anti-Negro feeling under the heading, "Do You Want Negroes or White Men to Run Chicago? Bye, Bye, Blackbirds!" The cartoons showed up frequently for the rest of the campaign, much to the discomfort of Dever. Thompson used them to his own advantage, always pulling one of the drawings from a pocket when he spoke to Negroes and yelling, "You see this? Dever and Brennan are circulating this vile thing! Dever and Brennan are the scum of the earth!"

At the armory meeting the Negro leaders pledged Thompson 60,000 votes. But not all Negro politicians were with him. Several were affiliated with splinter groups attached to the Brennan organ-

Big Bill and Mrs. Thompson

By Your Ballots
You Will Choose⁓

The man pictured above, the erratic judge (as designated by the Appellate and Supreme Courts, State of Illinois, which reversed his decisions twenty-eight out of twenty-nine times), who wears the Tribune halter, or—The man pictured below, "Li'll Arthur," who wears the Daily News halter, or — The man pictured on the page to the right, who wears no halter but is guided by the will of the people.

In this typical Thompson campaign circular in the bitter 1931 Republican primary, the man on top is Judge John H. Lyle and the other is Alderman Arthur F. Albert. Thompson won the nomination, but lost the election to Anton J. Cernak.

ization and at least one, Edward Wright, remained as obdurate as he had been in the primary. Informed that he would lose every bit of patronage he held as a county commissioner, he replied, "I was not born a slave and refuse to become one at this late day at the command of Thompson and his friends."

3

There were many other speeches, many other accusations.

A newly formed organization calling itself the Wage Earners' League staged a rally for Thompson in the Olympic Theater. Prominent among its organizers was Alderman Oscar Nelson, a rebel Democrat, who called Dever a "rubber stamp for the council" and charged that he had refused to install street lights in the wards of aldermanic foes. Thompson arrived with some 200 followers and they trooped onto the stage, upsetting scenery, shoving others from the stage into orchestra seats. Big Bill carried a big dinner pail with him. Banging heavily on it, he shouted, "I want everybody who is out of jobs to vote for me. I want all who may soon be out of jobs to vote for me. Let Brennan deliver the rest to Dever. Then Dever'll go to Europe."

In armories and meeting halls packed with bug-eyed listeners Thompson cried, "America First! The American who says 'America Second!' speaks the tongue of Benedict Arnold and Aaron Burr!" He sneered at Dever for wearing white collars and golf knickers: "Is he planning to graduate to knee breeches at the Court of St. James?" He declaimed steadily against the British: "There never was an Englishman who was the equal of an American and if there was he could make a million dollars in an hour and a half by beating that brave Gene Tunney, our world champion fighter!"

When Brennan repeated his charge that hoodlums were for Thompson, Big Bill twisted it to his favor. "My hoodlum friends," he once addressed a group of society women at the Opera Club. When the ladies gasped, he grinned and explained, "Well, George Brennan called my friends hoodlums and I hope you are all my friends. Well, my little hoodlum friends, just take one little hoodlum with you to the polls on election day. And remember what George

Washington said. He said, 'Keep out of foreign wars and make the King of England keep his nose out of our affairs!'" He printed a full-page advertisement in the *American*, with the key message: "VOTE FOR WILLIAM HALE THOMPSON AND AMERICA FIRST, a red-blooded American whose forefathers helped rock the Cradle of Liberty. Rid Chicago of British lackeys. Let them go to England, rally under the folds of the Union Jack and sing, 'God Save the King.' Let Chicago again take its place as the champion of true Americanism!" As an antidote to the subversive lyrics of "God Save the King," Thompson's poet laureate, Milton Weil, composed "Big Bill the Builder." At every meeting a quartet led the throng in its stirring words:

> "Scanning history's pages, we find names we know so well,
> Heroes of the ages—of their deeds we love to tell.
> But right beside them soon there'll be a name
> As someone we all acclaim.
>
> Who is the one, Chicago's greatest son?
> It's Big Bill the Builder!
> Who fought night and day to build the waterway,
> To stem the flood he stood in mud and fought for all
>   he's worth.
> He'll fight so we can always be the grandest land on earth.
> BIG BILL THE BUILDER, WE'RE BUILDING WITH YOU!"

4

His broad jaw outthrust, Dever responded.

Thompson was a buffoon and a clown, he declared, and he could have the King of England all to himself. "What an insult to the intelligence of the people of Chicago, the most marvelous city the world has ever seen, that the voters should be invited to meetings to listen to such claptrap about the British king! My opponent, seeking a laugh with his buffoonery, appeals in some districts on the color ground, in other regions on the religious ground—anything to divert the attention of the voter in the hope that in forgetfulness and laughter the wrong verdict will be given on election day. This is a critical time in Chicago's history and not one to be met by clowning!"

Picking up Thompson's cry of "Dever didn't do anything," the Deverites made capital of the charge. The accusation that "Dever Didn't" was true, they said. "Dever didn't appoint school trustees who were sent to jail. Dever didn't name a school-board attorney who was guilty of fraud. Dever didn't make fortunes for real-estate experts. Dever didn't force his employees to contribute to his campaign funds. Dever didn't sell promotions on the police force. Dever didn't have a whisper of scandal in the City Hall in the four years he has been mayor—a record for Chicago."

Cried Dever: "They accuse me of being a left-handed Irishman. I'm a right-handed Irishman and my grandfather was chased out of Ireland the day Robert Emmett was executed. My father's name was Emmett and that's my middle name. Nobody needs any blarney about 100 per cent Americans. We accept 100 per cent Americanism as part of the natural and ordinary existence, like air and food and clothes. We're all Americans first here, and nobody has any monopoly on that!"

He pleaded with his audiences: "Think of Chicago's future. Let the other fellow have the vaudeville and the clowning and the billingsgate. This is too serious a matter for Chicago. Think of the best interests of our city, and think upon matters of government." He demanded to know if Thompson was a "tool of the transit lines" and if Samuel Insull had contributed to his campaign fund. "Isn't it a fact that through your former corporation counsel, Samuel Ettelson, you were always in touch with the public utility companies?"

Edna Ferber, the novelist, paying a visit to relatives in the city, declared, "Thompson's election would be the greatest catastrophe." William Quinlan, head of the streetcar men's union, called him "a foe of laboring men." Professor Merriam asked, "Where was Big Bill Thompson in the Spanish-American war and in the World War? I'll tell you. He was playing football in the Spanish-American war and he hid under the bed in the World War!" Colonel Noble Brandon Judah, hero of the First Division, called Big Bill's "America First" slogan an "insult to the Chicago men now dead on the field of honor to whom he failed to say a word of goodbye. . . . The traditional right of citizens to 'America First' is a sacred thing and no demagogue has a right to claim it as his private property." A contingent of Gold Star Mothers, led by a Mrs. Mary Harrington, passed a resolution "officially resenting" Thompson. Raymond Robins charged that when Thompson first became mayor he issued an invitation to Negro gamblers and thugs to come to Chicago—"He speaks 'America First' but he thinks 'Africa First.'" Maclay Hoyne, in Washington on legal business, sent a telegram accusing Thompson of being responsible for the 1919 race riots by not allowing policemen to stop any disturbances in the Black Belt. The Reverend Philip Yarrow, the reformer who had praised Thompson in the days of the Sunday-saloon controversy, described a stag party Big Bill had thrown in the Chez Pierre night club at which nude girls gave indecent performances for members of the Good Roads Association. One hundred Protestant ministers issued a stolid statement describing Thompson as the worst mayor ever to rule any city. "Save Chicago!" cried the Deverites. "I want to beat that man and I will," cried Dever.

5

But Thompson slackened not a bit in the fury of his campaign. Instead, he broadened his attack on Dever's superintendent of schools, the stubborn William McAndrew.

Supplied with material by a group of anti-British Chicagoans who had been fervid supporters of Irish freedom, he charged that history books used in the city's schools were filled with false information. The group, calling itself the Citizens' Committee on School Histories, had attempted to lay its information before Dever, but he had delayed meeting with it. Now Thompson made full use of the data.

Citing two such standard works as William Fiske Gordy's *A History of the United States* and William Backus Guitteau's *Our Own United States*, Thompson accused McAndrew of condoning the use of these books in classrooms.

"Read these histories for yourselves!" he yelled. "The ideals you were taught to revere, the great Americans you were taught to cherish as examples of self-sacrificing devotion to human liberty, are subtly sneered at and placed in a false light so that your children may blush with shame when studying the history of their country. These men and others falsified and distorted facts to glorify England and vilify America."

This had all happened, said Big Bill, with the full approval of Dever. "When I went out of office, Washington fell out and the King of England fell in! This King George! If King George had his way there'd be a million American boys in China today to fight the battle for the dirty Englishmen and help the King make a billion dollars in the opium trade! And McAndrew is his lackey. Didn't he refuse to let our schoolchildren contribute their pennies to preserve noble Old Ironsides? You know why? Because Old Ironsides kicked hell out of every British ship she met and the King of England wouldn't like to have us preserve that ship! So he gave orders to his stooge, this McAndrew, and our children are not permitted to solicit pennies to preserve a priceless heritage. It's up to us, the red-blooded men and women of Chicago, to stand fast until the city is rid of pro-British rats who are poisoning the wells of historical truth!"

Unheeded went Dever's reply that the books of which Thompson now complained had been purchased when Big Bill was mayor. Before audiences in Polish neighborhoods, Thompson lamented that Casimir Pulaski and Thaddeus Kosciusko were not given proper credit for helping to win the American Revolution. Sometimes he was confused and called the heroes "Pulasko" and "Kosciuski" but his listeners understood what he meant. Before German audiences the neglected ones were listed as Baron von Steuben, Baron de Kalb and Christopher Ludwig, the latter appointed by Congress to be director of baking for the Continental Army. In Irish neighborhoods he howled that many Irishmen, including Mad Anthony Wayne and Light Horse Harry Lee, were slighted in the texts. "These Dever-violated school histories treat these nationalities with the contempt of silence and the venom of propaganda!"

McAndrew's service to King George had its advantages for the Dever administration, said Thompson. "Of course none of Mayor

Dever's school board were indicted. The King of England wouldn't let them be indicted. You take a chance on being punished when you're 100 per cent American!"

"The Same Old 'Bill,' " was the heading for a New York *Times* editorial when reports of his ranting reached the East "In some mysterious way he is running against King George. King George's head is always before him. . . ." And the Dever nonpartisan committee made a quick and logical analysis. "People are asking why Thompson accuses every person who opposes him with being a friend of King George of England. They are puzzled to understand why he continues day after day to rant about royalty in this mayoralty campaign. Some think it is due to a brainstorm, but we don't. We think it is because he hopes to win German and Irish and Polish votes and raise class distinctions in the minds of workingmen who he thinks hate the very mention of kings." The *News* had a neat evaluation of the anti-king furor—"the quintessence of piffle."

6

When he was not berating Dever and McAndrew for their abject allegiance to England, Thompson had other complaints about the schools, especially the ones built in Dever's term.

At a meeting in a hall on the West Side he displayed huge photographs which he said were enlargements of pictures showing cracks in concrete arches of these new schools.

"Disaster awaits your children in some of the schools built by Dever," he throbbed. "Concrete was poured for many of the arches during the winter and while the weather was cold the concrete was frozen and therefore unsafe. Now that spring is here these 200-ton arches are cracking and they are in danger of collapsing at any moment. Dever is afraid to close the schools or the people would find out how his builders grafted. So he has men working nights to bolster up these arches."

When some of the shawled women in the crowd wept and cried out, Thompson raised his arms and shouted, "I hope to God these arches hold up until election day. Because after that I will close these schools and keep them closed until they are made safe and find some place meanwhile to put your children!"

He did, of course, follow with his promise to respect personal liberty. "Those policemen who aren't poking into private homes are at breweries making sure that city officials get their five-dollar rake-off on each barrel of beer turned out. If I'm put in the mayor's chair I'll immediately use all my power to help repeal the Volstead Act. At this very hour there are police snooping about Chicago breaking down doors of homes to snoop around mattresses for a hip flask, or in the pantry for a little home brew, or in the basement or attic for a still. When I am mayor, I'll fire any cop who interferes with a citizen's personal liberty!"

"Hooray for Big Bill!" the audience cried. "Hooray for beer!"

"And I'll tell you someone else I'm gonna fire. One of the first things I'll do is fire King George's puppet, that McAndrew. I'll fire him and our schoolbooks will breathe patriotism again. On election day we'll snow this bird Dever so hard that he'll think George Washington has arisen from his grave to reproach him!"

7

While Thompson shot off his verbal fireworks, his associates prepared for the final assault at the polls. Crowe and Harding tightened their patronage rolls. Galpin, Pike, Snow and Ettelson raised campaign funds and warned recalcitrant party leaders and the city's Republican businessmen that a Democratic victory in Chicago would clear the way for a Democratic triumph in the nation.

Ed Brundage, with the approval of Deneen, was the first to swallow the many words of abuse he had hurled at Thompson. When, at a party love-feast in the Parkway Hotel, he announced this surprise, Thompson strode into the room. "Thank God, I have lived to see this day!" he murmured. Brundage offered sanctimonious reasons for his action. "I want to see this internal fighting in the party stopped. I want a united Republican party with leaders in whom the people have confidence, and I want to help in my humble way to secure good government for Chicago."

In a "loyalty rally" at Medinah Temple, Thompson shared the

stage with Deneen, Brundage, Litsinger and Louis L. Emmerson, a staunch Deneenite in downstate Illinois. Said Deneen: "Vote for William Hale Thompson because he is a Republican. If Dever is elected, he and George Brennan will be in a powerful spot to bring about the nomination by the Democrats of their friend, Al Smith, of New York, for President. Let us stand united!" Litsinger, whom Thompson had called "the biggest liar in politics," posed happily with Big Bill for photographers. Emmerson, whom Thompson referred to as "Lop-Eared Lou," praised Big Bill as the only man who could rid Chicago of its evils. Brundage, for whom Thompson's favorite appellation had always been "skunk," cried, "It's high time we Republicans got together and quit fighting among ourselves. I'm in politics and I'm a politician and I abide by the wish of the majority in our party!"

Arthur Evans, the *Tribune's* shrewd and witty political reporter, listened to the love-feast dithyrambs and promptly produced a fitting name for the alliance. He called it "The Republican Ananias Club."

8

Missing from these happy scenes was Fred Lundin. He was still behind his man, Dr. Robertson, and the independent Republican group calling itself the People's Ownership—Smash the Crime Rings Party, and he refused to budge.

"Big Baby Bill," Lundin called Thompson. Vehement in his denunciations, he also ripped into the Deneenites who, as Evans wrote, "have used mud dredges on each other in the past but have now sent their clothes to the dry cleaners while singing their harmony song." He challenged Thompson to tell the truth about the stag party of which the Reverend Mr. Yarrow had given unblushing details in a pamphlet: "If the story isn't true, Bill Thompson will be elected! If the story is true, then William Hale Thompson, you're unfit to touch the hands of a virtuous girl!" In Thompson's eight years as mayor, said the man who had helped put and keep him in office, he had accomplished nothing. "Big Baby Thompson was so busy crowning queens at street corners that he had no time to study the traction question. Instead of working on city problems and fulfilling his promises to the people, he organized a plaything, the Pageant of Progress, which furnished Big Baby Thompson a chance to parade the streets riding a police horse!" As for the caged-rat act of Thompson's, Lundin shrilled, "My only answer to Thompson for calling me a rat and for his other vile and untruthful references is that for eight years he lived most of the time in this rat's house and was willing and eager to gnaw at the rat's table!"

Another former Thompson adviser, William F. Mulvihill, one of the first members of his Printing and Publicity Committee, criticized Big Bill for using material in his speeches he had prepared years ago. "I wrote those speeches," cried Mulvihill, "when he was running for senator in 1918. Thompson didn't even know George Washington wrote a farewell address until I dug it up and brought it to him. And he has no more to do with the Illinois waterway than my sixteen-year-old boy!"

In the tradition of all independent candidates, Dr. Robertson flayed both Dever and Thompson.

"Mayor Dever is shooting the bunk and Thompson is tossing the bull!" was his theme. "Carfares in Chicago were five cents on the streetcars and five cents on the elevated when Thompson became mayor. Now they are seven cents and ten cents. Dever was elected on his promise to cut the straphangers' expenses and promote public ownership. But under orders from Boss Brennan he broke his campaign pledges and tried to put over a traction steal."

If either Dever or Thompson won, warned Robertson, crime would continue to thrive. He challenged Thompson to name the man he would appoint as police chief if elected. "He can't! If he gives the name of an honest man, the crooks will not vote for him. If he names Fitzmorris, Hughes or some other of their type, the decent people will refuse to support him. By his silence Thompson is giving the people a right to think he is yellow. By his silence he gives ample proof that he will not disappoint his underworld supporters. Every voter on election day will either line up with Thompson, Crowe, Fitzmorris, Druggan and Lake and Scarface Al Capone, or with Dever, Brennan, Collins and grafting policemen, or they will line up with John Dill Robertson. As you vote so must you pay!"

9

The fury increased in the campaign's final days.

Thompson took casual note of Robertson's campaign, just long enough to declare, "The doc is slinging mud. I'm not descending to personalities, but let me tell you that if you want to see a nasty sight, watch Doc Robertson eating in a restaurant. Eggs in his whiskers, soup on his vest. You'd think he got his education driving a garbage wagon!"

The race issue remained a heated one. In Lincoln Park appeared signs reading, "Do you want Negroes or White Men to run Chicago? Ask Thompson!" At Dever's meetings, bands played "Bye, Bye Blackbird!" Through Loop streets at the busy noon hour the Democrats sent a Negro in cocked hat and regimentals, riding a spavined horse and carrying a sign: "The British are Coming! Tell Bill!" Thousands of the cartoons depicting Thompson kissing Negro babies still floated through the city. Big Bill retaliated by distributing handbills with a photograph of Dever surrounded by Negro ex-soldiers in the 1923 campaign—"Double-faced Dever! He Would Strike Down Those Who Helped Raise Him Up!" Waving copies of the cartoons, Thompson raged, "Dever and Brennan are a disgrace to the Irish! They are trying to start a race riot to make white people hate Thompson and elect a crook mayor. I won't let them get away with it. I've had twelve men go into Dever headquarters and get copies of that dirty cartoon. If they succeed in starting a race riot I'll devote two years to putting Brennan and his pliant tool, Dever, in the penitentiary!"

As Bill persisted in his assaults on King George, speakers for Dever in strongly Catholic neighborhoods cried, "Big Bill says he means George of England, but he really means Cardinal George Mundelein. He's stirring religious hatred. He's mad because Mayor Dever kissed the cardinal's ring at the Eucharistic Congress last summer! Thompson's a Ku Kluxer!"

When Governor Small refused to indorse him, Thompson read him out of the Republican party. But a few days later he publicly thanked Small for not coming to Chicago to campaign for Lundin's candidate. Robertson immediately denied he had asked Small for aid and Small remained silent, so that Thompson found no difficulty in convincing doubtful Republicans that in effect the governor wanted him to win.

State's Attorney Crowe was assailed by the Democrats with "Who Killed McSwiggin?" and by Lundin with "The blood of your mur-

dered assistant is paging you and demanding justice at your hands!"
Crowe, no laggard in political strife, charged the Deverites were
seeking to cause riots and bloodshed. "If the efforts of the Dever
organization culminate successfully in destruction of property and
murder follows," he warned, "all persons engaged in the conspiracy
are equally answerable under the law." Despite this legalistic statement, Crowe could exhibit a sense of humor in all the bitterness.
Leaving the Hotel Sherman one night with Thompson, he found
that the tires on Big Bill's car had been slashed. "The Dever decent
element is giving rough treatment to us Thompson hoodlums," remarked Crowe. "I suppose some silk-hat highbrow from the Gold
Coast did this uplift deed with his umbrella."

Attorney General Oscar Carlstrom told a meeting of ex-service-
men, "I'm glad to see you here in behalf of a friend of mine, Big Bill
the Builder, who loves little children, Big Bill the American, who
stands for America First" and Judge Harry B. Miller of the Superior
Court laughed and said, "If Thompson wins, Chicago will have a
Fatty Arbuckle for mayor" and newspaper wits, aware of Capone's
interest in Thompson's victory, wisecracked, "Thompson's for
America First and Capone's for America's Thirst" and Thompson
yelled, "I'm wetter than the middle of the Atlantic Ocean," while
Dever insisted, "I'm for repeal of the dry laws too."

10

All through the campaign there were brief but bright glimpses
into Al Capone's alliance with the Thompson machine.

From the start Capone's money rolled into Big Bill's campaign
coffers. Some of it came through a porcine First Ward politician
named Daniel A. Serritella, a Capone protégé. Some came from such
West Side politicos as Morris Eller, the autocratic chief of the
"Bloody Twentieth" Ward actively allied with Capone district
leaders. Guesses on the amount Capone gave varied from $250,000,
which was too high, to $100,000, closer to the actual amount. Later,
the high-minded Illinois Association for Criminal Justice would
describe the Capone offering as "substantial" and Frank J. Loesch,

president of the Chicago Crime Commission, would estimate it had been $260,000.

From another gangster, an oily pimp and gambler named Jack Zuta, Thompson received at least $50,000. Zuta, a mysterious power on the West Side, had a shifty arrangement with Capone on underworld matters but agreed with him on the pressing need for Thompson's triumph. Zuta strutted about the Hotel Sherman headquarters of the Thompson faction. He held Card No. 772 in the William Hale Thompson Republican Club. "I'm for Big Bill hook, line and sinker and Bill's for me hook, line and sinker," Zuta boasted.

Other gangsters and gangland characters, Caponeites and independents alike, were seen regularly at the headquarters. "Big Tim" Murphy, bank robber and labor terrorist, served as a guide to visitors. Another was Abie Arends, an old Levee man who had managed Colosimo's cafe. Lurking in and around the campaign offices, too, was Vincent (Schemer) Drucci, once chief killer for Dion O'Banion, but now, with his revered leader lying in a Mount Carmel cemetery grave, a loyal Capone man.

In command of a squadron of gangsters assigned to quell or create trouble, Drucci was especially busy in the last week of the campaign. On April 4, the day before the fateful election, he and his men raided the offices of Alderman Dorsey R. Crowe, the Dever leader in the gang-ridden Forty-second Ward, intent on physically chastising the alderman for his anti-Thompson activities. Crowe had gone, however, so the hoodlums gave expression to their indignation by overturning file cabinets, terrorizing a secretary and kicking out a window.

Hearing of this raid, Chief Collins ordered a roundup of hoodlums and said he would consider asking for state troopers for the next day's election. Later in the day Drucci and two companions were picked up by a police squad and hustled to the Central police building, where Drucci was relieved of an automatic revolver. In half an hour his lawyer was in Criminal Court with a petition for a writ of habeas corpus. On the way to the courtroom, several miles from the police building, Drucci started an abusive argument in the police squad car with one of his guards, Policeman Dan Healy. After kicking and cursing and spitting at Healy, the gangster grabbed for the policeman's revolver. Healy got it first, and fired four shots into Drucci, killing him.

In the Thompson headquarters George Harding quivered with rage and demanded that he be permitted to make "sensational charges" in connection with Drucci's slaying. The only pro-Thompson paper, Hearst's *American*, asked, "Have the Brennan-Dever Democrats gone mad?" George Brennan ordered every City Hall pay-roller to be at the polls next day as watchers and guards. Chief Collins directed a "mobilization" of the police department, assigning 250 squads for election duty and rifle-bearing officers in every polling place. "Gangsters had better wear their heaviest armor tomorrow!" warned the chief. And Al Capone issued his own curt orders to his men to be at the polling places next morning to make certain that the election would not be stolen from Big Bill.

23 "Throw Away Your Hammer and Get a Horn!"

1

CONSIDERING THE WARLIKE PREPA-
rations, Chicago's election day was comparatively quiet.

In the early hours two Democratic precinct clubs on the North
Side were bombed, two election judges were kidnaped and beaten,
half a dozen voters were driven from the polls by pistol-waving
thugs, and five shots were fired into a West Side polling booth. Little
violence occurred during the rest of the day, with police squads
cruising the city, machine guns in their laps and tear bombs in their
pockets. At Randolph and Clark streets, center of the city's theater
district, the loungers and the wits had a joke whenever an automobile backfired—"That's not an auto, that's a machine gun going off."

In the early hours, too, the factions made the usual predictions.
Martin J. O'Brien, Dever's spokesman: "Mayor Dever will win by
160,000." Homer Galpin, the sly Thompson campaign manager:
"It's Big Bill Thompson by 150,000 or more." And Dr. Robertson,
speaking for himself with fantastic optimism: "My campaign has
been a success and my election is assured."

2

None proved himself a sure political prophet, although Galpin
came closest to the final truth. Thompson won his third term as
Chicago's mayor with 512,740 votes to Dever's 429,668 and the
hapless Dr. Robertson's 51,208.

A foe only of British monarchs, Thompson received the day's

returns standing beneath a huge painting of George Washington in
the Hotel Sherman's Louis XVI Room. He rolled an unlighted cigar
nervously in his mouth when the first results showed Dever in a slight
lead. He drank one bourbon highball after another and waved
wildly when the count turned in his favor. As the lead grew, he
grabbed a megaphone, stood on a table and shouted, "The lead is now
52,000! I thank you one and all, I thank you! Tell 'em, cowboys,
tell 'em! I told you I'd ride 'em high and wide!"

"Hey, Bill," someone shouted, "where's Fred Lundin?"

"He's gone to Russia!"

"Hey, Bill! How does old McAndrew feel?"

"He'll find out! I'm gonna kick him out!"

Someone shouted, "Thompson for President!" and another sang,
"Bye, Bye, Dever!" and then the gay crowd broke into Milton
Weil's song:

> "America first and last and always!
> Our hearts are loyal, our faith is strong.
> America first and last and always!
> Our shrine and homeland, though right or wrong.
>
> United we stand for God and country,
> At no one's command we'll ever be.
> America first and last and always!
> Sweet land of freedom and liberty!"

Soon State's Attorney Crowe arrived to beam at the crowd and
grasp Thompson's beefy hand. "This is a splendid victory!" he
declared. "With Thompson as mayor I know the police department
will give me the help in making Chicago a safe city for women and
children!" In a room adjoining the big hall sat Thompson's chief
counselors—George Harding, Sam Ettelson, Richard Wolfe,
Charles Fitzmorris, Gene Pike—and they talked softly and made
plans.

The festivities continued far into that night. At a jubilee aboard
the schooner headquarters of his Fish Fans' Club in Belmont Harbor,

Thompson offered his 1,500 listeners a new slogan. "Make Chicago hum!" he cried. "That's my motto in this administration! Open the waterway, to make Chicago hum. Settle the traction question, to make Chicago hum. Get rid of the bread lines, to make Chicago hum. Speed the great public improvements, to make Chicago hum. Chase out the crooks and gunmen, to make Chicago hum."

The cheering people stamped their feet so heavily that the schooner swayed and quivered. Before any of the celebrants could scurry off, the vessel settled into the six feet of water in which it was anchored, dousing hundreds of coats in the lower-deck checkroom. The spirits of the rooters were undampened as they filed out merrily, but the rickety vessel was no longer of use. For a long time after the demise of the gay club, those who remembered her frivolous days remained sentimentally devoted, an attitude expressed by William H. Stuart, the *American's* political editor and a steadfast Thompsonite. "To this day," he wrote years later,* "they mourn in Chicago the passing of the Fish Fans' Club, where plain folks enjoyed life and got a place in the sun in the exclusive Gold Coast."

On the next morning Thompson, bleary-eyed and tired, roused himself to speak his thanks to the citizenry over his radio station WHT that he and his backers had opened a few months earlier in the Wrigley Building. That night 3,000 rooters crowded into the Rainbo Gardens to pay him homage. "I'll strive for prosperity!" he promised. "I'll strive to make Chicago the greatest city in the world! We'll stop the bread lines! We'll put the police back on their beats and rid the town of crooks. We'll invite the blue noses and the internationalists to get the hell out of Chicago! Let's have teamwork! Once more let our slogan be—'Throw away your hammer and get a horn!'"

A committee celebrated the festive evening by leading Thompson outside and presenting him with a blue Lincoln sports coupe. He roared his thanks and seated himself at the wheel for the photographers. Later he would exchange the sports model for an open touring car with the rear seat raised, so that a spotlight installed in the front

---

* In his *The 20 Incredible Years* (M. A. Donohue & Co., Chicago, 1935), a voluminous account of Thompson's career, with many inside details of Big Bill's terms in office.

panel could shine on him when he toured the city at night. "The
people like to see their mayor!"

3

   While Thompson recovered his sobriety lost in explosive celebra-
tions and prepared for his inauguration, the country reacted with a
shock and a shudder and a bitter laugh. Not even in the days of King
Mike McDonald and his gambling empire, not in the buccaneering
days of Charles Yerkes, not in the wild era of Bathhouse John
Coughlin and Hinky Dink Kenna and the Everleigh sisters had Chicago been so derided, criticized and analyzed.
   Will Rogers, the cowboy humorist, seemed best to sum up the
attitude of the outsiders. "They was trying to beat Bill with the
better element vote," he joked. "The trouble with Chicago is that
there ain't much better element." In two indignant articles in *Forum*
magazine, Kate Sargent determined that Big Bill's election showed
Chicagoans suffered from "a blight of memory." Chicago, she
wrote, was a city with growing pains, easily led, easily beclouded,
full of immature judgment and with emotions that could be swiftly
and simply played on. Nels Anderson, in the *Century* magazine,
called Thompson's victory "the triumph of the gang."
   They made innumerable judgments on Thompson himself. In a
good-humored and astute portrait in *Harper's*, the brilliant Elmer
Davis called Big Bill "an artist, living by inspiration and not by reason, seldom riding an inspiration until it gives out, because he can
always get a new one, just as good." Davis felt Thompson would be
a roaring success in any large city: "He understands his people as
Sophocles understood the Athenians. Like Sophocles, he gives them
a catharsis of pity and terror, and like Sophocles he finishes off with
slapstick stuff that sends them home laughing. The art of politics has
a lot to learn from show business and William Hale Thompson has
learned it." Other eager students of the mayor-elect's personality
classified him as a realist in political conceptions and as a sort of
political bishop, never outraged at the shortcomings of his populace,
"a regular guy" and "a prince of good fellows." His powers, said
some, were not intellectual "but divination pure and simple."

The St. Louis *Post-Dispatch* thought Big Bill "Chicago's beau ideal" and the Indianapolis *Star* called his triumph "a striking example of the potency of demagoguery and appeals to prejudice in American elections" and the St. Louis *Star* was convinced that "Chicago is still a good deal of a Wild West town, where a soapbox showman extracting white rabbits from a gentleman's plug hat still gets a better hearing than a man in a sober suit talking business." *The Emancipator*, a Negro journal, predicted that Thompson would be proclaimed some day with Washington and Lincoln as a great leader in "the people's fight for democracy and human rights" and Hearst's *American* in New York called Thompson's election "a clear victory for the candidate of the people." Bitterest of the critics, Victor Yarros, in the *Independent*, called Thompson a "political blunderbuss ... indolent, ignorant of public issues, inefficient as an administrator, incapable of making a respectable argument, reckless in his campaign methods and electioneering oratory, inclined to think evil of those who are not in agreement or sympathy with him, and congenitally demagogical."

4

If he read any of the criticisms or heard the bitter imprecations, Thompson paid them little heed. He was too busy, he avowed, with details and ideas for driving out the crooks, building the Illinois waterway, ousting McAndrew, solving the traction problem, erasing the financial deficit, widening and paving streets. These promises he reiterated on his inauguration night of April 11, an event marked by the absence of Dever, still so embittered over Thompson's campaign tactics that he refused to attend. "He's a cheap sport and a poor loser," commented Big Bill.

"Officially we have arrived!" he roared happily on the next morning as he ambled into his City Hall office, tossed his sombrero on a couch, and settled his bulk in his chair. "Y' know, there's a hustling city near by named Detroit that is talking of surpassing Chicago. Now I have friends in Detroit, but they'd better tie on their hats, for they're going to get a ride. We'll give the old town the greatest ride for prosperity she ever had!"

Then he named the cabinet that would help him in his noble endeavors.

As his corporation counsel he chose Sam Ettelson again, despite criticism even inside his organization that Ettelson's legal tieups with Samuel Insull would lay bare the fact that Insull had contributed to the Thompson campaign and had a strong say in traction matters. Richard Wolfe, the master of pompous prose, became commissioner of public works. Michael Faherty, still fighting in court against the *Tribune's* expert-fees charges, won back his post as president of the Board of Local Improvements. Charles Fitzmorris, of the crime-cleanup days of 1920 and the fight with State's Attorney Crowe, was named to George Harding's old job of city comptroller, for Harding was still county treasurer.

As the man to combat the crooks—"I want them out in ninety days!"—Thompson chose Michael Hughes, who had resigned his post as chief of detectives under Dever to take a temporary job as head of the county highway police under the Thompson-dominated sheriff, Charles Graydon. A man with a reputation as "the best thief-catcher Chicago ever had," Hughes uttered brave and familiar words. "I'll do my best to make good the mayor's promise. When the crooks are convinced we mean business, some of them will volunteer to get out of town. I will do everything possible to put them in jail if they stay!"

On the same day Thompson gave Hughes his mighty mission, he appointed as city sealer Daniel A. Serritella, Al Capone's agent. Officially Serritella's duties were to see that Chicago citizens received honest weights from their butchers, grocers, and ice and coal dealers and other merchants. Unofficially this bulky fellow was in the City Hall to watch for Capone's interests there, to carry messages, to inform the high political command when favors were needed. Few questioned his appointment then for his close affiliation with Capone was not disclosed until several years later. He was known only as an up-and-coming First Ward politician who had once been a newsboy and founder of the Chicago Newsboys' Union.

Other deserving comrades were also slated for their rewards. Milton Weil, the composer of the immortal "America First, Last and Always" was given the privilege, as ace precinct captain in the First Ward, of running a card game in a hotel across from the City Hall, and when Captain George O'Connor, taking Chief Hughes at his word, raided the place, O'Connor was transferred to an outlying district. Later Weil was honored with a testimonial dinner in the Hotel Sherman where speakers hailed him as "one of God's noblemen" and paid tribute to Weil's other masterpiece, "Big Bill the Builder," as "the most inspiring song ever written about an individual." Morris Eller, whose first fame in the Thompson ranks came in 1915 when he won a gold cup for being the champion precinct captain, landed in the city collector's office, adding new power to that already established as overlord of the Twentieth Ward.

5

Once the appointments were out of the way, Thompson was ready for more specific action on his promises. As in previous years, he showed signs of confounding his critics.

At his first meeting with the city council, he announced formation of a 300-man committee of the city's leading businessmen and executives. "I want these men to help me do things for Chicago," he explained. Chairman was George Getz, a wealthy coal dealer, and other well-known members included James Simpson, president of Marshall Field and Company; William Wrigley; John Hertz of the Yellow Cab Company; A. Rupert Abbott, president of the Chicago Telephone Company; Elmer T. Stevens, head of Charles A. Stevens; and Silas Strawn and George M. Reynolds, leading bankers. One of Getz's first assignments from Thompson was to secure for Chicago the heavyweight championship prize fight between Jack Dempsey and Gene Tunney, a contest Getz was successful in persuading Tex Rickard, the promoter, to stage in July in the vast Soldiers' Field on the lake front.

The only irritating note in this first council meeting was furnished by Alderman William A. Meyering of the Third Ward, who had lost an arm in the World War when he picked up a German hand grenade and saved the lives of others in his trench. When Thompson

declared he was going to fight for the repeal of an ordinance calling
for the installation of water meters as required by federal regulations, Meyering complained, "That ordinance was passed for the
good of Chicago." The gallery, packed with Thompsonites, hissed.
Turning to the crowd, Meyering shouted, "Seven years ago you
didn't hiss me when I came back in uniform! I have lived in this town
a long time and I have listened to many kinds of bull, but never to
anything like I listened to in the recent campaign!" Then he sat
down while Thompson glared at him for disrupting the peaceful
meeting and the galleries snarled, "Put that bum out! Send him back
to the army!"

That same week Thompson and a merry crowd of 500 politicians
and well-wishers set out on two steamships, the *Cape Girardeau*
and the *Cincinnati*, on a Victory Cruise to New Orleans. Among
the guests was Jack Zuta, the West Side gangster, who invited
Thompson to stop over in his home town of Middlesborough, Ken-
tucky, where a lavish party was thrown for the travelers by Zuta's
uncle, a Colonel Ike Ginsburg.

After this festive visit, the expedition, originally designed to de-
velop publicity for the Illinois Waterway, ran into the crest of the
Mississippi River floods at Cairo, Illinois. Along the surging river
the ships stopped at many of the ravaged towns. In each Thompson
took up a collection and turned the money over to the flood refugees.
The *Tribune* scoffed at his Good Samaritan deeds, in a front-page
cartoon depicting him on a steamboat in the flooded region wiring
to Small, while farmers cried for help atop their house roofs, "Get a
speedboat and meet me at Cairo. We'll rescue somebody and I'll be
at the wheel of the speedboat myself."

The ships finally made their way to the outskirts of New Orleans.
Mayor Arthur O'Keefe met them and led Thompson and his party
into the beleaguered city. Together they drew plans for a flood-
control conference in Chicago to demand that the government build
stronger levees the length of the treacherous river. The conference
was held early in June. Thompson, as chairman, reported what he
had seen in the devastation of the flood area, saying, "What we saw
one might have expected in China, but not in rich America with our

boasted good government." Political leaders of both parties attended the meeting. Later Thompson went to Washington to lay his flood-control plans before President Coolidge and won a promise of co-operation.

Thompson worked hard in these early months. He encouraged organizers and supporters of the plans for the Century of Progress Exposition to be held in 1933. He helped to settle a strike of motion-picture operators. He traveled to Springfield to fight for a subway bill, and lost, and for legislation to increase the city's bonding powers, and won. With William Lorimer's help, he made peace with Governor Small. The wily governor discarded Lundin and turned over to Thompson all Park Board jobs. In return, Thompson promised his support in the 1928 governor's race.

So roseate was the surface of Thompson's new regime that he won plaudits as "Chicago's business mayor" from so seasoned and critical a political reporter as the New York *Times's* Arthur Krock. In June, Krock spent a week in the city and issued an interesting report. He wrote:

Big Bill Thompson, who went native many years ago, is beginning again to associate civilly with those Chicagoans whose families, like his own, constitute the aristocracy and culture of the Lake Shore.... Republican businessmen of large affairs and social consequence who swore only a few months ago, as they voted for Mayor Dever, that never, never should they hold up their heads again under the consulship of Big Bill, are working on his new committee "for the good of Chicago." ... The Crowe-Barrett faction and the Deneen faction are eating from his Brobingnagian hand, for that's where the food is now.... Well, something has happened. Maybe it was success. Maybe it was a new distaste, frequent in politicians growing old, for the base weapons employed in their advancement. Maybe it is a sudden determination to show that William Hale is as much of a Thompson, a North Shore Thompson, a Gold Coast, pundit-caste Thompson as any other member of the family.... Maybe the new habits of industry and constructive effort will be shed at the first false move from George V at Buckingham Palace.... For the present Big Bill is being a business mayor.

6

Al Capone was acting businesslike too.

Now he expanded his headquarters in the Hotel Metropole on South Michigan Avenue to fifty rooms on two floors heavily guarded by armed gunmen. In one of the pair of rooms he occupied was a long mahogany conference table at the head of which he sat when consulting with his lieutenants on which rivals to assassinate, which businessmen to terrorize, which politicians to pay off.

Despite Chief Hughes's frequent promises to drive out the gangsters and the crooks, Capone set up offices for his gambling empire at Clark and Madison streets, only a block from the City Hall. In charge were an old-time vice operator, Jake Guzik, and Jimmy Mondi, a hoodlum who was one of the original members of the Sportsman's Club that helped elect Thompson in 1915. Mondi summoned all owners of gambling joints to this office. "We're cutting in," he told them. "We'll get up to forty per cent of what you guys take in. For that we'll keep the cops off you. You take it, or else."

Capone gangsters roamed the corridors of the City Hall, collaring aldermen with requests for favors and threatening those who refused to vote their way. In June a series of murders occurred only a week after Krock's report that "machine gun murders, holdups and private assassinations have become rare, if not extinct." Capone's chief assassin, "Machine Gun Jack" McGurn, disposed first of one upstart rival, then another, then a third. Capone soon ruled the Unione Sicilione, federation of Mafia desperadoes, Italian businessmen and alky-cookers. "Mayor of Crook County," one newspaper columnist labeled him. Capone was strong, and growing stronger by the day, and his City Hall friends looked on and stuffed their safety-deposit boxes with his money.

7

In September the ninety days Thompson had allotted "Go-Get-'Em" Hughes to rid the city of all crime and criminals had grown to well over 120 days, and still crime thrived and criminals gloried in their ruthless power.

But Thompson was too busy with a new interest to remind Hughes of his order. President Coolidge had just announced: "I do not choose to run in 1928," and the field was open for Republican Presidential candidates. When Governor Small came to dine with Thompson at City Hall No. 2 in the Hotel Sherman, the reporters wanted to know if they had discussed a deal by which Small would insure delegates for Thompson if Thompson supported Len's bid for a third term at Springfield. William Lorimer spoke up in the hubbub to say that he favored Charles Deneen as the candidate, but if a deadlock developed he would be only too happy to see William Hale Thompson as the nominee. All Thompson would say was that he was as determined as in 1920 to prevent Frank Lowden from being nominated.

Having made this statement, Thompson immediately set out on a cross-country, 10,000-mile junket that showed every indication of being a tour to drum up enthusiasm for his candidacy. This trip was to be purely in the interests of flood control, insisted Big Bill, speaking as chairman of the recent flood-control conference. "Its purpose is to win support for a Congressional appropriation for flood control and for a Lakes-to-Gulf Waterway, and nothing else," he claimed.

With him, however, were not only such cronies as Judge Bernard Barasa and Charles Barrett, but Lorimer, to give sage advice, and Sergeant Frank McCann's police quartet to sing at every railroad stop, and two press agents, Frank Butzow and Robert Lyman, to keep each city's newspapers well supplied with releases about Big Bill Thompson and his important mission.

On the day before he departed, he was the guest of honor at the sixteenth annual Republican Labor Day picnic in Riverview Park. Factional fights were forgotten for the day as 65,000 cheered him. Throwing his gray sombrero to a barefooted boy near the speakers' platform, he declared: "I was criticized for my America First slogan because they said I was injecting a national issue into a municipal campaign. But my reply to that is this—What's the use of our working here at home, trying to make Chicago the world's greatest city, if someone's pulling down Old Glory at Washington by hooking us up with the World Court and the League of Nations?"

Advance agent for the tour, made in a private car festooned with ribbon signs reading WILLIAM HALE THOMPSON FLOOD RELIEF

SPECIAL, was Thomas J. Hill, clerk of New Orlean's city council, a
Southern Democrat. Was Thompson making the trip because of
Presidential ambitions? "No suh" was Hill's oft-repeated denial as
he came to city after city. "Would ah be with him if he were?"

In Omaha, Thompson spent a few nonpolitical hours with another
old cowboy, Mayor James Dahlman, who took him to the stockyards where, thirty years earlier, both had brought carloads of steers.
In Kansas City he spoke to Republicans at a luncheon, at Denver to
the Chamber of Commerce, at Cheyenne to stockbreeders. At Albu-
querque the *Journal*, noting his speeches and his publicity men, commented wryly: "Mayor Thompson may have a little political axe to
grind in making this tour of the West at this time, but the people of
this state will bear with him and overlook this if he succeeds in ac-
complishing the big objective he is after."

After a visit with William Randolph Hearst at the publisher's
massive ranch near San Luis Obispo, Thompson was greeted in San
Francisco by 1,000 devotees of flood control. His police quartet,
minus one ailing member, sang "America First, Last and Always"
and Thompson told the audience: "The reason there's only three
cops is that the other fellow's been called back to catch a murderer."
He talked briefly on flood control and then boasted that he would
soon be rid forever of William McAndrew. "He's the fellow you
may've heard of, the one that filled our histories with all that pro-
British trash. Now Bill Thompson is elected and George Washington is back and McAndrew is out!"

"Good boy, Bill! Good for you!"

"There are a lot of reports I want to be President. That's not
true. I want you to remember there were men of every party at our
conference in Chicago. I'm not interested in my or anybody's candidacy. My one ambition is to protect the people of the Mississippi
Valley from the floods of the future!"

Some skeptics in the audience stared down at their plates. There,
as at every luncheon in every city where the party paused, Butzow
and Lyman had placed copies of Thompson's eight-page pamphlet
on whose cover was a red-white-and-blue target around a bull's-eye
titled AMERICA FIRST! The pamphlet advised: "Don't scatter. Shoot
at the Bull's-eye for American Prosperity. To Hit the Bull's-eye

for American Prosperity we must have United Action." And to gain this Big Bill asked that each recipient urge the selection of delegates to the G.O.P. nominating convention who would be pledged to four Thompsonian principles—America First, farm relief, inland waterways and national flood control. With each pamphlet went a lapel button with AMERICA FIRST on it.

After a reception in Los Angeles, at which the Los Angeles police quartet serenaded him and such movie stars of the day as Monte Blue, Milton Sills and Irene Rich greeted him and where he spoke on "The Religion of the Cowboy," Bill headed back to Chicago. He was greeted by thousands at the Santa Fe Station, a reception arranged by two younger party officials, Edward F. Moore and Lou Golan. Then came a parade of 750 cars from the station to the Hotel Sherman, where State's Attorney Crowe expressed what many around Thompson felt at the moment, "He is a great American. He has done more for Chicago than anything that has happened in my lifetime. And he has, by this trip, reduced the prejudice that has existed in some localities, created by unfair critics of Chicago."

8

Whatever the intensity of his Presidential ambitions this time, he was slated for another failure, as in 1916. By the end of 1927 Thompson himself knew it. Speaking before the American Association for the Recognition of the Irish Republic, he decried the presidential talk.

"I don't want to be President," he said. "I'm a peace-loving man and I'm afraid if I were President I'd plunge this country into war, for I'd say 'Go to Hell' to any foreign nation which attempted to dictate the number of ships we could build or which tried to flood in propaganda as is being done now!"

His audience laughed, and he laughed too. But there was a hollow tone to his laughter. By this time he was involved in a battle in Chicago that had set most of the world cackling and laughing at him, and national Republican leaders were in no mood to look favorably on a man who inspired jeers.

24 ||| The Trial of William McAndrew

I

BALD AND TOUGH, J. LEWIS COATH
gloried in his nickname of "Iron-Handed Jack."

Irregular in his loyalty to Thompson in his earlier days as a mere member of the Board of Education, the cocky businessman became fanatic in his devotion when Thompson, soon after his 1927 victory, chose him the board's president. To Coath was assigned the big job of ridding the schools of its stubborn superintendent, William Mc-Andrew.

Coath relished the assignment. He quickly ordered the board's attorney, James Todd, to study the law books for a technical charge to be made against the bearded educator. With Big Bill's sanction, he asked a former Congressman and professional Anglophobe named John J. Gorman to undertake a full examination of McAndrew's links with the British empire. "We'll get that guy," snapped Iron-Handed Jack.

In the weeks before any action occurred in McAndrew's case, Coath had several chances to practice the role he would play later. When Charles H. English, the schools' playground director, objected to loading his pay rolls with Thompson precinct captains, Coath fired him. Allan B. Pond, former president of the City Club, called Coath "that unspeakable insect in the president's chair." Later Coath summoned 280 principals of elementary schools to a meeting, upbraided them for making speeches before Kiwanis Clubs and threatened to install time clocks in every school. "You're all egotists!" he raved. "You educators must understand that teaching is a business. You are salesmen. Your commodity is education. Some of you are unbearable. You must remember that you are no more than a small cog in a great educational machine!"

By the end of August, all was ready for the grand assault. The charge was insubordination. McAndrew, asserted Attorney Todd, had defied the board and a Supreme Court ruling that clerks in the school offices were to be placed under civil service. "This is the most astounding insubordination," Todd said, "and brands the superintendent unfit to hold his important office."

Todd had more accusations, based on a fat report prepared by Gorman after studying textbooks, speeches of professors at the University of Chicago and of British statesmen, pamphlets issued by the local branch of the English-Speaking Union, records of the Carnegie Foundation, and the files of the anti-British Citizens' Committee on School Histories. McAndrew, stated this voluminous indictment, had recommended certain textbooks that contained pro-British propaganda and omitted the names and exploits of many foreign and native-born heroes of the Revolutionary War, "all for the purpose of promoting propaganda for the English-Speaking Union." He had removed from the school walls the famous picture, "The Spirit of '76," to carry out "his purpose of perverting and distorting the ideals and patriotic instincts of our schoolchildren." He had entered a conspiracy with Charles E. Merriam and Charles Judd, professor of history at the University of Chicago, to "destroy the love of America in the hearts of children by encouraging teachers to attend special classes at Chicago University at which a textbook was used which pictured George Washington as a rebel and a great disloyalist." (Replied Merriam: "This is very funny, but I find the comic strips more amusing.") He was insolent, insubordinate and domineering in his attitudes. He repeatedly absented himself from his office without leave. On these trips he made speeches at never less than $100 a day.

By a vote of six to five, the board voted to dismiss the superintendent, pending a formal trial. McAndrew's lawyers, Francis X. Busch and Angus Roy Shannon, called the charges "preposterous" and declared their client guiltless. They demanded an immediate hearing but Coath, banging with his gavel, set the trial for the next month. Then he hurried to tell Big Bill of the action and Big Bill found occasion to remark, "Those who stand for American ideals are going to run Chicago's school affairs. They represent the will of the people. I have no private war with the King of England, but I want him to keep his nose out of our schools."

The stage was ready for the weird and raucous events that again turned the world's attention to Chicago and its Cowboy Mayor.

2

In the first weeks of the trial there was little excitement. Coath brought a white-silk pennant, with AMERICA FIRST! sewn across it, to the board rooms and affixed it to a staff above the American flag, a step promptly protested by American Legionnaires. Asked what "America First!" meant, Coath grinned and replied, "Gosh, I don't know. You'd better call up Bill. He knows all about such sentiments."

In these early sessions McAndrew sat in the front row of the spectators' section reading a newspaper while minor witnesses droned on and on. His dark eyebrows twitched now and then when someone accused him of arrogant behavior, but mostly he remained unemotional, and once or twice he dozed off.

To set the tone of the trial, Coath summoned Frederick Bausman, a former Washington State Supreme Court justice. Bausman spoke not of McAndrew at all. Instead, he railed at England's efforts to conquer America "not by shot and shell but by a rain of propaganda." Since his retirement from legal duties, said Bausman, a little man with pince-nez spectacles and tousled gray hair, he had traveled all over the country. "I've noticed a lack of patriotic verve," he reported. This was due, he loudly insisted, to British propaganda at Columbia University, the American Library Association, Princeton University, among many others. When Shannon demanded that the peppery little man's testimony be stricken as irrelevant, Coath refused. To set everyone's mind at rest, Frank Righeimer, the former county judge now serving as the board's attorney, announced that despite Bausman's Teutonic name he was born in Pittsburgh and his mother was British-born.

Then, a few days later, came the zealous Gorman. He told of his extensive probing and of the horrendous discoveries he had made and duly reported to Thompson. "The result, Mr. Gorman tells Mayor Thompson, is the uncovering of a plot to feed the American eagle to the British lion," quipped the *Tribune*.

Of all the volumes he had studied, only one, Carl Russell Fish's *History of America*, was good. As for the others in the hands of the schoolchildren—David Saville Muzzey's *History of the American People*, Carlton J. Hayes's *Modern History*, Andrew McLaughlin's *History of the American Nation*, *Story of Our Country* by Ruth and Willis Mason West, William H. Mace's *School History of the United States* and Arthur M. Schlesinger's *New Viewpoints in American History*—they were all filled with sinister alterations and distortions. They minimized, cried Gorman, characters and events and ideals sacred in American history. They contained "the insidious teachings of alienism." "From my examinations I am firmly of the opinion that the purification of our histories and the dissemination of American patriotism can be successfully attained only by the compilation of an entirely new history," declared Gorman.

In vain did Charles N. Noderwell, board president under Mayor Dever, refute most of Gorman's charges. Many of the books had been purchased, said he, in Thompson's second administration. Muzzey's book was not used at all in the schools. Gorman had lifted passages out of context to distort the meanings. The one book approved by Gorman had only six pages on the American Revolution. Day after day Gorman returned to read from the dangerous volumes. Often the sound of his voice lulled board members to sleep and once Coath roused himself to complain, "Something's gotta be done to pep up this trial. I'm beginning to get tired of all this history-book stuff." But Gorman had other things to say.

"Mayor Thompson's fight against these objectionable histories," he orated, "is the fight of a courageous American to restore love and admiration for those who established this Republic. He is not anti-English. He is pro-American. This is not a fight against England or her people. It is a fight for America."

In one curious assertion, Gorman insisted that the history of the American Revolution as written fifty years earlier was the exact truth and that it was impossible to find any facts since that would change matters. He hinted darkly at reasons for Andrew Mc-Laughlin's pro-British sentiments as head of the University of Chicago's history department. "First, he's the brother-in-law of James Angell, president of Yale University. Second, he visited in England a lot. Back in 1918 he went there and although he was not regarded as an important individual by his shipmates, when the vessel docked he was met by a large concourse of people and during his visit he was wined and dined everywhere, even in Windsor castle. The only explanation is that his writings were favorable to the British!"

Professor McLaughlin maintained a dignified silence, but Muzzey, professor of history at Columbia University, slapped a $100,000 libel suit against Gorman. He was descended, cried Muzzey, from a long line of American patriots and two of his ancestors were slain at the Battle of Lexington. Gorman had made fraudulent distortion of paragraphs and sentences to throw Muzzey's writings into a British-favored light. Citing Gorman's charge that Muzzey's book asserted that the capital of Massachusetts during the Revolution was "a center of vulgar sedition," the suit emphasized that Muzzey's actual statement was "To George III's eyes the capital of Massachusetts was a center of vulgar sedition." Muzzey listed other distortions and "canards and unwarranted allegations" made against him, to which Gorman replied loftily, "The professor's libel suit is the last refuge of the coward."

3

On the same day of Muzzey's suit Big Bill swung into the battle on another front.

Now his victim was the Chicago Public Library. He had been informed, he said, that hundreds of books on the shelves in the main building and thousands more in the branch libraries were soaked through and through with British propaganda and un-American statements. He was therefore appointing his good friend and fellow yachtsman, Sport Herrmann, to check into these books and root out all subversive volumes.

Herrmann, the robust sportsman, leaped to his assignment with

Vote for Big Bill the Builder
He Cannot Be Bought, Bossed or Bluffed

CUT OUT THIS PICTURE AND HANG IT IN YOUR WINDOW

(Courtesy, Chicago Historical Society)

Thompson's favorite campaign portrait, by John Doctoroff.

Big and bulky, Thompson makes one of his last campaign speeches.

fists cocked and eyes blazing. If his pal Bill Thompson wanted the library cleaned up, Sport Herrmann, learned member of the library board, was just the man for the job. "I'm gonna burn every book in that there library that's pro-British!" he announced.

"Will you ask for a historian's help in finding the books?" the reporters asked.

"No! I'll be my own judge, after conferring, of course, with Mayor Thompson or with who's gonna be on the investigating committee with me."

"Do you think there's any objection to what you're planning to do?"

"Not a bit of it. The library's supported by public taxes and if this thing of undermining Americanism isn't stopped, the country'll go to pieces, that's all!"

Any book that made less than a hero of George Washington or Abraham Lincoln, thundered Sport Herrmann, would be taken to the shore of Lake Michigan and burned. "There must be thousands of propaganda books in the library system. I'll hunt them out and when I find them I'll burn them on the lake shore."

Carl Roden, head librarian, frowned at this talk, but when he was asked if he would resist Herrmann's plan, he replied, "Resist Mr. Herrmann? Of course not. I am employed by him and the rest of the board, of which he is a member."

Herrmann's promise to burn the books was issued on a Friday and the investigation to determine which volumes were to be the victims was to start Monday. Meanwhile, Clarence Darrow quipped, "When Thompson gets through throwing out books written with a bias in favor of England, in the end he'll have nothing left but fairy tales." The Chicago Methodist Ministers' Conference passed a mock resolution of sympathy for King George III and King George V for "the terrible ordeal through which they have been called to pass by an outrageous asininity." Another resolution was adopted by the Federal Business Association recommending that a language other than English, preferably "Esperanto, without Cockney or English accent," be used in transacting its affairs. Half a dozen Canadian and British mayors wired Thompson to send the undesirable books to them for their libraries. The American Association for the Recognition

THE NEW LEARNING

of the Irish Republic and several German-American organizations sent resolutions of praise. Gail S. Carter, grand dragon of the Illinois Ku Klux Klan, croaked his pleasure and urged Thompson to set out after Catholics and Jews.

Over the week end Herrmann's only trouble came from the county jail's warden, Edward Fogarty, who announced that he would not set the torch to books, as Herrmann had said he would in his capacity as official hangman. But on Monday Herrmann had objections in a stronger form, this time from a lawyer, Edward Bohac, who filed suit for an injunction to restrain the book-burning. Bohac's action brought a denial from Thompson that he wanted a literary pyre on the lake front. Herrmann admitted the book-burning was his own idea and agreed to discard it.

But the damage had been done to the city's reputation, and the legend still persists that Herrmann burned hundreds of books that autumn. He did finally seize four volumes he had heard were seditious. One was *The American Nation,* by Harvard's distinguished historian, Alfred Bushnell Hart; it was dedicated to Theodore Roosevelt but Herrmann insisted it was "dictated by King George." Another was *Practicer of American Ideals,* by Hart and C. H. Van Tyne, and dedicated to George Washington. The two others were Van Tyne's *The Causes of the War of Indepedence* and *The Story of American Democracy,* by Willis Mason West.

How had he come to pick these four? "A fella tipped me off," whispered Sport Herrmann in his best side-of-the-mouth manner. "I can't just remember who the guy was that told me about them but he said these are pretty bad. I haven't got time to read them myself. But I'll turn them over to the Patriots' League or something and let them mark the passages they think are pro-British. Then we'll have something to go on."

The volumes lay unclaimed for several days on his desk, while reporters irritated him with more questions. He was grateful to Roden when the head librarian suggested that perhaps such books could be kept in the library's "inferno," a closet in which obscene books were stored as unfit for general circulation. Herrmann held his post as official censor of books for a few months more, then gave it up to devote more time to his yachting and night-life activities along Randolph Street.*

One more assault was made by Thompson on the library. To the board members he sent a lengthy letter asserting that one of the

---

* In 1930 Herrmann and a friend and business partner, Eugene McDonald, contributed $250,000 to buy books for the library.

library's pamphlets, Herbert Adams Gibbon's "Reading With a Purpose," listed four books that were "biased" and "unfair" and "insulting." He complained that "propaganda pipelines are led out of that reservoir to poison the minds of American citizens."

The reply of the board's president, Andrew J. Kolar, was direct and enlightened. "Even taken at their worst," Kolar wrote, "we believe these books should be supplied to the library patrons so that they may be acquainted with every shade of opinion. In this, the Chicago Public Library is like all other libraries of the world, a depository of human thought. Consequently, much of its contents are contradictory. This exchange and freedom of thought we consider the primary function of a library and in keeping with the American ideal of a free press. Any other course would lead to an arbitrary censorship as detrimental to American political liberty as to American academic thought."

Thompson retorted to this sensible statement with a demand for the trustees' resignations. To a man they refused, and he backed down.

4

He was soon up again, louder than ever, trumpeting a nationwide appeal for all governors, members of Congress, and mayors of cities of more than 20,000 to join his newly launched America First Foundation.

For a membership fee of ten dollars, the prospects could become part of Thompson's movement to "build the coming generation, native and foreign-born, into sturdy defenders of American ideals." The replies came back swiftly. They ranged widely, from enthusiasm to distrust to mockery to anger.

"Were you not so enthusiastically misguided in your campaign against anything British and were it not for your raid on the Chicago Public Library I might consider your proposal seriously," wired Congressman Emanuel Celler of New York. "But your anti-British mania has made you ridiculous in the eyes of intelligent people."

At Davenport, Iowa, Mayor Louis Roddewig said he was in favor of such a foundation and was sending his ten-dollar bill. Cornelius

Vanderbilt, Jr., hearing of the foundation, sent his money and his applause.

"I quite endorse the proposed object of your new crusade," wrote Mayor Elvin Swarthout of Grand Rapids, Michigan, "but I am wondering whether your career guarantees proper leadership. Your persecution of my old college mate, McAndrew, gives me pause. Your proposed holocaust of pro-British literature makes me think of the experience of Charles V with Luther's writing. Then I've been told you are no valiant supporter of the Eighteenth Amendment. Can the blind lead the blind? I'll think further before I send my ten dollars."

From Beloit, Thompson received a reply over the signature of Mayor John Magill: "Wisconsin's pro-British Conservation Commission protects English pheasants introduced into this state to make our loyal Germans dissatisfied with their spareribs and sauerkraut. In the name of 100 per cent Americans, can't you do something about it? Under your starry banner we will fight for the complete extermination of English pheasants, English sparrows and English bulldogs. Don't let King George buy you off!"

Urged to join, too, were Chicago's 6,500 police, the urging gently done at station roll calls.

5

As a respite from the clamor, Thompson journeyed to Washington early in November for a flood-control conference with President Coolidge and a mass rally with delegations from other states enlisted in his flood-control program.

The Chicagoans packed themselves into a ten-car train, each car wrapped with red-white-and-blue bunting. As they departed the Chicago Police Quartet sang, the Tripoli string trio played, and the Murray sisters danced on the train platform. All the delegates— "They're my national legislative assistants," chortled Thompson— wore America First badges. In the capitol they jammed the Mayflower Hotel, singing "America First, Last and Always," cheering Big Bill and shifting lobby furniture about. Thompson showed Coolidge two thick volumes of information about flood-control measures and was cheered when he entered a hearing room where a House committee on flood control was in session. At the conference, Mayor Arthur O'Keefe of New Orleans shouted, "We'll never forget what Bill Thompson did for us," and Leroy Percy, former senator from Mississippi, cried, "Big Bill Thompson, as his friends love to call him, has made some enemies, but he'll never make an enemy in the Mississippi Valley!"

Pleased and gratified, Thompson continued his travels. In Boston, his native city, he made his customary statements about the British before a meeting of the American Association for the Recognition of the Irish Republic. Visiting Bunker Hill, he said, "This little hill? Why, out West we wouldn't even call this a knoll. If the redcoats couldn't get up here, there must have been some tough guys at the top." In New York he whacked at Rupert Hughes's new biography of George Washington. "Hughes is a damned liar. He is a cheapskate trying to get some personal publicity. No, I haven't read his book, but I understand he has a lot of stuff about Washington being a ladies' man and having a lot of affairs. I don't know if he was or what he did, but I do know he won the Revolution and he is the man responsible for our liberties. You can't slam him to me!"

Chicago was free of crime, he insisted. Murders and killings? "That's a lot of newspaper talk!" His city, he said proudly, "is the best city in the whole world. There's no use even trying to compare Chicago with New York."

6

Back in the best city in the whole world, the trial of McAndrew picked up new speed.

Charles Grant Miller, identifying himself as the founder of the Patriots' League to Perpetuate American History, cited hundreds of instances in which he declared that American history writers had taken erroneous views and pro-British views of the principal events of the American past. He named books in which John Hancock was described as a smuggler, Samuel Adams as "a hard-boiled politician" and "the first American political boss" and Patrick Henry as "a gay, unprosperous and unknown country lawyer." Such culprits as David Muzzey and Carlton Hayes and Willis Mason West and Andrew McLaughlin had been wined and dined by the British many times and had promised, over the clink of champagne glasses, to do their best for Great Britain. "Here in Chicago," commented Miller, "I hear that Mayor Thompson's kind of patriotism is sneered at as 'politics in the schools.' Well, I want to see politics, patriotic, virile, American politics active enough to wipe British politics out of our schoolbooks."

One teacher after another, filled with hostility toward McAndrew, the man their union's leader, Margaret Haley, had called a "stooge of the Union League Club and the Chicago Association of Commerce," filed before Coath and the board. In a single day seventeen teachers appeared against McAndrew, while Coath munched pretzels. Some called the superintendent a Simon Legree, a faker and a cruel taskmaster. One said he used flippant language and swore at her. Another told of a visit he paid to her room to give her pupils a music test. After he left she had asked the children to write their impressions of him, and the most frequent were "insolent" and "unkind" and "ungentlemanly." Another testified that McAndrew himself had ordered her to remove from her classroom wall pictures of the Boston Tea Party and the figures in "The Spirit of '76." (Later McAndrew took the stand to say, "I think that pictures showing soldiers in action or appealing to the martial spirit are a bad influence on children, just like cannon and captured war trophies in public displays.") Others criticized his demand that students had to get a grade of 100 in special arithmetic tests before being advanced. When they were finished, Coath glowed. "I cannot but remark," he said, "on the beautiful sentiment of simplicity, honesty of purpose, and integrity demonstrated here today in the hearts of the men and women who testified. It is one of the most gratifying spectacles in the history of my school board experience and I thank God for the real, human, honest people in the Chicago public schools!"

On November 2, Thompson issued his list of Revolutionary War heroes who, by his reckoning, had been neglected and ignored in the

books used in the city's schools. He ordered that the board of trustees advise all teachers of history to give verbal instruction about
these heroes, until such time as a properly revised text could be written. For the Poles there were Pulaski and Kosciusko. For the Germans Von Steuben and De Kalb. For the Irish there was a longer
list, including General Richard Montgomery, who commanded
Washington's northern army, and Commodore John Barry and
General Joseph Reed and Mad Anthony Wayne. Even two American-born heroes had been neglected, said Thompson. One was
Nathan Hale and the other was no less a personage than George F.
Harding's "heroic ancestor," General Abner Clark. "To treat these
and other heroes with the 'contempt of silence' or to desecrate their
memories with the short, slurring references of anti-American historians is an affront to patriotic Americans!"

Next morning McAndrew attempted to present to Coath a
lengthy statement demanding that he be tried on the charge of insubordination and that all other irrelevant matter be discarded.
Coath angrily refused to accept the statement. McAndrew glared,
smoothed his beard and walked out of the hearing room.

This sparked a heated fight between Walter S. Raymer, one of
the pro-McAndrew minority, and Attorney Righeimer. Raymer
promptly asked that the board proceed to prove the charges on which
McAndrew had been dismissed. "I'm tired of being lectured to by
a long-haired gentleman from Seattle and another gentleman from
New York! Let's get to the real concrete propositions!"

"Do you believe that the omission of Kosciusko and Pulaski from
the history books was accidental?" yelled Coath.

"I believe that if these patriots were overlooked it was an error.
We are all human and all of us commit errors."

Righeimer spoke up with a snarl. "Are you willing to omit such
a patriot as Ethan Allen, who said, 'I regret that I have but one life
to give for my country!'"

Loud laughter swept the room. "I object! I object!" cried Attorney Busch. "That was Nathan Hale, not Ethan Allen!"

Unperturbed, Righeimer continued, "When a man teaches that
the revolutionary soldiers were smugglers, bums, pettifogging lawyers and loafers, the Board of Education should refuse to be cowed!"

On this note the hearing adjourned to give the trustees time to make a decision on whether to continue without McAndrew.

7

Throughout the McAndrew trial there reverberated a constant rumble of comment, protest and criticism from all parts of the country and the world.

Many professors and historians struck back, with hard facts and with wit. Professor Frank Cole Babbitt, head of Trinity College's Greek department, informed Big Bill he was on a wrong scent in stressing English influence in the United States: "It's insignificant compared to Greek influence. They're responsible for our texts on mathematics, astronomy and medicine, all our tragic drama and free verse, most of our architecture, our ABCs, not to mention oratory and democracy." Princeton University's Dana Carleton Munro accused Thompson of distortions and quoting parts of statements. "Does he want honest historians to tell lies about the great men of our country?" he asked. Hendrik van Loon saw Thompson as a "dangerous hero," a creature of America's own making, appealing to people who had grievances, "people who are therefore the best of all possible constituents." But he felt there was some logic in Thompson's rantings about the British influences: "As long as one part of the country insists on singing 'Rule Britannia' another part is going to sing 'Deutschland Uber Alles.' As long as one part of the country insists that the Teutonic hymn must not be shouted from Milwaukee beer barrels, it must also refrain from indulging in sentimental ale feasts where George Washington is revered as a British gentleman rather than a first-rate and highly successful rebel."

Tangling with Thompson in a debate in *Forum* magazine, Rupert Hughes, prime exponent of the current history-debunking school of biographers, scoffed at Big Bill's insistence that such words as "rebel" and "traitor" must not be applied to the heroes of 1776. "He might as well have pledged himself the heresy that two and two are four. If you repeat what Washington, Jefferson and Adams actually wrote, you are treason-tainted. But you are a good citizen as long as you stick to Parson Weems. . . . Shall we teach truth or lies? Shall we

teach both sides of great questions or only one? Shall we try to find
out facts and teach them or shall we go on promulgating silly fables?
Shall we try to breed prigs, hypocrites and cads in the name of patriotism, or shall we give to our young the benefits of wisdom,
scholarship and impartiality? Shall we lift education out of politics
or leave it to the mercy of party ferocity? Shall we try to put history alongside arithmetic, geography, astronomy, geology, biology,
chemistry, and physics, or shall we have it written fresh from every
campaign by the aldermen and the bosses? Shall we encourage gentlemen desirous of winning as many votes as possible to plaster with
slander scholars whose one purpose is to recite the facts of the past
for the education and guidance of the present and the future?"

In Great Britain the furor was shrill and often sardonic. All London grinned at a half-page drawing in the *Evening Standard* by the
great David Low depicting "A grand pageant of 100 per cent American history, dedicated to Mayor Thompson of Chicago, who thinks
America has now enough history of her own to dispense with British
assistance." In the pageant, led by "Prohibition" bearing the American flag, marched a long procession of characters including Barbara
Fritchie, Harry K. Thaw, John D. Rockefeller, a Ku Klux Klans-
man, Sacco and Vanzetti, Felix the Cat, the chorus of the Ziegfeld
Follies, Leopold and Loeb, an original "Tin Lizzie" with Henry
Ford at the wheel, and Lon Chaney, then a popular movie star.
Thompson's charges against McAndrew, gasped the newspaper, had
"a distinct element of the fantastic, not to say the grotesque."

William T. Stead, an old authority on Chicago and Chicago politicians—his famed "If Christ Came to Chicago!" had caused a political upheaval in the 1890s—called Thompson, in his *Review of
Reviews*, "the Chicago Farceur." He denied that history taught in
America was pro-British; if anything, it kept alive in the American
mind the conception of Great Britain as "the hereditary enemy." In
Glasgow, university students renamed Thompson "Big Bull" and
dragged him in effigy through the streets.

In the London *Daily Express* the author J. B. Priestley quipped
ironically that Thompson was perfectly right in what he was doing.
"Of course Chicago must be kept 100 per cent American! As long
as you are casting your eye on pro-British books, you had better

throw out Dickens and Shakespeare, an out-and-out King George man of his day. As a thinker you are an anachronism. Your attitude is really an insult to your own country and not ours. Why this deep suspicion of a little praise of another friendly nation? Does it not suggest a lack of confidence in your own country? If the sturdy defenders of American ideals must be kept from any praise of another country, from any knowledge of others and different points of view, there is something very queer about their sturdiness, and about those ideals that they are only ready to defend by being ignorant about others."

In the United States H. L. Mencken, the caustic editor of the *American Mercury*, wired his regrets to Thompson's invitation to come and help fight the British in Chicago. "That is certainly a good show Mayor Thompson is running over there in Chicago," he commented. "I would like very much to go over and see it, but I can't possibly spare the time now." The New York *Times* coined a word to describe the events—"Bigbillism." When the Bronx Chamber of Commerce planned to invite Thompson to be guest of honor at a dinner, the organization's founder, Albert E. Davis, balked the invitation in protest against "Chicago's mountebank mayor." In reply to Thompson's request for support in his purge, the Massachusetts branch of the American Legion, still bitter as in the days after the war, replied with a letter:

You ask our support, you, who in 1918 by your actions would have in political glee seen the supporters and defenders of our national integrity sold out into slavery? You, who in 1918 by your actions gave vent and leadership to that opinion which would have put crepe on our honor door?

You a defender of American institutions? You a patriot? You a defender of the America of yesterday, today and tomorrow? You, who had a great chance in the world's greatest crisis, and failed?

In Chicago, where every newspaper except the *American* deplored and deplored, Rabbi Louis L. Mann of Chicago's Sinai Temple spoke the thoughts of many fellow clergy when he called the McAndrew trial "a farce." "The mayor has made Chicago in its intellectual humiliation second only to Dayton, Tennessee, with its evolution trial." A young editor of the Parker High School newspaper, David Keniston, was nearly suspended for writing in a humor column:

> Rid our city high schools of that horrible British taint.
> Make the history textbook tell things as they ain't.

In a blistering report, the Public School Emergency Committee summed up the opinions of scores of citizens:

Never in so unblushing and brutal a fashion has the spoils system dared to lay its hands upon our public schools. Never have proceedings been so hypocritical and insincere. Never has patriotism been so brazenly invoked to cover up the designs of a plundering crew of political pirates. When they say "America First" they mean "Chicago Last." A crew of political buccaneers, lost to all sense of sportsmanship and fair play, has made a bonfire of the bill of rights while hoisting aloft the picture of George Washington to detract attention from the blow directed at the vitals of real Americanism!

8

Into Chicago, as the board prepared for its final meeting on the McAndrew case, came the young English writer, Beverly Nichols, to see for himself the phenomenon he had heard so much about.

He was ushered into Thompson's suite in City Hall No. 2 on the Hotel Sherman's sixteenth floor. He saw several photographs on the wall of his host's waiting room: one of Thompson as a young man, football tucked under his arm; another with a large pink face above a starched collar; a third of Thompson superimposed on the roof of the City Hall looking down benignly on his constituency; and the fourth a plain and simple photograph of the White House. Near Thompson's starched-collar picture was one of Charles A. Lindbergh and beneath that one a framed poem:

> They asked how I did it
> And I pointed to that Scripture text,

"Keep your light a'shining
A little in front of the next."

When Nichols was led into Thompson's office his eyes noticed a phonograph on a near-by table, and a variety of porcelain figurines on the big desk, little elephants, a Moorish dancer in china—blue, yellow and red—and two girls, in bunchy frocks tied at each waist, a miniature fly on each chest.

Nichols asked questions about King George and Thompson parried. Suddenly the mayor leaped up and pointed over his head. "A friend of mine said it was about time I had a telepho-radio set so I could ring up Buckingham Palace whenever I felt like talking to King George. Here it is! Three rings for the palace. Listen!"

He pressed a button on the small cabinet. There were three rings, then a tinkling tune. The doors flew open and Thompson reached for a bottle of bourbon and two glasses. "Ho! Ho! What a joke on you!" he bellowed.

After Nichols had a highball, he got up to leave. Thompson shook hands, pressed an "America First" pamphlet on him, and yelled, "Nail Old Glory to the masthead and keep her there!"

Later that day Nichols was given a quick insight into the feelings many Chicagoans had for their strange mayor. He had dictated some 300 words of his story about the visit when the hotel stenographer leaped to her feet, threw down her pencil and shut her notebook. "You think I'm going to take down that sort of bunk? I happen to be a one hundred per cent American, and I can tell you that Mayor Thompson's little finger is worth more to me than any Englishman that ever came over here!"

9

On March 14, 1928, Coath's board held its final hearing in the McAndrew case. Only nine spectators lounged in the board room as Attorney Righeimer ended his oration. McAndrew had purged the history books of Light Horse Harry Lee, of Mollie Pitcher, of Ethan Allen and the Green Mountain boys. "And he taught little children to tell falsehoods!" said Righeimer.

A week later the board, by a vote of eight to two, officially ousted McAndrew. Coath smacked the desk with his gavel. "So be it!" he cried, and the case was declared at an official end.

But there were interesting aftermaths.

McAndrew filed suit for $6,000 in back salary and a $250,000 libel suit against Thompson. He dropped them both in 1929 when Judge Hugo Pam officially overturned the board's ruling and declared that McAndrew had been neither insubordinate nor unpatriotic. Until he died in 1937 McAndrew traveled here and abroad. Occasionally he lectured to groups of educators and although he rarely discussed in any detail his Chicago experience he always related an anecdote that Thompson, when asked if he opposed George III or George V, cried, "What? Are there two of them?"

Iron-Handed Jack Coath's powers began to wane shortly after he went on a publicized trip to New York to see a publisher of "patriotic books." In the following May he was through, after trying in vain to persuade the board to award a $1,600,000 contract for a new high school to a firm in which his son, Virgil, was a vice-president. He was replaced by H. Wallace Caldwell, a young Thompson booster, and quickly faded into political obscurity.

And Big Bill? For a while he gloated over his victory. He had won his fight against "American society snobs who would kiss the hem of royalty" and against "international bankers who would make stupendous profits by the cancellation of foreign debts owed America" and against Rhodes scholarships and the "new" historians and all his enemies. In triumph, he ordered that no lions, those symbols of the British empire, should ever be carved on new school buildings while he was mayor. But for the rest of his years his attack on McAndrew would plague him, and he would explain and rationalize and defend and cry out that the "lying newspapers" had used the trial to make Chicago the object of ridicule and laughter all over the world.

25 ||| Thompson's "Jonah Years"

I

IN THE TEEMING OLD NINETEENTH
Ward, home of scores of Italian workers and shopkeepers and alcohol cookers for the infamous Genna clan, the humble ones always spoke lovingly of Guiseppe Esposito, their "Diamond Joe."

All agreed that he was a man of princely benevolences. No child was born or christened without a gift from Diamond Joe. No wedding, no funeral, no street or church festival was complete without the presence of Diamond Joe. On Christmas Day no one went hungry, for in Diamond Joe's famous Bella Napoli Café were miles of spaghetti and tons of hot bread.

A handsome, smiling fellow, and the protector, too, of the Gennas, a fixer for gamblers and vicemongers, and the devoted representative in the murky district of Senator Charles S. Deneen. Such a hold did Esposito have on his voters that in Big Bill's great anti-Deneen triumph of 1920 he was the only Deneen ward committeeman to retain his post.

Now there was to be another primary in this rainy April. Already Esposito had received threatening telephone calls: "Don't run. You'll be sorry." Already two Capone gangsters had visited him in his restaurant: "Get out. Don't do it."

But Esposito had shrugged and replied, "I got to. The senator wants me to run."

He continued his electioneering, paid more calls to the dead and the relatives of the dead, to the new mothers and the hungry ones. And on the night of March 21, 1928, three men in an automobile cut him to pieces with poisoned bullets from sawed-off shotguns. In a gutter in his beloved Nineteenth Ward lay what remained of Diamond Joe. The corner street lamp picked out the glitter of his $5,000 solitaire diamond ring, his belt buckle with his initials in diamonds, and his diamond tie pin and diamond shirt studs.

For whatever reason Diamond Joe was slain—many whispered that he was enmeshed in double crossing and intense rivalry with Al Capone over bootleg profits—his murder set off new violence in an election campaign that came to be forever known as the "Pineapple Primary," and inspired one newspaper cynic to write:

> The rockets' red glare the bombs bursting in air
> Gave proof to the world that Chicago's still there.

In Washington, Diamond Joe's liege lord, Senator Deneen, vowed that when his candidate for state's attorney, Judge John A. Swanson, defeated Bob Crowe in the primary and went on to win from his Democratic rival, he would run down Diamond Joe's killers and send them to the gallows. Swanson affirmed that his zeal would be heavily applied to doing this.

Five days after Esposito was done away with, two bombs were exploded. One, filled with dynamite, demolished the front of Deneen's three-story home on the South Side. Another was hurled outside the home of Swanson. The "Pineapple Primary" grew hotter.

2

Until this final week in March, Big Bill, virtual ruler of a domain of more than 100,000 political jobs in city, county and state, had been cocky about the future.

Only a few months earlier, in the midst of the McAndrew trial, he had taken another junket with Sam Ettelson, the inevitable Chicago Police Quartet, and a crowd of partisans to New Orleans for a flood-control conference. After gaiety and speeches and songs, Louisiana's new governor, Huey Long, had spoken fondly of

Thompson and presented him with a handsome scroll inscribed
to "one of the greatest living Americans."

In drawing up the primary slate when he returned to Illinois
Thompson had great success, forcing a place for Len Small despite
Crowe's protests that he was a weak candidate and for Frank L.
Smith despite the cloud of the Reed investigating committee. The
Deneenites seemed to be without funds and without force. A full
conquest in April seemed certain.

But these bomb explosions now shook the entire Thompson-
Crowe edifice.

"The criminal element is trying to dominate Chicago by setting
up a dictatorship in politics," charged Senator Deneen. "The
'pineapple' industry grew up under the Thompson-Crowe administration," said Swanson. Senator George Norris seriously suggested
to President Coolidge that the Marines then involved in warfare in
Nicaragua be dispatched to Chicago.

His Irish temper up, Crowe issued a statement. He was "satisfied
that the bombings were done by leaders in the Deneen forces . . .
and were done mainly to discredit Mayor Thompson and myself."
And Thompson echoed the accusation, adding the interesting
explanation that Esposito had been slain because he had been unable
to call off federal prohibition agents raiding stills and speak-easies in
the Nineteenth Ward. Among the side-of-the-mouth wiseacres,
some growled that Crowe was right, that the bombs had been thrown
by none other than Ben Newmark, whom Crowe had finally fired
from his job as chief investigator.

3

The bombings and Crowe's astounding statement raised the fever
of the campaign.

The Chicago Crime Commission, which earlier had endorsed
Crowe, now scurried from its own endorsement and called the pugnacious prosecutor "inefficient and unworthy." Businessmen who
had publicly thanked Crowe when he presented figures showing a
decrease in crime during his regime now stood up in their clubs and

denounced him. This minister and that civic group and this rabbi and that former judge arose to accuse him.

At one meeting Edward R. Litsinger, now running for the County Board of Review against Thompson's good friend, Judge Bernard Barasa, asked his audience, "It costs $243,000,000 to run Chicago, and what are we getting?" And the crowd replied "Bombs! Pineapples!" Litsinger, of all the Deneen men, was most vitriolic. When Thompson accused him of moving to the Gold Coast and leaving his aged mother in their old home on Goose Island, a patch of land occupied by low-paid laborers, Litsinger purpled with rage and spoke these words: "This lowdown hound who degrades himself and the city of which he is mayor, is guilty of as false and malicious a lie as was ever uttered in a political campaign. This man, who claims to possess the intelligence and instincts of a human being, digs down in a grave that was closed twenty years ago, and blasphemes the memory of my dear old German mother. This man with the carcass of a rhinoceros and the brain of a baboon!"

Still confident, Thompson hammered at the old issues. He was the standard-bearer for the cohorts of America First! He was for personal liberty and freedom of the individual! He was champion of the waterways, friend of the working man, savior of the weak and the downtrodden! Deneen? "He made deals with the forces of vice when he was state's attorney!" Crowe? "The greatest state's attorney you've ever had!" Litsinger? "The greatest mud-slinger in town!" And always he bellowed that he loved his Chicago!

"We have the biggest city of her age in the world!" he cried. "We have the best people in the world. We have the best health record of any big city. We have the most wonderful parks and the most wonderful playgrounds and the most wonderful school system. Business is good and getting better." When reporters, visiting him only a week after the Deneen and Swanson bombings, asked about crime in Chicago, he puffed smoke from a big cigar and said airily, "Sure, we have crime here. We always will have crime. Chicago is just like any other big city. You can get a man's arm broken for so much, a leg for so much, or beaten up for so much. Just like New York, excepting we print our crime and they don't." Bombings?

"There'll always be bombings just as long as there is prohibition."

He talked of the day when the Lakes-to-Gulf waterway would be finished. He revealed a plan to bring 500,000 excursionists to Chicago in summer: "We'll put them on busses and show them Chicago. Let them come and see for themselves what we are and go home and tell their people Chicago is not the crime-ridden capital of the universe but a fine city to work and live in and going to be still better!"

Albert R. Brunker, head of the Swanson Business Men's organization, complained that Capone gangsters were smashing windows of merchants who refused to join "protective associations." Crowe was introduced at one of his own meetings as "the man who put crime on the run" and loud laughs mingled with the applause. At that, Crowe was the only Thompson man brave enough to speak to members of the City Club, where both he and Big Bill had been roundly denounced. Voters were reminded that even when the homes of Charles Fitzmorris and another Thompsonite, Dr. William Reid, had been bombed a few months back no one was arrested. The Chicago Bar Association recommended that Crowe be beaten, a decision that later caused Crowe to resign from the lawyers' group. Someone with a bent for statistics tallied the number of violent crimes in 1926 and 1927 and found that of the 720 murders in the city and the rest of Cook County, 130 were gang murders, all unsolved. Len Small was blasted for permitting the Ku Klux Klan to hold a meeting on the State Fair grounds and circulars noting his action were distributed by Deneenites to Negro voters. "Ours is a government of bombs, of bums, of grafters and crooked politicians," cried the clergymen. Sam Ettelson was denounced as "Sam Insull's luggage" and Ettelson replied with a reminder that Big Bill Thompson had saved the schools from King George V. And Swanson cried, "Who killed McSwiggin?"

Under the barrage, Thompson quailed. He warned ward committeemen who showed signs of skittering to the Deneen crowd that they would lose all city patronage. He called those who voted for Deneen "damned suckers" and pleaded, "If you think there is something wrong with this town, for God's sake don't swap horses now!" And he growled a new threat. "If Deneen's candidate, Swanson, wins in this election I will resign! I ate regular before I became mayor and I will eat regular after I'm mayor!''

4

All over the city on primary day of April 10 there were reports of sluggings, vote thievery, intimidation and stuffing of ballot boxes. The Thompsonites complained that the Deneenites had imported thugs from Capone's Cicero stable. The Deneen forces retorted that the men coursing the city terrorizing plain citizens bore the unmistakable features of authentic Caponeites and were working for Thompson. In the Bloody Twentieth Ward, domain of Thompson's city collector, Morris Eller, there was murder. Octavus C. Granady, a Negro attorney and war veteran and candidate for ward committeeman against Eller, was standing, toward the end of the day, near a polling place. A car with four men passed. A shot was fired at Granady. He jumped into his automobile and sped away. The assassins and another car with three men pursued him. More shots were fired. Granady's car crashed into a tree. When the police arrived they found a dozen shotgun slugs in his body.*

That night a listless Thompson sat by the telephones in his headquarters. A cigar was clenched between his teeth, his shirt sleeves were rolled high to show elbow-length underwear. No shouting now. No caroling of "America First, Last and Always." Only vote reports, all bad. Small had lost to Louis L. Emmerson, Thompson's "Lop-Eared Lou." Plurality: 440,000. Smith, beaten by Otis F. Glenn by 244,000. Crowe? Swamped by Swanson by 200,000. Even in his own ward, Thompson was defeated for Republican committeeman. Someone asked Big Bill to smile for the news photographers. "Smile? You'll have to tell me a funny story!"

Immediately the reporters wanted to know if he would abide by his threat to resign.

"No, I won't!"

"But you said definitely you'd get out if Swanson beat Crowe."

"Well, now I'm saying definitely that I'm not getting out!"

---

* Four policemen and three gangsters, including James (King of the Bombers) Belcastro were later tried for the murder, and acquitted.

THE WOODSHED

The *Tribune*, of course, insisted that he keep his promise to quit. His defeat, it crowed, was "the work of an outraged citizenship resolved to end the corruption, the machine gunning, the pineappling, and the plundering which have made the state and city a reproach throughout the civilized world." Others hailed the Swanson-Deneen victory as "the dawn of a new day" and "good news for all America." "Chicago may now write 'Paid in Full' across her Big

Bill," jested the New York *Post*. And the Omaha *Bee-News:* "Pardon the query, but will Mayor Thompson proceed now to sing Small and eat Crowe?"

5

This year, which had started with a ruddy glow, was destined to be what Thompson himself called his "Jonah year."

A special grand jury investigation into election violence and crime sprang up with Frank J. Loesch, the grizzled old crime fighter, in charge. Loesch sought to tear into the tangled alliance between the criminals and the politicians and sometimes ripped open a seam that showed that not all the wrongdoers were in the Thompson camp. He wanted to know if Al Capone had helped the Thompsonites, but got no really satisfactory replies. Homer K. Galpin, head of the County Republican Central Committee, chose to evade all questions and fled the city, spending his summers in the Wisconsin north woods and his winters in Florida until he acquired the nickname of "Homeless Homer."*

In June Thompson went with other delegates to the Republican National Convention in Kansas City, determined to draft the reluctant Calvin Coolidge for the Presidential nomination. His determination exceeded his meager influence and he frowned heavily as the convention named Herbert Hoover, a man he considered too internationalist-minded for his patriotic tastes.

After returning from the convention, Bill had less than a week to reflect on his low state when Judge Hugo Friend in Circuit Court announced he was ready to hand down his decision in the *Tribune's* long-fought expert-fees suit. The case had been on trial for over two years, had involved over 100 witnesses, 11,000 pages of testimony and 3,000 exhibits. Those who had attended or read of the case in detail learned secrets of how the Thompson machine had functioned. They heard that for a short time after Thompson had been elected in 1915 he paid the usual $50 daily fee to qualified experts

---

* He finally returned in 1932 and was named a state tax commissioner.

who examined properties for condemnation in connection with civic improvements. But soon new arrangements were made, by which the appraisers received a percentage of the value of the property they examined. Experts hired by Thompson began to raise the values to garner higher fees. Arthur S. Merigold, a realtor who was a friend of Thompson's father, managed to get nearly $600,000 in two years under the new system; Merigold had been carried on the pay rolls, said witnesses, as "Mary Gold." Other experts on such big projects as the Ogden Street highway had averaged $1,500 a day. Invariably, said witness after witness, they presented their bills to the city whenever the Thompson political organization was pressed for funds. Paid with vouchers signed by George Harding, then city comptroller, the experts—at least the five involved in the suit—had pocketed part of the money and used the rest to pay bills owed by the Thompson organization.

In a lengthy decision, Judge Friend traced this conspiracy. He found that in their quest for power and political control of the city, Thompson, Harding and Michael Faherty had employed certain men who were used as conduits for passing money to Thompson's political machine. "All were working for one purpose, to build up the organization and elect men who would support the policies of William Hale Thompson. . . . As a result, certain of the defendants and political adherents of Thompson were personally enriched and the heavy obligations for political purposes incurred by Thompson, Harding and their associates . . . were reduced by the vast amounts contributed by the experts, directly and indirectly, to the Thompson organization."

In view of all this chicanery, Thompson and his codefendants, declared the judge, were obliged to return to the city the sum of $2,245,604.

Thompson grew hysterical when he heard of the ruling. "They've ruined me! They're going to take everything I've got! The sonsofbitches have ruined me!" Harding, a cooler man, arranged with a bank to use his and Thompson's real-estate holdings as collateral for a $3,000,000 bond while their lawyers, confident of a reversal in the higher courts, filed an appeal.

6

Shaken by the decision and unnerved by the strain of other woes since the devastating defeat of April, Big Bill reacted as other such men of bravado and bluster often do. He broke down physically and mentally. He drank constantly, gabbled hysterically and spoke irrationally, stared through rheumy eyes at men he had known for years and called them by wrong names, raged against enemies who had long ago faded out of politics. Alarmed, friends spirited him away to the secluded estate of his friend, Carter Blatchford, in the heavy forests of northern Wisconsin.

In the City Hall Samuel Ettelson now became "unofficial mayor." He immediately touched off resignations and rumors of resignations.

First to leave the cabinet was Comptroller Charlie Fitzmorris. He quit early in July to become an executive for George Getz's coal company. Although he issued no explanation for his action, it was well known that he had been able to see Thompson for conferences only four times since the first of the year, that he had refused to sign vouchers to permit Mike Faherty to spend $647,948 for preliminary work on a proposed subway, that Fitzmorris and Ettelson bitterly hated each other.

Then Ettelson, obviously in a maneuver to placate the *Tribune*, forced the ouster of Police Chief Hughes, who was in a hospital with arthritis. He sped to Thompson to secure the shaken Big Bill's approval before laying on Hughes's hospital bed a statement of resignation. Hughes signed it and in his place went Captain William F. Russell, known as an "honest cop" and a devoted friend of Alfred (Jake) Lingle, a police reporter for the *Tribune*.

During his regime "Go-Get-'Em" Hughes had been criticized for big talk and little action. For a man with public orders to drive out the criminals in ninety days, he was in a frustrating position, since the very ones who had issued the directive were least interested in his attempts to carry it out.

Only once had Hughes asserted himself in his anti-criminal campaign. This occurred late in 1927, while the Thompsonites were scrubbing their America First slate of candidates to present them clean and angelic to the populace. When Capone, barred from visiting Los Angeles on a vacation trip, announced he was returning, Hughes snapped, "Capone can't come back to Chicago." He posted a twenty-four-hour guard at Capone's Prairie Avenue home and Capone was obliged to stay away for nearly a year, establishing meanwhile a lavish residence in Miami. His lieutenants carried on ably for him. In Chicago they forced more and more businessmen to join their associations. In Brooklyn his gunmen disposed of Frankie Yale, the professional assassin who had dared to doublecross Capone by supporting a pretender to the throne of the Unione Sicilione, presided over by Antonio Lombardo, Capone's man. In this summer of 1928 Lombardo himself was made the object of Yale's avengers, for on a warm September day they killed him at State and Madison streets, the world's busiest corner.

7

Slowly Thompson recovered from his breakdown. He stopped all drinking and smoking. He took walks with Blatchford and rare visitors. He read no newspapers, took long naps, seldom discussed politics. Only one reporter from Chicago succeeded in reaching him in his exile, the *Herald-Examiner's* John Dienhart.

"I feel fine now," Big Bill told Dienhart. "I'll be back soon to make Chicago hum again. I'll have to prove to the world that we don't have a crime-ridden city. Have to build more schools, more playgrounds. Need clean alleys. When I get back to Chicago we will organize the team and start down the center to the goal—and that goal is to make Chicago the greatest, the most prosperous, the most beautiful and happy city in the world."

In September he returned. "There is a lean look to his jaw and a freshness to his countenance," reported June Provines in the *News*, "that reflects the outdoor life of the last two months." He ate breakfast in the Hotel Sherman's Celtic Room, returning the stares of other diners with a quick smile. He posed willingly for photographers, waving his sombrero, picking up his telephone, shaking hands with well-wishers. "I'm back to build the town and work for prosperity. I'll be going in and out of town, but I'll always be working for the prosperity of Chicago."

But the lassitude continued.

There were a few bright spots—his new schools superintendent, William J. Bogan, officially eliminated all of the "pro-British" history books of which Thompson had complained except Gordy's, and President Coolidge signed a bill appropriating $300,000,000 for flood-control measures. But when his 300-man business committee disbanded in November, Thompson merely shrugged. When Swanson became state's attorney with nearly 165,000 votes over Judge William Lindsay, Thompson uttered no comment. When Emmerson defeated Floyd E. Thompson, he mumbled, "Well, Lou'll make a pretty good governor, I guess." When a vast scandal, redolent with graft, pay-roll padding and looting, was discovered in the Sanitary District, Thompson reminded any who cared to listen that he had nothing to do with that governmental unit. When Mike Faherty's $26,000,000 bond issue for local improvements was rejected by the voters, Thompson expressed his bewildered regrets to Faherty. When Al Capone, on St. Valentine's Day in 1929, finally consolidated his fantastic empire by slaughtering seven henchmen of his last major rival, George (Bugs) Moran, Thompson expressed little interest, except to remind the new state's attorney of his pledges to wipe out crime and murder. When ninety-five clubs on the city's North Side presented a joint resolution that he resign, he bristled and rumbled, "No, not me."

8

Early in 1930 Big Bill had to bestir himself to the ugly reality that Chicago was in a desperate financial state. The Great Depression was under way and the city's debts far surpassed its income. An audit by a bankers' committee headed by Silas Strawn, former president of the Chicago Bar Association, reported that the city had spent $23,000,000 above the income it could expect from taxes. Another contributing factor to the weakened condition of the city's finances was the recent reassessment of property in Cook County, which had deprived the local governments of income for over a year and, worse yet, had lopped off some $300,000,000 in valuations on buildings and land in the Loop.

The reassessment was, in Thompson's eyes, the prime reason for the crisis. "This huge sum which was lifted off the Loop was crushed down upon the bungalows and small stores in outlying districts," he told the city council.

Whatever the reason, teachers, policemen, firemen and public employees faced payless paydays. Delegations of workers visited Thompson's office but failed to find him in. A demonstration of local Communists, carrying signs reading SOCIALISTIC PROSPERITY IN THE SOVIET UNION and POVERTY IN CAPITALISTIC COUNTRIES, was broken up in front of the city hall by mounted policemen yelling, "Move along, you're tying up traffic. We want wages, too!"

Strawn's committee of bankers set up a $20,000,000 emergency pool but refused to let the city have access to it unless the committee could control expenditures. But Thompson made no reply. H. Wallace Caldwell, his president of the Board of Education, attacked Strawn for his "hidden motives." Finally, however, Thompson was forced to yield. He agreed to Strawn's plan to sell tax anticipation warrants totaling $74,000,000, and thereby surrendered part of his jealously held power. "The reformers are responsible for it all," he muttered. "They're trying to wreck my administration."

Again he became ill. He stayed in bed for weeks in his home, sometimes leaving it to ride in his open touring car from which he waved weakly to people on the streets. Even mention of King George failed to excite him. "I don't care about King George. I just agree with George Washington that we ought to keep out of foreign entanglements and mind our business."

9

Thompson was not yet free of the shadowy links between his City Hall and Al Capone's underworld.

After the slaying of Moran's men on St. Valentine's Day—"Only the Capone gang kills like that," the terrified Moran had mumbled—Chief Bill Russell intoned ancient words: "It's a war to the finish. I've never known of a challenge like this, but now that the challenge has been made, it is accepted. We're going to make this the knell of gangdom in Chicago."

Gangdom was unimpressed. Not long after "Machine Gun Jack" McGurn, Capone's ace killer, won his freedom in a trial stemming from the Moran gang massacre, there occurred a new murder to challenge the hapless Russell.

This was the slaying of his close friend, Jake Lingle, the *Tribune* reporter, on June 9. When he was shot to death in the Illinois Central Station underpass at Randolph Street and Michigan Avenue, he was instantly portrayed as "an arch enemy of the underworld." But this picture was soon smeared completely as investigation revealed Lingle to be a good friend not only of Police Chief Russell, but Gang Chief Capone, the man whose Yes or No was final to underworld supplicants for special favors. Jake, a $65-a-week reporter, was discovered to have a real income of $60,000 a year, an $18,000 summer home, heavy investments in the stock markets and an elaborate suite of rooms in one of Chicago's best hotels.

Bill Thompson could derive little satisfaction from the uproar created, for the *Tribune* itself published the exposures of Lingle's activities and demanded a full investigation. When the inquiry into Lingle's death* further disclosed him to be a kind of "unofficial police chief," Thompson was forced to demand Russell's resignation. Then he appointed John H. Alcock, known as the police department's "Iron Man," and, as if the idea had just occurred to him, issued an edict: "Drive the crooks and criminals out of Chicago." Before long Alcock had his hands full trying to find the three robbers who held up Mrs. Thompson and escaped with $10,000 worth of jewelry after beating her chauffeur. Thompson demanded that Alcock arrest the thieves. Through underworld sources, the chief managed to get the gems back and finally put three men on trial for the crime, but all were acquitted.

One other gangland affiliation was laid open before the summer ended. In the St. Valentine's Day massacre, Capone had given warning to every Moran ally. One of these was Jack Zuta, who had switched his allegiance from Capone to become general manager of all brothels and dives in Moran's domain. For a time Zuta also was

---

* In 1931 a St. Louis gunman, Leo Brothers, was sentenced to prison for fourteen years for Lingle's murder. He was released after ten years, and died in 1950.

suspected of having planned Lingle's slaying. Gunmen tried to cut him down in State Street while he was being escorted by police from an interrogation into the Lingle murder on July 1. A month later, they succeeded. Zuta had fled Chicago, but his enemies found him in a summer hotel in Delafield, Wisconsin. As he stood in the hotel's dance pavilion, dropping nickels into an electric piano, five men strode in. One carried a machine gun, another a rifle, and three had pistols. Zuta was riddled with bullets and slugs. In his desks and safety-deposit boxes, police found his membership card in the William Hale Thompson Republican Club of Chicago, a canceled check for $500 paid to the club, a deputy sheriff's card, records of loans to judges, including Emmanuel Eller, son of the boss of the Bloody Twentieth Ward, to Republican ward committeemen and minor city officials, to the mayor of suburban Evanston.

Again there were demands that Big Bill give up, resign, leave forever. Again he replied, "No, I won't quit. I'm not finished yet, and don't let anyone think I am."

26 ‖‖ The Beginning of the End

I

RUMORS AND COUNTER-RUMORS CON-
tinued to flit through the city. To halt them, Sam Ettelson proposed
that Thompson declare his intention to run again for mayor—or not
to run. With a boy's petulance, Thompson refused to commit himself. He argued that he had to wait for the Supreme Court ruling on
the experts-fees decision, that he wanted to see the results of the
November Senatorial contest between Medill McCormick's widow,
Ruth Hanna McCormick, and the pink-whiskered Democrat, J.
Hamilton Lewis. "Let's wait a while," he grumbled. "Maybe I'll
know better."

Meanwhile he busied himself with other activities. He went sailing more often and made frequent use of the Illinois Athletic Club
swimming pool. He went to Nantucket with his wife, returning
with a story of having caught 150 pounds of bluefish in three hours
with a hook made by Mrs. Thompson from an ordinary hairpin. He
staged a "Chicago Day" for his philosophical mentor, William Randolph Hearst, after the publisher had been expelled from France for
printing the details of an Anglo-French treaty in his newspapers;
"one of the foremost patriots in our land," Thompson called Hearst.

Late in September he strolled into the Republican headquarters.
"I've come back ready to scrap side by side with my fellow Republicans to do my part for the election of our whole ticket," he announced. "I'll lift every pound, every ounce that's in my power,
and if we all do that there can be no doubt of the result."

Within a month he reneged on his promise. Earlier, in the primary

318

contest between Deneen and Mrs. McCormick, he had worked hard for her in spite of his violent antipathy toward the *Tribune* and any member of the *Tribune* family. In her hour of victory Mrs. McCormick said she did not want the vote of Thompson or any of his friends. This statement infuriated Big Bill, and now despite the protestations of George Harding and other party chiefs he publicly bolted from the McCormick supporters and announced his support of Lewis. He gave as another reason for his defection Mrs. McCormick's support of the Prohibition laws. "Hundreds of thousands will join me in casting their votes against anyone who indorses such vicious and insane legislation which has brought such terrific suffering on the people of the nation!"

Among those who disagreed with Thompson was his inveterate adherent in the Negro districts, Oscar de Priest, by now the only man of his race in the House of Representatives. He threw doubts on Thompson's sanity. "I will pay no attention to the ravings of Bill Thompson and I shall advise the voters to do the same. I propose to spend the rest of the time until election advising our people to pay no attention to his ravings. No sane man, unless ill advised or sick, would ask the colored people to vote for a Democrat."

Thompson, alienated from his old supporters and cronies, was a pathetic figure as he shuffled, day after day, into the Hotel Sherman's Celtic Room, where the Democratic strategists gathered for lunch. Once, as he passed their round table, he smiled at them through their cigar smoke, and said, "Hello, boys, I'm for J. Ham and I'm wet." But the politicos stared back and someone replied, "Well, who cares?"

2

Into this bleakness came flashes of welcome light.

On October 23, Michael Faherty, who had entered a separate appeal from Judge Friend's decision in the experts' fees case, was absolved of all conspiratorial guilt by the Illinois Supreme Court. The high justices ruled that nothing in the prolonged trial had proved Faherty received any of the money personally, and that the experts who had contributed heavily to the Thompson political organization had a perfectly legal right to do so.

Two days later the court made a similar reckoning in the appeal of Thompson and Harding. Neither, stated its unanimous decision, had actually conspired to milk the city of funds for political purposes: "All the circumstances relied on as proof that Thompson and Harding were members of an alleged conspiracy and were guilty of intentional, deliberate and wrongful conduct, fall short of the mark."

Technically and legally, Thompson and his associates were guiltless. But, in carefully chosen language, the high court chided them for their negligence, indifference to reports of waste and extravagance, and failure to stop mishandling of city funds: "Reviewing the proof in its strongest light, it can only indicate that these defendants after notice should have known that a large amount of fees was paid to the experts and that they should have taken some action to prevent further payments. The proof amounts to . . . nonaction on the part of these defendants in their failure to prevent further payment being made."

The *Tribune* had lost its strenuous fight in the courts. Thompson exulted, and in this moment of exultation he spoke precisely the words his political teacher, the now hated Fred Lundin, had uttered when he was found not guilty of graft and plunder of school funds in 1923. "Truth crushed to earth shall rise again!" thundered Thompson, and again and again he lifted his highball glass to toast the day when he would see the end of his newspaper foe.

So wild was his jubilation that he dictated a long and vitriolic speech against the *Tribune*, intending to deliver it at a Lewis rally. Before he could make the address, he was stricken with appendicitis. But he refused to be moved from his hotel to a hospital until Richard Wolfe, over the objections of Sam Ettelson, agreed to read the speech. "Atta boy, Dick," grunted Thompson. "I'm ready to go now," he said, turning to his doctors.

All that day banners and placards in the Loop advertised that Thompson would "pay his respects to the Chicago *Tribune*." An atmosphere of excitement pervaded the Olympic Theater when Wolfe appeared, manuscript in hand, to announce that he would read the sensational speech. The diatribe, long and rambling and

filled with half-truths and innuendo, was considered so vituperative
that no newspaper printed it in full. Among other things, it accused
the *Tribune*, by inference, of responsibility for the assassination of
Abraham Lincoln, repeated apocryphal stories about the *Tribune's*
founder, Joseph Medill, narrated the troubles other mayors had with
the newspaper, and challenged the *Tribune* to try to harm him. "I
leave the matter in your hands and I will accept the consequence of
telling the truth, and from my nine years' experience on a cow ranch
and my ability to handle a gun I confidently believe that I will not
go alone should one of their cowardly attacks be made upon me. . . . "

Big Bill, recovering from his operation in Passavant Hospital, was
certain he had struck the *Tribune* a serious blow, and soon his "death-
bed speech" appeared in pamphlets which were sold for a dime
each. He was still in the hospital when Lewis overwhelmed Mrs.
McCormick by nearly 750,000 votes, and he chortled to his visitors
that he and his speech had helped the Democrat win.

3

When Thompson left the hospital, he had a scheme for bringing
"unprecedented prosperity" to Chicago. This was to be done, he
proclaimed, through a lottery by which tradesmen and public
alike would profit. By this plan tradesmen would buy coupons
from the city and give one with each twenty-five-cent purchase
in the four months of a "prosperity drive." Holders of the
numbered coupons could win $100,000, $50,000, $25,000, or one of
16,500 prizes of $50 each, for at least $1,000,000 would be raised
through the merchants' immense business in the specified period.
He proposed that three sixty-foot glass towers be built in Grant Park
to hold the coupons, but Judge Walter P. Steffen refused permission.

Then Horace J. Donnelly, Federal Post Office Department solici-
tor, called the plan a lottery and barred any coupons from being sent
through the mails. Thompson dispatched two young aides, Samuel
J. Golan and Carl J. Appel, to Washington and this pair induced
Donnelly to reverse his judgment. When Colonel Isham Randolph
criticized the plan, Thompson elected the members of the Chicago
Association of Commerce, which Randolph headed, to "the vicious

circle of those who would put our people on the British dole." Early
in December, with the drive progressing feebly, he clashed with
Superintendent Bogan because that dignified gentleman refused to
let schoolteachers distribute handbills advertising the drive to children. Denouncing Bogan as "heartless and with a head filled with
impractical ideas," Thompson assigned policemen to pass out the
handbills. They read: "Come on, boys and girls! Let's go for Chicago! It's teamwork that counts! We will pull the old town out of
the rut she is in and bring back good times!" A few days later, with
response to his plan fading fast, he declared he would enlist the aid
of the occult to spur the campaign. "I'm going to go to a medium
who's in touch regularly with the spirit of Grover Cleveland. I'll
tell the medium to get in touch with Cleveland and I'll tell him,
'Grover, you were President of the United States during a hard-time
period. We're going to have our drawing here in Chicago in our
million-dollar prosperity drive. Now I want you to pick the winning numbers.' I'll get the numbers and I'll write them down on a
piece of paper. And nobody but me will know what those winning
numbers are!" This brought a ready and indignant reply from
C. A. Burgess, president of the Illinois State Spiritualists Association. "No recognized medium will do this!" he snapped. "Our organization won't permit interfering in family affairs or love affairs
or giving tips on the races or promoting games of chance."

In the end, which came within a few months, the drive fell some
$950,000 short of the one-million mark. Not a single Loop merchant
would participate. Sadly, Thompson called the whole thing off and
postponed its resumption indefinitely "until such time as the opposition has been withdrawn and the prosperity drive may be the success that we planned it to be."

4

All through the uneven, uncertain months of 1930 his loyal city
prosecutor, James W. Breen, had sounded out ward committeemen about supporting Thompson for another term. Thirty-three
of the fifty powerful individuals leaned toward Thompson. "I

will lay my record down along with that of any candidate," Big
Bill told these worthies on December 20. "Who has a better
right to be the World's Fair mayor? Has anybody built as many
bridges? Has anybody widened more streets? I promised to stop
them teaching in the public schools that George Washington was
a rebel and a traitor! I promised to straighten the Chicago River
and settle the traction problems! I kept my promises!" And the
committeemen, loyally overlooking the discrepancies, shouted,
"You tell 'em, Bill!" Eleven days later, Big Bill officially filed his
petition for candidacy. His slogan, said he, would be: "Jobs, not
charity, for the unemployed!"

Thompson's action sent angry tremors again through the Republican ranks. Even George Harding, loyal for so many years, deserted and drew in line behind Municipal Judge John H. Lyle, who
had opposed Thompson as a member of the city council. The
Deneen forces, weakest of the factions, chose a young alderman,
Arthur F. Albert, who also had fought Thompson in the City Hall.
Charles Barrett, the powerful member of the Board of Review, had
aspirations too but quickly withdrew when Thompson, reading of
his ambitions, issued an open letter starting: "Tie on your hat,
Charlie! You're going for a ride!"

Declaiming against his onetime ally, Bernard W. Snow, new chair-
man of the party's central committee, for joining Harding in Judge
Lyle's behalf, Thompson cried, "Thank God! I'm rid of the bosses!"
With his old style and old enthusiasm, he tore into the fray.

From Thompson's first meeting on January 17 in the Hotel Sherman it was evident he would fight the hard, flamboyant and snarling
fight. And it was clear that Chicago was in for another political
supercircus, an extravaganza that would becloud the basic issues and
raise another world-wide chuckle at the antics of her windy politicians. Prior to the rally rumors had spread that Thompson was too
ill to appear, that he would appear to announce his withdrawal, that
he had already withdrawn and left for the north woods again. Yet
here he was, more wan than usual, in a neat gray suit with a scarlet
necktie setting off his tan shirt.

"I am not dead yet, and I am not sick any more!" he bawled, when
the 5,000 men and women in the crowded ballroom had ceased their

cheering. "I am not withdrawing yesterday, today or tomorrow, no matter how many lies you'll hear about me! I have 250,000 loyal friends in Chicago! Dead or alive, they'll vote for me!"

"Hit 'em hard, Bill! Give 'em hell, Bill! Come on, you cowboy!"

Thompson grinned. He picked up from a near-by table a leather horse halter and held it up to the audience. "Some say your mayor is a circus man. Well, I'd rather be a circus man than an undertaker!" Holding the halter aloft, he continued, "What's the real issue of this campaign? It's whether you're going to elect a mayor who is subservient to the people, or whether you're going to elect a mayor who wears a newspaper collar!"

He swung the halter. There were cheers and whistles.

"Tell me the name of the candidate who won't take orders from a newspaper!" he howled.

"Bill Thompson!"

"Where would this cheap judge be without his newspaper publicity, his cheap newspaper publicity?"

"In the sewer!"

Swinging the halter, Thompson asked, "Where will this halter lead if Lyle's elected?"

"The *Tribune!*"

"And now—" he pretended to pick up another halter—"here's a halter for Lil Arthur! He's against all Thompson ever did! Well, if you want a wrecker for mayor, take Lil Arthur! If he's elected, he'll put this halter around his neck and where will it lead?"

"The *Daily News!*"

"Good! You know more about this business than I do. But you're right! You can fool some of the people some of the time, but you can't fool any of the Thompson people any of the time!"

Furnished with ideas by Wolfe and adding a few of his own, Thompson made full use of the stage of Sport Herrmann's Cort Theater. Not content with mere speeches, he used animals in his noon rallies. Outside the theater paraded an elephant with a sign: STAMP PROHIBITION OUT OF THE G.O.P.! VOTE FOR WILLIAM HALE THOMPSON. Behind the elephant was a shaggy camel, its sign reading: I CAN GO EIGHT DAYS WITHOUT A DRINK, BUT WHO THE HELL WANTS TO BE A CAMEL! Two side-show barkers shrilled, "Spend twenty-five cents! Come inside and see ten acts of swell vaudeville and learn the real issues of the campaign!"

The customers who thronged inside first saw a movie. Its title was "Chicago, the Home of Thompsonism," and it displayed the wonders Thompson had wrought in the building of bridges, paving of streets, establishment of playgrounds, and digging of sewers. It ended with a scene of an old-style saloon with a jovial bartender dispensing schooners of beer.

Then the "vaudeville" came. First, a scrawny youngster astride a burro, sent to Thompson by Republican well-wishers in New Mexico; the beast was led by a seedy man bearing a sign: CHICAGO DAILY NEWS. Then a pale man on a mule, led by a tramp in tattered clothes, his sign reading: CHICAGO DAILY TRIBUNE. Finally out rode Big Bill himself, atop a sleek black charger; he was dressed in a cowboy suit and a ten-gallon hat, and a long cigar stuck out of his mouth.

As the trio lined up the boy chirped, "I want to be mayor! I'm against Big Bill and everything he's done, but I don't care. I know he reduced milk one cent a quart! But I don't care! I know he widened the boulevards and built bridges and increased land values. But I don't care!"

Big Bill removed the cigar and jerked his thumb at the boy. "Why, he must have been running around with Eva Tanguay when she sang that song, 'I Don't Care!'"

The pale man whined, "I'm the judge, but I wanna be mayor. I've rid the city of all the crooks!"

"You have?" exploded Thompson. "Well, where are the crooks?"

"Why, they're with the politicians!"

"And where are the politicians?"

"Why, they're with me!"

At some of the theater meetings he was confronted by hecklers. During one of his speeches he finished his act with the halter, then said, "Thank God, we have got one real friend in the newspaper business! He's a Democrat and his name is William Randolph Hearst!" A man threw two eggs at him, missing with both, but yelling, "And he's got a halter around your neck, you lying skunk!" The man was pummeled by those around him until he was finally rescued by policemen.

At every meeting the first one hundred women received silk sofa pillows with stenciled pictures of Big Bill. Each time there was denunciation not only of Lyle and Albert, but, of course, of King George—"Who benefited from Prohibition? Did you ever hear of an Italian or German or Spanish or Scandinavian rum fleet? Who owns the rum fleets which are peddling hundreds of million dollars worth of poison booze off the American coast? The British! In Canada they tell the people to vote wet and let Uncle Sam pay the taxes! Let us change the situation and tell the King to go to hell!" At each rally there stood the Chicago Police Quartet to sing "America First, Last and Always," and "Big Bill the Builder" and a new ditty that went:

> "Happy days are here again,
> The gang is feeling swell again.
> The mayor's coming back again,
> Happy days are here again.
> He was out for a while,
> But now he's back with a smile.
> And he'll shove the others all about,
> Just like they took his appendix out!"

5

Of Thompson's two rivals, Lyle was the more vociferous and the most active.

In his courtroom he had started a campaign to classify gangsters as vagrants and had ordered their arrest on sight. Most of the big leaders and many of the minor ones simply scurried out of town, to homes in Florida or California. "The idea of these crooks walking around Clark and Randolph streets and through the City Hall with revolvers sticking in their pockets, free from molestation, is an insult and a challenge to the citizens of Chicago," stormed the indignant jurist.

He charged that Al Capone had contributed $150,000 to Thompson's 1927 campaign and was doing as handsomely in this one. He waved machine guns, bombs, revolvers and sawed-off shotguns at his meetings and cried, "Look at these! They are the fruit of William Hale Thompson's administration!" He threatened to arrest Capone if the gang leader showed up in town. "I lay at the door of the Thompson administration every murder by gangsters in the last twelve years," he declared. "The gangsters are gnashing their teeth and frothing at the mouth. They are stopping at nothing to defeat my election. They are using dastardly means to discredit my candidacy."

When a Charles S. Smith filed a suit charging that Thompson had turned over to the American Red Cross only $18,000 of the $140,000 collected from schoolchildren and their parents for the victims of the 1927 Mississippi flood, Lyle said, "I charge that Jumbo, the flood-relief quack, cannot and dare not explain what he has done with the money." Thompson slapped Lyle with a $100,000 libel suit, and angrily replied, "I don't care about name calling but he has attacked my integrity and I'd like to knock this loony judge down, kick him in the face and kick hell out of him!"

This expression of Thompson's strong feelings evoked from Lyle a bitter description of his adversary. "The people have grown tired of this blubbering jungle hippopotamus defending his gangsters and crooked contractors by slobbering insults against the people of Chicago. He calls me loony. Did you ever see a lurching, shambling imbecile with the flabby jowls of a barnyard hog, whose diseased brain didn't defend its own lunacy by snarling at others?"

Such an outburst prompted the Baltimore *Sun* to comment, "Why does not Chicago rise as one man, push all the aspirants into the drainage canal, and select a man from a deaf and dumb asylum, if only as a measure of ear drum conservation?" A psychiatrist, Dr. John W. Hall, offered to serve on a commission to test the sanity of each. "I could serve because I agree with both of them. Their speeches would serve as fine clinical material."

6

Soon Thompson picked up his enemies' cry of "Beat Thompsonism!" and distributed thousands of handsome rotogravure sections labeled THOMPSONISM!

"If Thompsonism is the issue, it is the greatest asset the city possesses today. While others talk, Thompson ACTS. Others promise, he PERFORMS. Many start things, he FINISHES them. Thompsonism means progress, growth, development. It has been the greatest single force in the progress of this great city and, in spite of the efforts of two powerful newspapers, Thompsonism will carry Chicago to a position of power and influence second to no other city in the world." Page after page pictured bridges, new streets, schools. "WOULD YOU vote to do away with the modern schoolhouses and put the children back in portables? WOULD YOU KILL THE BOOSTER SPIRIT AND HELP THOSE WHO KNOCK YOUR CITY?" There were photographs of Albert, haltered to the Daily News building, and of Lyle tied to the Tribune Tower, and an idealized portrait by John Doctoroff, a noted Chicago painter, of Thompson: "The man who wears no halter but is guided by the will of the people."

Against the *Tribune* Thompson issued a booklet called "THE TRIBUNE SHADOW—Chicago's Greatest Curse." In it was a statement by Daniel A. Serritella that Al Capone helped to settle a pending strike of delivery men and that the *Tribune's* editor and publisher, Colonel Robert R. McCormick, had thanked him. (Replied Colonel McCormick: "I arrived late at a publishers' meeting. Capone walked in with some of his hoodlums. I threw him out and after that I traveled around in an armored car with one or two bodyguards. Capone didn't settle anything. And he didn't take over the newspapers as he wanted to do.") An especially interesting display in this document were three photographs of Thompson, loose-lipped and sleepy-eyed and jowly, that had appeared in the *Tribune*, and three by commercial photographers. The latter, greatly retouched, showed Thompson as smooth-faced, handsome, with hair neatly combed, not the slightest trace of a jowl, no double chin, no lines of dissipation. At the time a reporter for the Kansas City *Star* caught Thompson in a relaxed moment and described him as "a picture of sluggish content . . . ponderous, pot-bellied, heavy-jowled, and saggy from ruddy, mottled cheeks, with puffiness beneath twinkling eyes and with soft, fat hands."

Above the hubbub the most eulogistic appraisals of Thompson came from the Negro wards, where many still regarded him as a great man. In vain did Harding, now campaigning for Lyle, try to

remind his listeners there of the obvious fact that the only Negroes
Thompson had always been interested in were those who could do
him service on election days, or gamblers with campaign contributions, or ward workers. But most of the people in the Negro wards
were of a mind with the Reverend J. C. Austin, who delivered an
oration at one meeting that finished with the evaluation, "God made
just one William Hale Thompson and forgot the mold. Truth,
courage, consecration, ideas of right, ideas of justice, let there be
righteousness. Let it come to earth. Call it William Hale Thompson. . . . When history is written, they will write in the blue sky
high above all of them the name of William Hale Thompson. . . . "

7

When the noise died down long enough for the ballots to be
counted on election day, Thompson had come out ahead of Lyle by
70,000 votes, with Albert far behind.

In the Hotel Sherman, Thompson drank a highball, posed for
photographers, and sent a high-sounding telegram to Hearst: "I won
through on our principles of driving internationalism and prohibition out of the Republican party!" Before the publisher received
the wire he was already on the long-distance telephone, congratulating Thompson on his victory. Even after the click of Hearst's receiver signified the call was over, Big Bill pretended still to be talking.
"Well, fine, Bill, you bet I do. I'll be glad to, Bill. Good to hear
from you, Bill. Thanks for calling, Bill."

There was a telephone call from Huey Long and one from New
York's mayor, Jimmy Walker. For Walker's benefit, Bill called in
the Chicago Police Quartet. "Jimmy," he yelled, "I wanna have you
listen to the song I've written for my campaign against Tony Cermak. He's the winner for the Democrats. Just listen to this." And
the weary policemen bawled into the mouthpiece:

> "Tony, Tony, where's your pushcart at?
> Can you picture a World's Fair mayor
> With a name like that?
> What a job you're holding!

And now you're trying for two.
Better start thinking of one for me
Instead of two for you!"

8

At one time in his turbulent life, Anton J. Cermak had indeed
been a pushcart peddler. Years back, when he was twenty years old
and poor, he had come to Chicago from the mining town of Braidwood, in southern Illinois, where his immigrant parents had brought
him as an infant from Bohemia. To make extra money he collected
waste wood from industrial plants and factories and peddled it for
kindling among his neighbors on the city's West Side.

Tony Cermak, of course, had gone far since those indigent days.
Under the tutelage of the Democratic boss, George E. Brennan,
whom he had first met in Braidwood when Brennan was a teacher
in a school for miners' children, he developed into a politician, and
a skillful one. From a precinct captain in his Lawndale district,
where lived thousands of foreign-born, Cermak advanced through
the political grades. He served four terms as an alderman and was
bailiff of the Municipal Court. From 1922 to 1931 he was the powerful president of the Cook County Board, responsible for the building of a new Criminal Courts Building and jail, for the acquisition
of the forest preserves, for additions to the gigantic Cook County
Hospital. Reform groups charged that graft and favoritism had
been involved in the purchase of the forests and the land for the
Criminal Courts Building, but none of the money involved had ever
been traced to the president of the County Board.

He was a canny politician, a master of organization and detail.
He could be ruthless, and often was, with those who defied his orders. He thought fast and made decisions quickly. He spoke un-
grammatically, but he never failed to make his meaning clear,
whether he spoke to rival politicians or gamblers in his district seeking favors, or bankers. He was determined that he would be Chicago's World's Fair Mayor when the vast Century of Progress
Exposition—which Thompson had boosted when it was only an idea
in the minds of a few enthusiasts—would be held in 1933.

Cermak had clashed with Thompson before. As secretary of the United Societies for Local Self-Government in 1915, he led the fight against Big Bill's order closing saloons on Sunday. He threatened legal action and organized that gigantic parade of 40,000 wets down Michigan Avenue. As an alderman, Cermak found himself attacking Thompsonian legislation, sometimes for valid reasons, sometimes because George E. Brennan wanted him to. When Brennan died in 1928, Cermak had become the boss of Cook County Democracy.

9

Thompson was certain he could defeat Cermak with his customary tactics. He was certain, too, that Dr. Herman N. Bundesen, who had served him and had been fired by him as health commissioner, would run as an independent Democrat, thereby drawing votes from Cermak. But Bundesen, who had collected 950,000 votes when he was elected coroner in 1928, decided not to run. And, to add to the complications, most of the big men of the Republican party were still too embittered over the primary to come to the aid of Big Bill now. Of all the leaders who had supported Lyle, only George Harding returned to help Thompson.

In customary style, Big Bill blustered through the campaign. Not only had Tony Cermak been born in Europe—"You want a bohunk for mayor?"—but he was, of all unlikely things, "an ally of King George." This fatuous reasoning derived from the fact that one of Cermak's backers was Melvin Traylor, president of the First National Bank and an organizer of the World Bank. "If Cermak is elected, he would make Traylor a most powerful ally of the King of England, which would be to the detriment of the American people!" The multimillionaires were for Tony Cermak, but the working people were for him, said Big Bill. "Tony Cermak is the biggest crook that ever ran for mayor!"

Bristling at Thompson's sneers at his background, Cermak was ready to reply in kind. But a wise newspaperman, John Delaney, warned him against it. "Thompson's a master at that sort of stuff. Take it easy. You can't compete with him, so don't try." Instead, Cermak made dignified speeches, promising to clean up crime, to keep politics out of the school system, to bring prosperity to Chicago. He also made strong appeals to Republicans to cross party lines and oust Thompson. He called attention to the rise in city taxes under Thompson and the reduction in county taxes under his own reign as county board president.

Thompson's meetings were poorly attended. Each week a new defection of a party regular occurred, so that at one gathering Thompson, rambling on and on in a long anecdote about his cowboy days, looked over at Bertha Baur, national G.O.P. committeewoman, and one of the few who remained with him, and muttered, "We're all mixed up, I guess." A week before the election State's Attorney Swanson hit him a hard blow. His police raided the offices of City Sealer Daniel A. Serritella and seized mounds of records. Serritella was quickly indicted with his chief deputy, Harry Hochstein, for conspiring with merchants to short-weight housewives all over the city and threatening other merchants who refused to join their plot.* "Tony Cermak's state's attorney has violated his oath and will be punished," croaked Big Bill. "I expect to win by the greatest majority I have ever received."

10

On the night of the election Thompson sat and stared at a poster on the wall of his hotel headquarters. FIGHT FOR THOMPSON—HE FIGHTS FOR YOU! There were no tinkling pianos, no gay callers, no long-distance telephone calls. By seven o'clock, little more than an hour after the polls had closed, he received his first big jolt: he was running 150,000 behind.

He walked into his inner office, sat for a few minutes chewing convulsively on a big cigar. When he came out again, he had his message to Cermak: "The people of Chicago have spoken. I cheerfully abide by their decision. I congratulate you on your victory." Someone brought in a microphone and asked him to make a speech. Wearily, he said, "I will redouble my efforts for the completion of

---

* Both were found guilty by a jury but the convictions were later reversed by the Appellate Court on grounds of insufficient evidence.

the waterway, to bring to Chicago a greater prosperity and work for the unemployed. . . . I shall continue to uphold the teachings of George Washington and fight foreign entanglements. . . . "

He jammed his hat on his head and turned to wave to Ettelson and the other few who remained. "I'm tired of working for 3,500,000 people. Now I'll work for myself for a while."

II

On the next day, Thompson set out for a waterway trip down the Mississippi River on the *Cape Girardeau*. With him were Len Small and Frank L. Smith. They were jovial, these three, as if the defeat of Big Bill was only a passing slight. With them they carried a five-piece jazz band and at every stop along the river they invited the townspeople to come aboard and dance to the music. At every stop someone asked Big Bill what his plans were now, and always he replied, "I'm not through yet, believe me. They'll be hearing a lot more from Big Bill Thompson!"

But wherever he went he carried the memory of the *Tribune's* editorial on the morning of Cermak's victory, the bitterest ever penned and, tragically for Thompson, the one with which Chicago had agreed on that election day.

"For Chicago, Thompson has meant filth, corruption, obscenity, idiocy and bankruptcy," read the strongest portion. "He has given the city an international reputation for moronic buffoonery, barbaric crime, triumphant hoodlumism, unchecked graft, and a dejected citizenship. He nearly ruined the property and completely destroyed the pride of the city. He made Chicago a byword of the collapse of American civilization. In his attempt to continue this he excelled himself as a liar and defamer of character. He's out.

"He is not only out, but he is dishonored. He is deserted by his friends. He is permanently marked by the evidences of his character and conduct. His health is impaired by his ways of life and he leaves office and goes from the city the most discredited man who ever held place in it."

III ‖ The Last Years

27 ⫴ No Friends, No Foes

I

THE SHOCK OF HIS DEFEAT JOLTED Big Bill. All geniality went out of him for a time after he returned from the trip. He was angry, sullen, filled with hate for those he deemed his enemies. He was bitter at what he considered a betrayal by friends he had helped make rich through his favors and influence. He was irritated with a populace that had refused to send him back to the City Hall: "I spent plenty of my money to help build up this town and they double-crossed me!" He raged against Wall Street financiers and bankers who backed Cermak: "It's elemental political philosophy that when a man in public life gets too strong, like I did, there arrives a time when it's worth somebody's while to spend a lot of money to beat him." Sometimes he said that he was finished with politics forever, but mostly he vowed to avenge his beating and make a triumphant comeback. He had no organization, many of his associates had retired or taken jobs with the Democrats, and the Republican party was shattered. But Thompson spoke of the day when he and Len Small and those still loyal would take over the statehouse again, and the G.O.P. County Committee, and the City Hall.

In these rantings, Thompson failed to realize that his showman's tactics had tarnished. He gave no sign that he understood the meaning of Cermak's victory. This was not a fleeting Democratic triumph, like Dever's in 1923. Cermak had built a machine on the lessons of George Brennan—and Billy Lorimer and Fred Lundin. Like them, he believed in rigid organization from the top of the

337

party to the lowest ranks, with all final authority vested in Tony
Cermak. In their wards, the party committeemen were the Big
Powers. They gave orders to aldermen and police captains, they
helped name judges and public officials. Cermak made the over-all
policies and carried out the major maneuvers necessary to strengthen
the party's hold on the city and state. He maintained the alliances
with the underworld syndicate, and even when Al Capone was sent
to the federal penitentiary for income-tax evasion, the empire he had
constructed remained intact as new leaders, with suaver ways and
smoother speech, moved in to make their arrangements with the
politicians in power. Cermak engaged in flagrant bipartisan deals
with Republicans who hungered for position. He built and continued to build his organization into such a force that only the reckless or the foolhardy would strive to destroy it.

Big Bill was one such man. When the lull following his defeat had
passed he set out to plan Len Small's campaign for governor. "We
do that first, then we get the county committee back from Charlie
Deneen, and four years from now," he chortled, "we got Tony
Cermak back on his pushcart."

2

But when, early in June, Thompson sent out a call for his Cook
County leaders, the response was discouraging. Some had joined
Deneen, some had their own factions and candidates, some had
simply quit. A few came to Thompson: Jim Breen, his lawyer; old
Morris Eller, of the Bloody Twentieth Ward; Patrick Sheridan
Smith, former city clerk; Thomas V. Sullivan, one of Thompson's
school-board lawyers; Sam and Lou Golan, a pair of bright young
lawyers with political knowledge; Charles Burmeister, only pro-
Thompson member of the party's county committee.

Aboard his yacht, *Doris*, Big Bill transported these men and some
fifty other minor party politicians to a picnic rally near Zion, Illinois.
He presented Small as "Illinois' best governor and Illinois' next governor" and just to show the younger men he was still alert he tied
Burmeister for first place in a trap-shooting contest. "Our keynote

NOW THAT THE SLOW FREIGHT IS PAST——

is going to be to drive out the internationalists, the prohibitionists and the depressionists!" he cried. "Let's vote out the wreckers and the robbers! Let's elect Len Small governor and Calvin Coolidge president!" He proposed a $5,000,000 Prosperity Loan to hire the unemployed on needed public works. "Vote for a Prosperity Ticket!" was his slogan.

Thompson spoke the sentiments of most Illinois Republican leaders, but his foes did not intend to let him regain control of the party.
While he returned to Chicago and set up campaign headquarters
for Small in the Conway Building, the rival factions picked their
own candidates. The favorite was Omer N. Custer, a former state
treasurer, who was stamped with the official approval of Deneen
and the party's county central committee. Oscar Carlstrom, the
former attorney general, was another factional hopeful, and so were
Ed Brundage and William H. Malone, once Small's chairman of
the Illinois Tax Commission.

To Custer's aid went none other than George Harding, that long-
time ally of Thompson, Homer Galpin, and Oscar Nelson, who had
been Thompson's floor leader in the city council. Harding's defection particularly infuriated Big Bill. "I'll nail his political hide to
the wall!" he roared. To help Small, Thompson dipped into his own
funds for sound trucks, radio time, printing bills and rallies.

Near the end of the primary campaign, Custer horrified his professional supporters by declaring himself to be a confirmed dry.
This was a boon for Small, since in Illinois, as in many other states,
there was growing sentiment for prohibition repeal. Small polled
110,000 votes more than Custer and the other candidates, and
Thompson howled, "We're gonna win in November!"

But he was howling out of desperation rather than confidence.
The Democratic nominee was Probate Judge Henry Horner, of
Cook County, a man of dignity, learning and fine reputation. Not
only was Horner a formidable opponent, but the victory of Herbert
Hoover at the Republican Presidential convention in the Chicago
Stadium convinced Thompson that the Republicans would lose the
national election. Recklessly he played the bigot's role as he campaigned for Small. Because Judge Horner was Jewish, Thompson
told downstate farmers, "Elect Henry Horner and the price of pork
will go down to nothing." He repeated his derisive statements about
Cermak, calling him "Tony Baloney," and listed some of Cermak's
associates, then snarling, "Yah, Cermak to Szymczak to Zintak—the
Irish are out!"

A group of Thompson's Jewish friends called on him in protest.

Big Bill gazed at them in bewilderment. "You know I've been a friend to Jews," he told them. "Look at the record of my appointments. I'm saying what I've got to say to make Small win. That's the only thing that's important here. Len Small has got to win!"

He was willing to agree to any deal that might help Small. W. W. O'Brien, a shrewd criminal lawyer, devised a tricky plan. He and a smart young press agent, Lou Kent Fink, traveled to Sinissippi Farm to see Frank O. Lowden. They convinced him that thousands of citizens wanted him to run for president on an "Independent" ticket. When Lowden started to decline, they asked him to withhold any answer for twenty-four hours. Lowden agreed. The following day the newspapers carried the announcement that O'Brien would be the Independent Party's candidate for governor. And the announcement went on to say that Lowden was "considering" acceptance of the party's nomination for the presidency. Before the deadline for Lowden's disavowal arrived, O'Brien and Fink hustled to Thompson's rooms in the Congress Hotel.

"I'll campaign like hell," said O'Brien, "but in the last week I'll withdraw and throw my support to Len Small. I'll be giving the Democrats hell in the meantime!"

"What's the deal? What do you want?" asked Thompson.

O'Brien's eyes sparkled. "We want 100 pardons, $50,000 in cash and payment for radio time."

Thompson pondered a moment. "No cash. You get money for the radio time and I promise you you'll get the pardons."

Unfortunately for the sly lawyer, Small was defeated. Judge Horner's plurality of 556,000 was more than twice the margin of victory achieved by the Democratic Presidential candidate, Franklin D. Roosevelt, in the state. The heaviest blow to Thompson was in Chicago, giving blunt testimony of the power of Cermak and the quick dissolution of Big Bill's popularity. Even the Negro wards failed to produce a big vote for Small. Cermak had helped see to that by ordering his police to close policy stations and racing handbooks in those districts. When the policy chiefs protested and asked Cermak what he wanted, they received a simple answer: "More Democrats in your wards."

3

Small's defeat sent Thompson into a temporary eclipse.

He had no comments to make on events political, either when Cermak died from an assassin's bullet meant for President-elect Roosevelt in Miami, or when Edward J. Kelly, the hard-boiled and politically shrewd party treasurer, replaced him, or when Roosevelt put through his first New Deal measures. Nor did any reporters ask Thompson about his thoughts on these happenings. He was ill, depressed. For the first time anyone could recall, he decided to join a church. At an Easter Sunday Evangelical meeting in the Thoburn Methodist Episcopal church, he prayed with other penitents before the altar. When someone asked him if his church membership would change his convictions about prohibition, Big Bill solemnly replied, "I am a wet and I am going to stay wet, because the Bible is wet."

In this period Thompson received comfort and solace from a dark-haired young woman named Ethabelle Green. She had been hired as a stenographer in the 1931 campaign and had stayed on after Thompson lost to Cermak. At the time Thompson was not living with his wife. Their married life had been unhappy and from time to time he had moved out of their North Side home to live in either the Hotel Sherman or the Congress Hotel. After his defeat, he asked Miss Green to be his companion, secretary, nurse and "daughter."

"You are just a kid and I am getting on in years," he told her. "I am separated from my wife. I am lonely and I am sick. I feel you can give me the happiness that has never been mine. I am confident that it will pay dividends to both of us."

Ethabelle agreed. She took a room near Thompson's suite in the Congress and ministered to his needs. When he went to Mount Clemens, Michigan, a favorite health resort town for Chicago politicians, she accompanied him. He called her "Dear Kiddy" and paid her thirty-five dollars a week for the first few months. Soon she received no regular salary but Thompson provided her with food, shelter, clothes and "pin money." He was full of promises: "I'm going to some day draw a will making you heiress to half my estate, the same as a daughter of my own blood."

4

But not even Ethabelle Green's soothing attentions could keep Thompson from thinking of politics when the Democrats began to act like Republicans and engaged in bitter internal feuds.

In 1935 Mayor Kelly easily trounced an obscure lawyer, Emil Wetten, the only Republican brave enough to oppose him. Kelly and his county chairman, Pat Nash, immediately set out to strengthen their position in their party. They ran into stubborn opposition from State's Attorney Thomas J. Courtney, who, also trained in the political ways of Cermak, had mayoral ambitions. When Kelly and Nash tried to force passage in the state legislature of bills legalizing betting handbooks in Chicago, Governor Horner rose against them, too, and now there was an alliance of Horner and Courtney against Kelly and Nash.

Early in 1936, Big Bill rumbled out of his hotel room to announce his return to politics. "I'm shooting at one target," he told reporters. "I'm going to put over Tommy Sullivan, who used to be our school attorney, for attorney general and he'll stop vote frauds and thieving. Me? I'm not running for anything right now. You'll remember that a lot of people said a lot of things about me when I was in office. Well, I was in public life and I took it on the chin. Y' know, a fellow was here the other day who commented on Grant Park and the boulevards and the bridges and the playgrounds, and he said it must be gratifying to me to sit here and see the evidence of what I had done. Well, of course, I didn't do it. I put the projects before the people and they voted for them. . . . I'm not looking for any office in this campaign. Later? Maybe."

Thompson called on Sam Golan for help, and Golan arranged a conference with Small, again a candidate for the governorship. Small agreed to support Sullivan in the primary, but when the vote was counted it was clear that Small had walked out on his agreement. Sullivan was badly beaten.

"Double crossers!" Thompson bellowed, and took steps to set up a third party. He was sure he could draw enough votes to engineer the defeat of Small. By June he was ready. He formed the Union Progressive Party, had himself declared its candidate for governor.

In his angry ranks were some old Thompson loyalists, professional dissidents, radical Republicans, and a conglomeration of Harrison Parker's Co-operative Party, Father Charles E. Coughlin's followers, Newton Jenkins' anti-Semitic Unionists, visionaries, crackpots and rabble rousers. Senator William E. Borah was designated the party's patron saint. Thompson sent him a letter declaring that his party stood firm against the League of Nations and the World Court, against "the vicious monopoly assailing our financial system and taking hold of our party machinery" and against the Democrats' vote thievery in Chicago. He was supporting, he said, the North Dakota irregular Republican, William Lemke, for President. "We are all together," he assured Borah. "Lemkeites, Townsendites, Huey Longites, Thompsonites, Laborites, and the American people are going down the pike together!"

The American people refused to go down the pike with these forces, and in Illinois the results for Bill Thompson were disastrous. Everywhere he went the crowds were small and apathetic. They listened to his denunciations of the regular Republican nominee, C. Wayland Brooks: "Curly Brooks claims to be a farmer, but he can't even ride a horse. I pledge here and now that if Curly Brooks will get on a horse and ride it, I'll withdraw from the race!" They heard him pay his respects to Len Small, who died suddenly in May. They yawned when he made his promises.

In the election, Thompson received only 108,614 votes. Governor Horner, despite his primary campaign cry that "One of my greatest mistakes was supporting Kelly for mayor!" received the full support of the mighty Kelly-Nash machine in the election and he defeated Brooks by nearly 400,000 votes. In Chicago Thompson could get only 80,000 votes to Brooks's 574,000. Now he had no political friends—and no political enemies. He was ignored.

5

And still he craved the attention he needed.

He became ill early in 1937, so seriously that Dr. M. W. Samuels informed Ethabelle Green that he feared for Thompson's mental condition. But by spring he appeared to have recovered. He was soon in the midst of a new conflict.

For years water from Lake Michigan had been diverted at a rapid rate into the Chicago River. When their water levels dropped drastically, other Great Lakes cities sued to force Chicago to construct locks at the river mouth and costly sewage-treatment works. Now the Supreme Court had ruled that Chicago would have to limit the flow of water from Lake Michigan to 1,500 cubic feet a second, and Chicagoans were protesting.

Thompson promptly started a series of speeches supporting Congressional bills for greater lake diversion. He picked on Mayor Daniel Hoan of Milwaukee, a leader in the antidiversion fight. "Pay no attention to him," snapped Hoan. "Bill Thompson wants to be the big savior of Chicago and Illinois. He wants to run for mayor again."

When Thompson went to Washington to plead for the legislation the reporters asked him about the rumored mayoral ambition. "I might run," said a humbled Bill, "if the people indicate they want me."

"And what," asked one reporter, with a laugh, "do you think of the British now?"

Thompson grinned and lighted his cigar. "Y' know," he said affably, "I've got a place in Canada. I'm learning to sing 'God Save the King' with my Canadian neighbors. I never had anything against the English, really. There were just more Irish in Chicago— and they had the votes. I've changed. I've cut out all that stuff now. I just shake hands. It gets the same results. I like the English. One of these days I'll take a trip over there and see my friends."

But two months later he was denouncing the English as loudly as ever. Again he cried, "The British want us to fight their battles!" and "Let's never forget what George Washington warned us about!" and "Friendly to all, entanglements with none!"

Late in 1937 he incorporated the William Hale Thompson Association to Keep America Out of Foreign Wars, with himself as president, Richard Wolfe as vice-president, James Breen as treasurer, and Ethabelle Green as secretary. This group, he declared, would sponsor in the coming state elections a public policy measure to be voted on in a special ballot: "Shall the people of Illinois approve the

William Hale Thompson public policy proposal which provides that all members in the Congress of the United States from the State of Illinois shall vote 'No' on all legislation for the drafting of American boys to fight on foreign soil?"

Critics of Thompsonism quickly pointed out that the proposal had no legal standing, that it was merely advisory. The *News* called it a cheap political trick devised by Thompson to get publicity. The *Tribune,* which had dropped all mention of Thompson's name and called him only "a former mayor of Chicago," ignored his proposal. Yet many persons who deplored Thompson's politics and his methods but were sincerely against war felt that the measure had merit. Churchmen endorsed the plan and Thompson, despite his rabble rousing in the previous campaign, was invited to speak at churches and synagogues.

In the middle of his antiwar crusade, he was caught in a flurry of lawsuits, some started by Democratic-appointed receivers for bankrupt printing and campaign supply houses. They sued him for $250,-000 in unpaid bills and he managed to settle for $50,000. Then, to end a long legal battle that had started in 1931, he was ordered to pay to the American Red Cross $72,794, the balance of a fund collected by his Waterway and Flood Control Association for the relief of the Mississippi River flood victims of 1927. The organization had collected $139,772, but the Red Cross had received only a small portion of this. Thompson had insisted he never knew where the rest of the money went, but now he accepted responsibility and paid in full.

In the midst of his public policy campaign his name flashed, for a day, over world cables and radio. The German government news service, taking cognizance of an anti-Nazi statement by Chicago's George Cardinal Mundelein, asserted that the prelate had been the man meant when Mayor William Hale Thompson had inveighed against King George a decade before.

Thompson at once denied it. "To say I meant Cardinal Mundelein when I assailed King George is an absolute falsehood," he declared. "What I said was, 'King George has got to keep his snoot out of Chicago's schools.' I meant the King of England. And right now I say that the American people must not let King George lead us into another foreign war."

He continued to work hard for his public policy measure. His office in the Conway Building was packed with people bearing anti-war petitions and with some old followers from his golden days in the City Hall. He spoke at three or four meetings every night, lost weight and grew hoarser. Finally he stood by a truck loaded with bundles of petitions for Springfield. An American Legion color guard came to attention as the driver started the motor. "This is the happiest day of my life," mumbled Thompson.

He was elated when, in the state election that November, the William Hale Thompson public policy proposal won by a vote of 1,700,000 to 958,000. Throughout Illinois the Republican political ticket collapsed. In Cook County not a single Republican was elected. Only. Bill Thompson, of all his party, had a winner and could bask in the sunshine of victory, however meaningless. He was seventy now and his once full face was mottled and loose and his eyes were lusterless and tired. But he grinned, waved his hat in old-time style and wheezed huskily, "Bill Thompson's not counted out yet. He'll be heard from, wait and see!"

28 ||| End—and Epilogue

WITH THE STUBBORN INSISTENCE OF a cranky old man, Big Bill placed fantastic importance on the success of his public policy measure. Those who had voted for it had done so as an expression of fear that America might be drawn into a major war. Many among them would not have cast a ballot for Thompson if he were the only candidate on the only ticket for the only office in the state. But Thompson refused to realize this. He saw the vote as a summons for him to return to save the people from rapacious Democrats and Republican bosses. "They went for it because they went for me," he boasted. "They still remember me, they still want me."

Holding such notions, it was inevitable that he should declare himself a candidate for mayor in the 1939 elections. He was certain that he had no powerful enemies in Republican officialdom. Charles Deneen was in ill health. Ed Brundage was dead, by a revolver in his own hand in the basement of his home. Fred Lundin had finally made good his promise to quit politics and was traveling all over the world. Bob Crowe was in a fast bipartisan alliance with the Democrats. For a long time, Thompson had been obsessed with the desire to prove to these onetime friends and onetime enemies that he could win and rule without them. "This is my chance to show them all!" he cried to steadfast Jim Breen.

Breen tried to dissuade him. He pointed out the need for an efficient organization of precinct and ward workers. If Tom Courtney and Ed Kelly, as seemed likely, engaged in an all-out war for control of the Chicago Democrats, perhaps a Republican could be elected. But first he had to be nominated in the primary and that, should the official Republicans now led by Edward F. Moore refuse endorsement, required a city-wide organization, promises with potentiality of being fulfilled, willing and eager workers, a lot of money. None of these was in sight.

Breen sat outlining his views to Thompson in the Congress Hotel suite one early January afternoon in 1939. He was gaining mutters of acquiescence from Big Bill when the telephone rang. Thompson took the call, listened for a moment, then roared, "Gene! You bet I will!" He winked at Breen. "I've never been fitter in my life. I will, and we'll give them the fight of their lives. We'll give them the fight of their lives! And, say, give my regards to George."

The caller was Gene Pike. "He's in George Harding's house, and they want me to run in the primary. Gene'll manage, George promises money and the whole South Side. I'll get that nomination and I'll beat any Democrat, no matter if it's Kelly or Courtney!"

Pike had told him, said Thompson, to start his preparations. "He and George are going down to Florida and they'll be back in two weeks. Then they'll jump in with both feet, and by then we'll be rolling!"

That afternoon Breen rented an office at Clark and Madison streets, putting down $800 of his own for a month's rent. News spread of Thompson's bid for the nomination. Other old-timers showed up. There was a call from William J. Balmer, another South Side leader, and from Ed Litsinger, once such a rabid foe, and from Oscar de Priest and from Dan Jackson. The local Hearst newspapers, friendlier than ever since Thompson's antiwar crusade, sent reporters who wrote that Big Bill had recovered the form that made him famous as a spellbinder.

To visitors who came to see for themselves, Big Bill rasped, "They say over on that county committee of double crossers that I've got one foot in the grave. Ed Moore, who's only a stooge for Ed Kelly, says I'll drop dead. Let me tell you, they've got both feet in the grave over there. They've been dead since 1931. It's about time the Republicans of this city stop following the hopeless leadership

of this Ed Moore. My friends have asked me to run for mayor and
I will make the race. Together we will go to victory!"

2

Ed Moore's leadership was by no means hopeless. He gathered
together small splinter groups who showed no eagerness to join
Thompson and built the semblance of a united party front. To
counter the threat raised by Thompson he put forward the party's
candidate in Dwight Green, the Assistant United States District
Attorney who had been helpful in sending Al Capone to the penitentiary. A mild, soft-spoken lawyer, Green now was given a strong
build-up as a fearless foe of gangsters, the friend of businessmen, the
epitome of political decency. Readily available was the support of
the *Tribune*, Thompson's implacable foe, and the *News*, whose new
publisher, Colonel Frank Knox, had aspirations of his own to be the
Presidential nominee in 1940.

While he awaited the return of Harding and Pike from Florida,
Thompson moved swiftly ahead in the familiar pattern of the campaigns of earlier years. Rebellious Republicans, smarting under this
or that rebuff from Moore, flocked into the small office. A loud-
speaker blared into the busy street: "Let's elect Big Bill again!"
Richard Wolfe, thesaurus at hand, was turning out hyperbolic
speeches designed to turn the hair of Thompson's adversaries.

The inevitable monster rally, complete with balloons and tin
horns and sirens, was staged by Breen and Balmer in the Medinah
Temple. Papier-mâché sombreros were distributed to the crowd of
3,000 who chanted, clapped and whistled as in the old days. When
Thompson strode out on the stage, he raised his familiar plainsman's
hat high, eyes glistening as the throng roared, "We want Bill!"

He called them his trusted friends. He thanked them for their
support. He denounced, in a louder, hoarser voice, his familiar
enemies. "The corrupt and rotten Kelly-Nash machine has brought
government in Chicago so low that State's Attorney Courtney and
Governor Horner, who were put into office by that machine, cannot stomach it!" he shouted. "And what does the *Tribune*-Moore

outfit propose to do about it? They want to put into office a pip-squeak errand boy who claims he helped put Capone behind bars! Who killed cock robin? I want to know! Why do these forces that have always been beholden to Ed Kelly now want to foist on honest Republicans a complete unknown? I'll tell you why! They want Ed Kelly to win. They want the Kelly-Nash machine to go on bleeding Chicago!"

"Atta boy, Bill! Give it to 'em, Big Bill!"

"I'll give 'em hell, all right. Then I want you to go out and give 'em hell!

"In 1917 they called me pro-German because I was against the war! I was right then and they tried to crucify me. I was right then, and I am right now! It is the poor man who pays the cost of war. It is the poor man who is robbed of his right to raise his voice against it! Bill Thompson gave you the right to speak in November and you spoke in a voice of thunder! I want you to join with me in a cry next primary day that will be heard all the way to Buckingham Palace! I want you to join me in telling our English friends that we will gladly die to preserve and protect the glorious old American flag but never again, never again will we send a single American boy to be slaughtered on a European battlefield."

Men and women rose and yelled. Arms high, Bill asked them to join in singing "The Star-Spangled Banner." When they finished, he cried, "Yes, my good friends. I am going to be your mayor again. But it won't be easy. We've got to fight like we've never fought before. Are you with me?"

"Yes! Yes!"

"Will you go out and tell the people all the truth about Bill Thompson's record?"

"Yes, we'll tell 'em! We'll tell 'em!"

"Will you go out to man the precincts?"

"We will, we will!"

"Will you keep at it night and day until we win?"

Thompson grinned at the din of the shouted promises. "Then we'll win, we'll win. My hat is in the ring!" He sailed his sombrero into a pile of papier-mâché hats on the stage. "We'll win together!"

3

It was a brave show, one of Big Bill's best. But even as he spoke, he was fighting a losing fight, with no chance of getting the nomination.

From the moment it became known in Republican circles that Harding and Pike had urged Thompson to run, pressure had been exerted on Harding to recant. He was reminded that he had been elected national committeeman in 1936 with the support of the men now backing Green. Before he could publicly disavow Thompson, he was stricken with a gall bladder infection and rushed to Passavant Hospital for an operation. All visitors were barred, and for days neither Thompson nor Green could get a statement from him. Pike refused to go to Thompson's side without Harding. At once the ardor of some of the lesser Thompson ward representatives chilled when the Harding-Pike support and funds failed to materialize, and they scurried off to make their deals with the Green forces.

Thompson struggled to maintain the illusion of political fight. Even Maysie Thompson, although estranged from him, loyally came to his aid. She graciously permitted herself to be interviewed by a *Times* reporter writing a series on "Who'll be Chicago's Next First Lady?" It was the first time in years that she had allowed such an interview, and she carried it off well. She told of preparing lunch each day for her grand-nephews, William Hale Gehl, Jr., and Hale Thompson Gehl. She told how much she loved her home, now an eleven-room apartment on Lake Shore Drive, but gave no hint that Big Bill rarely spent any time there. She told of the trips she and Thompson had taken to Honolulu and to Europe. "Mr. Thompson," she said quietly, "is the most interesting and fascinating person I have ever known. He has a magnetism that I have never met in another human being. He always dominates the situation wherever he is. My greatest interest is to see him re-elected so that he can continue rebuilding Chicago as he started."

It was a valiant gesture and, under favorable conditions, could have been a real help to Thompson. But he had lost his zest for the campaign, once Harding and Pike had failed to carry through the promises he claimed to have received. He canceled all speeches in outlying wards, appearing only in his own district to a crowd that half filled a small meeting hall. In one corner a pianist and saxophonist played a dismal "Happy Days Are Here Again." He cried out against his foes, but the familiar accusations fell on inattentive ears. His lower lip drooped at the end of his sentences. Spittle flecked his mouth as he snarled his hackneyed charges—"Green is Kelly's stooge and the hand-picked candidate of the La Salle Street Republican bosses!"—and his trite promises—"A vote for Bill Thompson is a vote against foreign war and against the drafting of American boys for European service!" The cheers were weak, the crowd's spirit listless.

For the rest of the primary, Breen and Balmer worked loyally, although each knew Thompson's cause was hopeless. Big Bill ordered expenditures cut to the preposterous figure of five dollars a precinct—in the roaring days each precinct was flooded with money for him. His few remaining workers ground out their press releases, defies to Ed Moore and Dwight Green and wildly optimistic predictions. When reporters asked why Thompson was making no speeches at ward meetings, they were told curtly that he was so well known everywhere that further campaign oratory was quite unnecessary. When Harding, three days before the primary election, sent Green a note wishing him well and complimenting him on the vigor of his campaign, Thompson was too depressed to make any comment on this final act of treachery.

On primary night he isolated himself in his hotel suite, playing cards with Ethabelle Green and listening to voting results on a table radio. In the heavily Democratic wards both he and Green had fared equally bad, of course. When he heard the results in the Twenty-fourth Ward, stronghold of the politically astute Alderman Jacob M. Arvey—17,355 for Kelly, 1,817 for Courtney, 396 for Green and 246 for Thompson—he growled, "Why didn't they steal 'em all?" Breen's ward, the Fourteenth, went to Thompson, and so did the Negro wards, where he was still Big Bill the Magnificent Benefactor. But when the final tally was in, he had received only 62,000 votes to 212,000 for the man he had derided as a pipsqueak.

4

This was defeat, humiliating and complete and final.

Thompson had no words for the reporters, and they pressed him for none. He had nothing to tell his friends, no new promises to offer, and they went their separate ways, some into lasting obscurity, some to plead for small favors from the triumphant Green. Although Green would need every bit of aid in his fight against Ed Kelly, victor over the rebellious Courtney in the Democrats' primary by nearly 300,000 votes, he made not even a token bid for help from the defeated Thompson.

Once again, as in other years of defeat, Thompson declared he was through with politics. There was no solace for him even in Green's eventual defeat by Kelly. He had no public comment to make as he watched Kelly solidify his power by the same methods Lundin had taught him. Where Thompson boasted of Chicago as a "wide-open town," Kelly now spoke of it as a "liberal town." Like Thompson, Kelly sought full control of the Board of Education, and denounced his critics with such Thompsonesque terms as "busybodies" and "snooping reformers." Like Thompson, Kelly boasted of his many achievements, picturing the city as a miserable shambles before he came into office. Like Big Bill, Ed Kelly had his tie-ups, through many underlings, with the powerful men of the underworld syndicate built by Capone, and when he was assailed for condoning the operation of betting handbooks and widespread gambling, he lashed at his assailants as "defamers of Chicago's good name" and "bluenoses."

Another development of deep irony came after Adolf Hitler's invasion of Czechoslovakia touched off war in Europe that September. The slogans and the accusations, the propaganda and the counterpropaganda were all too familiar to Thompson as America split into those who cried, "America First!" and those who cried, "Defend America by Aiding the Allies!" Newspapers which for years had fought Thompson on every issue now printed editorials which restated the very ideas he had espoused on nationalism, foreign entanglements, British and French policies, involvement in Europe's old conflicts, self-protection for America. Orators who would have shuddered to know that they were spouting the Thompsonisms of 1917 inveighed against sending supplies to Great Britain and France, against selling them arms and munitions, against lending them ships, against entertaining their heroes, against drafting young Americans into the armed forces, against passing any legislation that held the slightest chance of involving the country in the war.

In all this new hubbub the voice of Big Bill remained unheard. He was part of the past now, an old man discredited and forgotten, with a dark-haired woman to keep him company and a case of whisky in his closet. He kept gloomily to his hotel suite, dressed in a bathrobe or pajamas, sucking on a briar pipe and staring out of his window at Lake Michigan. Occasionally he stirred himself and took long drives or went to a baseball game. For the first time in his hyperactive life, he began to read regularly, mostly books about the glories of the Napoleonic era and of colonial days in New England. A few old friends sometimes got past Ethabelle Green. But most of the time she kept a close watch on him, playing gin rummy with him, preparing his meals, nursing him when he fell ill, tending to his financial affairs with the help of Jim Breen. And once a month she dutifully mailed a check to Maysie Thompson.

Sometimes Bill granted an interview to an old newspaper friend. One was Charles N. Wheeler, now of the *News*, who found him gray, thinning, haggard. "What about England now, Mr. Mayor?" Wheeler asked. Bill's answer surprised many who recalled his earlier attitudes. "I am for helping England in this hour because I believe that in so doing we are helping the defense of this country. We should extend to England in every way we can, short of sending our boys to foreign battlefields, every possible aid."

Politics? "No more politics. What's the use? No one understands what you're trying to do. No one tries. They only want to get on the bandwagon if you look like a winner. . . . Maybe I was theatrical. I was trying to sell good ideas. The ideas were okay. But what has come of it all? Look at the Loop. Look at the local transportation service. Why all this stagnation? Taxes? Discouraging, isn't it?"

It was one of his last public statements. Each month found him more listless, less interested in life. When America finally entered the war, Bill Thompson and his era were completely pushed into the past. The Congress Hotel was taken over by the Army and he moved into a small suite in the Blackstone Hotel, faithful Ethabelle Green by his side. There he kept a cabinet well stocked with liquor, a refrigerator, a few mementos of his days in the West, two suits of dress clothes. He gave up reading books. He grew forgetful, often bellowing for Ethabelle Green to take down his letters to people named Lundin and Deneen and Hearst and Pugh.

In February 1944, Thompson roused himself from his lethargy. He bought a Canadian hunting and fishing license and announced a trip to his lodge near Little Current, Ontario. Before he could carry out his plan, he caught cold. Soon he was in an oxygen tent. His wife, his brother Gale, and his sister, Helen Pelouze, were summoned from their homes. Jim Breen came too, and to him Big Bill whispered, "Everything is all set, Jim." Breen nodded; Thompson's affairs, as much as he knew of them, were in order. "That's right," Big Bill said with a sigh, "that's right."

He had spoken his final words. He lapsed into a coma and never emerged from it. Four nights later, on March 19, Big Bill Thompson was dead.

5

There were, of course, headlines. And there were estimates and evaluations.

From his old newspaper foes, there came grudging praise and expected criticism. "He was a master of mass psychology," declared the *Tribune*. "He lived in action, not introspection, and he had the color of the frontier and the western plains. His genius for the spectacular made him an international figure. He might produce dismay and ridicule, but he was a force to be reckoned with. Cowboy Bill— Big Bill the Builder was always on the front seat of the American bandwagon." The *News* made its keen analysis: "In the death of William Hale Thompson, Chicago and the nation have lost a practical politician of first magnitude. Big Bill was not a great man; he was a highly successful man in his field. He was not a statesman, he was a consummate politician. His success was based on deception and distraction. He was the most amazingly unbelievable man in Chicago's history."

Ed Kelly, who had improved on Thompson's political techniques, called Big Bill "a good friend—he lived a full life and certainly was dynamic in his public efforts." Dwight Green, now Illinois' governor, hailed him as "a fine citizen—he was a good warrior." And the *Tribune's* Colonel McCormick: "Too many people made the mistake of underestimating Bill Thompson. He was a demagogue, true. But he was intelligent, clever and a fighter. I can remember the times he made monkeys out of us."

For two days and nights, Big Bill's body lay in state in a near North Side funeral parlor, and only the tiniest fraction of those who once had cheered him by the many thousands deigned to come. On the second night, Jack McPhaul, a *Times* reporter, found only a handful of the faithful in the chapel, a sorrowful contingent led by Jim Breen. McPhaul waited several hours, then went away to write: "Just thirty-two persons stopped at the chapel last night. Mayor Thompson lay in a solid bronze casket. There was not a flower nor a fern to be seen."

The city's politicians hastened to make amends. On the day of Thompson's funeral, workmen hurriedly draped the entrances to the City Hall with somber crepe, and the city council held a memorial service. Old enemies and old friends stood with young aldermen who knew of Thompson only through the tales of others. They put on their most sober expressions as Oscar de Priest, for so many years a Thompson loyalist among the city's Negroes, spoke fervently of how those of his race felt about the man who had convinced them he was their greatest champion since Abraham Lincoln. "He had real love for my people in his great heart," said De Priest. "We will never forget him."

Then they trooped to Thoburn Methodist Church on the South Side for the funeral service. A crowd of 1,000 filled the church, another 2,500 packed the street outside. There were senators and Governor Green among the mourners, such men of Thompson's past as Carter Harrison, Gene Pike, Carter Blatchford, Mike Faherty, Bob Crowe, Charles Fitzmorris. But no Fred Lundin.

The Reverend John H. Williamson, a steadfast friend since the days when he had been directed to lift the city's moral standards as Thompson's law-enforcement commissioner, delivered the final eulogy. He cited the public improvements completed during Thompson's three terms, reviewed the tumultuous life that had ended in its seventy-seventh year, and hailed him as one of the great men of the world. "Thompsonism is just another word for Americanism as he saw it," he concluded. "He had his mind and heart and spirit behind his peculiar methods."

6

There was, as seemed appropriate for one who had lived such a fabulous life, an interesting epilogue.

Five days after his death, Thompson's estate was estimated at only $150,000 by Jim Breen, filing petitions to make Maysie Thompson administrator. For five more days a routine search was made through Thompson's desk and papers for a will. Then, on March 30, Breen, Mrs. Thompson and Probate Court officials went to the American National Bank and Trust Company safe-deposit vaults to continue the search for a will. No will was found in either of the two boxes Thompson had rented there since 1931, but instead the boxes were crammed with old-style gold certificates, currency, and bundles of stocks and bonds. In this hoard were $1,466,250 in cash, the certificates in denominations of $50, $100, $500 and $1,000, and $20,000 in stocks. A week later another cache was uncovered in the vaults of the First National Bank: $112,000 in stocks and bonds. And finally two more safe-deposit boxes in the Boulevard National Bank yielded $220,000 in securities and $22,000 in bills of $50, $100 and $500. All this, plus his real-estate holdings, brought Big Bill's total wealth at the time he died to $2,103,024.

Everyone seemed to have a ready explanation. There was plenty of talk of bribes and graft and payoffs, and many recalled Al Capone's heavy contributions in the 1927 campaign. Some said that Thompson had been given over $1,000,000 by grateful contractors and businessmen when he was appealing the vast judgment against him in the experts' fees case, and when the higher courts had ruled he did not have to pay he had simply failed to return this handsome sum. Others had their side-of-the-mouth answers: Thompson had kept a percentage of every campaign contribution for himself; he had refused to return unexpended funds after his victories; he had stuffed $1,000 contributions into his pockets in the haste of electioneering; he had dipped into the party's till indiscriminately when he was supreme in the City Hall; he had retained most of the $500,-000 raised during the hectic 1931 primary. Breen loyally denied that the cash came from any political transactions legal or illegal during Thompson's regime, and some remembered that Big Bill, heeding Fred Lundin, had sold 10,000 shares of Commonwealth Edison Company stock in 1915 for $1,230,000 because Poor Swede felt that ownership of such stock would make his protégé vulnerable to attack as they went onward and upward in their political conquests.

No one had the complete answer, and no one ever would.

7

Whatever the source of the fortune, there were scores of claimants besides Maysie Thompson. From Pembroke, Ontario, came a letter of a George Thompson, Jr., who insisted that Big Bill was a close relative because George Thompson, Sr., had a similar habit of hoarding money in safe-deposit boxes. A man in Wisconsin claimed to have once saved Big Bill from bleeding to death by pressing a dime against his nostrils during a severe nose bleed, and for this feat he wanted $20,000. A woman wrote that she believed she was Thompson's foster daughter and was entitled to a modest $200,000.

Breen, handling Mrs. Thompson's legal action for the major share of the estate, rightly scoffed at these claims and some 200 others like them. But there was one strong claim. It was made by Ethabelle Green. In a suit demanding half of the estate, she brought into public light her relationship with Thompson. She admitted she had occupied suites with him in the Blackstone and Congress Hotels for twelve years, had traveled with him, and had been a combination secretary-nurse-housekeeper-daughter. When her own health failed, she said, Thompson sent her to Florida to recuperate and promised to make a will giving her half the estate. In the tradition of all such relationships, she insisted she had given Thompson the best years of her life—she was thirty-six now—and she demanded rightful payment.

Angrily denying every allegation, Breen set out to fight Ethabelle Green's claims. He accused her lawyer, Joseph T. Harrington, of plotting to use her as a means of getting Thompson's money. He filed an answer in Mrs. Thompson's behalf charging that Ethabelle had taken a wallet from Thompson as he lay dying and removed $1,700 from it. He denied Ethabelle's charge that two trunks filled with her clothes had been removed from Thompson's suite immediately after his death.

But he was waging a losing battle. In the midst of hearings before Probate Judge John F. O'Connell, he had no reply to Harrington when, in one heated argument, Harrington shouted, "Well, what if she was his mistress! What is it worth for a millionaire to have a mistress?"

The case ended abruptly on January 10, 1945, when Ethabelle Green accepted $250,000 in an out-of-court settlement. Breen, insisting that he wanted to keep fighting her claim, said he was acceding to the wishes of Mrs. Thompson, ill and distraught over the litigation and the prospect of a wearying trial. Ethabelle Green took her money, paid her lawyers and the tax officials and, scurrying back into oblivion with the $100,000 that remained, sputtered, "I hope Mrs. Thompson has a speedy recovery and lives long enough to enjoy the fortune Mr. Thompson has left her." Maysie Thompson received the major share of the estate, went to Europe on an extended trip, and eventually returned to live in subdued comfort on Chicago's Lake Shore Drive.

There was little more to add now to the story of Big Bill. In many places in his city, on bridges, playground entrances, parks, boulevards and widened streets, Chicagoans found bronze plaques to remind them of Big Bill the Builder. Some saw only the glories of that era, remembering that Chicago, as the age of great cities is reckoned, was then young and immature, and they forgave and condoned. Some saw inflated tax bills, remembering a time of waste and corruption, and identified Big Bill with Al Capone, gangsters and carnage.

His name quickly became wrapped in political legend and myth. To the loyal ones he was still the hero, the lover of his town, the man whose faithfulness to friends he had chosen unwisely had led to his greatest mistakes. To the others he became increasingly the clownish symbol of all that had been evil in Chicago in its most evil days. New epithets were invented to describe him, new phrases of praise were devised to glorify him, and stories wild and untrue and fantastic were told of his long reign. And this is the final irony, since neither myth nor legend can ever match the fact and reality of that lusty and uproarious life.

Bibliography

BIBLIOGRAPHY

Books

Allen, Frederick Lewis, *Only Yesterday.* New York, 1946.
Allen, Robert S., *Our Fair City.* New York, 1947.
Andreas, A. T., *History of Chicago.* (3 vols.) Chicago, 1884.
———, *History of Cook County, Illinois.* Chicago, 1894.
Asbury, Herbert, *Gem of the Prairie.* New York, 1940.
Battles and Leaders of the Civil War. (Vol. 4) New York, 1888.
Beard, Frances Birkhead (editor), *Wyoming from Territorial Days to Present.* (Vol. 1.) Chicago, 1933.
Bennett, James O'Donnell, *Chicago Gangland, the True Story of Chicago Crime.* Chicago, 1929.
Bright, John, *Hizzoner Big Bill Thompson.* New York, 1930.
Bross, William, *History of Chicago.* Chicago, 1876.
Burns, Walter Noble, *The One-Way Ride.* New York, 1931.
Clay, John, *My Life on the Range.* Chicago, 1924.
Davis, John McCann, *Breaking the Deadlock.* Chicago, 1904.
Dawson, George Francis, *Life and Services of General John A. Logan.* Chicago, 1887.
Dennis, Charles H., *Victor Lawson, His Time and His Work.* Chicago, 1935.
Dobyns, Fletcher, *The Underworld of American Politics.* New York, 1932.
Dunne, Edward F., *History of Illinois.* (5 vols.) Chicago, 1933.
Ericsson, Henry, *Sixty Years a Builder.* Chicago, 1942.
Goodspeed, Weston A., and Healy, Daniel D., *History of Cook County, Illinois.* (2 vols.) Chicago, 1929.
Gosnell, Harold F., *Machine Politics: Chicago Model.* Chicago, 1937.
———, *Negro Politicians.* Chicago, 1935.
Guernsey, Charles A., *Wyoming Cowboy Days.* New York, 1936.
Hamilton, Henry Raymond, *The Epic of Chicago.* Chicago, 1932.
Harrison, Carter, *Growing Up with Chicago.* Indianapolis, 1944.
———, *Stormy Years.* Indianapolis, 1938.
Hastings, Frank, *A Ranchman's Recollection.* Chicago, 1921.

Hough, Emerson, *The Story of the Cowboy*. New York, 1898.

James, Will, *Cowboys North and South*. New York, 1924.

King, Hoyt, *Citizen Cole of Chicago*. Chicago, 1931.

Kirkland, Joseph, and Moses, John (editors), *History of Chicago*. (2 vols.) Chicago, 1895.

Kohlsaat, H. H., *From McKinley to Harding*. New York, 1923.

Landesco, John, *Organized Crime in Chicago*. (Illinois Crime Survey.) Chicago, 1929.

Lasswell, Harold D., *Politics: Who Gets What, When, How*. New York, 1936.

———, *Psychopathology and Politics*. Chicago, 1930.

Lewis, Lloyd, and Smith, Henry Justin, *Chicago, The History of Its Reputation*. New York, 1929.

Linn, James Weber, *James Keeley, Newspaperman*. Indianapolis, 1937.

Logan, John Alexander, *The Volunteer Soldier of America*. Chicago, 1887.

Masters, Edgar Lee, *The Tale of Chicago*. New York, 1933.

McCormick, Robert R., *Memoirs*. Chicago, 1952.

Merriam, Charles Edward, *Chicago, A More Intimate View of Urban Politics*. New York, 1929.

Morris, Richard B., *Encyclopedia of American History*. New York, 1953.

Olson, Ernest W. (editor), *History of Swedes in Illinois*. (Vol. 1) Chicago, 1908.

Pasley, Fred D., *Al Capone, The Biography of a Self-Made Man*. New York, 1930.

———, *Muscling In*. New York, 1931.

Peake, Ora Brooks, *The Colorado Range Cattle Industry*. Glendale, Calif., n.d.

Pelzer, Louis, *The Cattleman's Frontier*. Glendale, Calif., 1936.

Peterson, Virgil, *Barbarians in Our Midst*. New York, 1952.

Pierce, Bessie Louise, *History of Chicago*. New York, 1937.

Poole, Ernest, *Giants Gone*. New York, 1943.

Prather, Donald Fry (compiler), *There Will Always Be a Mackinac*. Chicago, 1925.

Randall, Frank A., *History of Chicago Building*. Urbana, 1949.

Reckless, Walter, *Vice in Chicago*. Chicago, 1933.

Robertson, Mrs. Harriet M. (editor), *Dishonest Elections and Why We Have Them*. Chicago, 1934.

Rollinson, John K., *Wyoming Cowboy Days*. New York, 1936.

Shumway, Grant L. (editor), *History of Western Nebraska and Its People.* (Vols. 1-2.) Lincoln, 1921.

Smith, Henry Justin, *Chicago's Great Century.* Chicago, 1933.

Stackpole, Everett S., and Thompson, Lucian, *History of the Town of Durham, New Hampshire.* (2 vols.) Durham, n.d.

Steffens, Lincoln, *Shame of the Cities.* New York, 1904.

Stimpson, George, *A Book about American Politics.* New York, 1952.

Stuart, William H., *The 20 Incredible Years.* Chicago, 1935.

Sullivan, Edward Dean, *Chicago Surrenders.* New York, 1930.

———, *Rattling the Cup on Chicago Crime.* New York, 1929.

Thrasher, Frederick, *The Gang.* Chicago, 1927.

Wallis, J. H., *The Politician, His Habits, Outcries and Protective Coloring.* New York, 1935.

Washburn, Charles, *Come into My Parlor.* New York, 1936.

Weber, Harry (compiler), *Outline History of Chicago Traction.* Chicago, 1936.

Wendt, Lloyd, and Kogan, Herman, *Lords of the Levee.* Indianapolis, 1943.

Werner, M. R., *Privileged Characters.* New York, 1935.

Wilson, Samuel Paynter, *Chicago and Its Cess Pools of Vice and Infamy.* Chicago, 1910.

Winsor, Justin (editor), *The Memorial History of Boston.* Boston, 1881.

Wish, Harvey, *Society and Thought in Modern America.* New York, 1953.

Wooddy, Carroll H., *The Chicago Primary of 1926.* Chicago, 1926.

———, *The Case of Frank L. Smith.* Chicago, 1931.

Zorbaugh, Harvey W., *The Gold Coast and the Slum.* Chicago, 1920.

NEWSPAPERS

Chicago *American* (1901-1948)
Daily Drovers Journal (1891-1893)
Daily News (1890-1948)
Democrat (1901-1902)
Evening Journal (1900-1929)
Evening Post (various dates)
Examiner (also *Herald and Examiner*) (1902-1939)
Inter-Ocean (1890-1914)
Record-Herald (also *Herald*) (1901-1918)
Sun (also *Sun-Times*) (1941-1948)

The Voter (1903)
The Day Book (various dates)
The Republican (1915-1917)
Times (1929-1947)
Tribune (1880-1948)
London *Herald* (1927-1928)
Times (1927-1928)
New York *Times* (various dates)
Stockholm, Sweden, *Dagens Nyhetter* (article by Jan Olof Olsson "The Life of Frederic Lundin," translated by Kay Martin)

DOCUMENTS, MANUSCRIPTS AND PAMPHLETS

Burleigh, D. R., "William Hale Thompson, Nebraskan." (MS, Nebraska State Historical Society, Lincoln).
Campbell, Mary R., "Evaluation of a Mayor." Chicago, 1915.
"Chicago: Eight Years of Progress." Chicago, 1923.
Evans, Arthur, "Rise and Fall of Thompson's Machine." Chicago, 1931.
Estate of William Hale Thompson, Sr., (Files of the Cook County Probate Court).
Estate of William Hale Thompson, Jr., (Files of the Cook County Probate Court).
"Thompsonism." Chicago, 1931.
The Tribune Company *vs.* William Hale Thompson, et al, Circuit Court of Cook County.

MAGAZINES

Annals of the American Academy of Political and Social Sciences
Cherry Circle (Magazine of the Chicago Athletic Club) (1888-1898)
Chicago Yacht Club Bulletin (various issues)
Christian Century, 1931
Current History (Esp. "Big Bill Thompson of Chicago" by Robert Morse Lovett, June, 1931; also articles on Thompson school policies by Rupert Hughes, Albert Bushnell Hart, Dana Carleton Munro, Elbridge Colby, Lyon G. Tyler and William Hale Thompson, February, 1928)
Collier's (Esp. "They Can't Beat My Big Boy," by William Allen White, January 18, 1927)

Forum (Esp. "Patriots and Propaganda," April, 1928)

Harper's (Esp. "Portrait of an Elected Person," by Elmer Davis, July, 1927)

Nation (Esp. "Thompson the Cowboy Rides In," by John Flynn, April 20, 1927)

New Republic (Esp. "Tammany in Illinois," by Charles Merz, April 19, 1919)

The Rudder (1900-1913)

The Sphere, London (1913)

Journal of the Illinois State Historical Society (Esp. "How Big Bill Thompson Won Control of Chicago," by George Schottenhamel, Spring 1952)

During the many years in which we gathered information for *Big Bill of Chicago* we interviewed scores of persons who knew Thompson and his times. Some were his friends, some his enemies, a few were neutral. Many requested that their names be omitted from any list of credits for personal reasons.

We are grateful for especially valuable interviews to the following persons who appear in the book and are part of the Thompson story: Frank C. Heinz, manager of Thompson's Nebraska ranch; Leslie (Ike) Volz, for years secretary to Fred Lundin; Clyde Morrison, Deneen campaign secretary and later a Thompson publicity man; Colonel Robert R. McCormick, editor and publisher of the Chicago *Tribune;* Samuel Golan, a Thompson aide in his later years; James M. Breen, Thompson's lawyer and friend; Judge Hugo Friend; Lou Kent Fink. Before their deaths we interviewed Senator J. Hamilton Lewis, Senator Otis F. Glenn, Mayor Edward J. Kelly, and Patrick A. Nash.

Others who provided aid include Nelson Algren, Robert Perbonner, close associate of Thompson; Bernard Fink, publisher of *The National Republican;* Thelma E. Drayton, publisher of the Ewing, Nebraska *Advocate* and Jack Spittler and Henry Drayton, of Ewing; Miss Helene M. Rogers of the Illinois State Historical Society; James C. Olson, superintendent of the Nebraska State Historical Society; W. C. Dannenberg, Leonard C. M. Johnson, Cornelius Kelly, Virgil Peterson, managing director of the Chicago Crime Commission and Walter Devereux, its chief of investigators; Herbert M. Carlin, Laughton Crosby and Charles Washburn.

Many newspaper people, some of them close observers of the Thompson era from its beginnings, were especially helpful. They include Elston

Bradfield, James Doherty, Arthur M. Evans, Joseph M. Garrett, Frank Hinman, Johnson Kanady, John A. Menaugh, Marie O'Connor, Ray Quisno, Charles Smutny and Percy Wood of the *Tribune;* Milburn P. Akers, David Anderson, Leona Bender, William J. Block, John Dreiske, Richard J. Finnegan, Robert E. Kennedy and Virginia McEachern of the *Sun-Times;* A. T. Burch, David Keniston, Clem Lane, Everett Norlander, Thomas Sayers and the late Charles Wheeler of the *News;* Harry Reutlinger, Ernest Tucker, the late Justin Forrest and the late A. L. Sloan of the *Herald-American.*

Each Chicago newspaper made available to us all its reference material on Thompson and his associates, as did Chester Lewis, head of the New York *Times* reference department. We are grateful to Mrs. John T. McCutcheon and the Chicago *Tribune* for permission to reproduce cartoons by the late John T. McCutcheon, and to the Chicago *Daily News* for permission to use those of Vaughn Shoemaker.

In our research, we also received invaluable aid from Herbert H. Hewitt, chief of the reference division of the Chicago Public Library, and his staff, and from Frederick Rex, head of the Chicago Municipal Reference Library. We also wish to thank the staffs of the library of the Chicago Historical Society, Newberry Library, the University of Chicago Library and the Library of Congress.

Index

INDEX